CHILDHOOD WELL-BEIN AND RESILIENCE

CU00892225

This book examines the ways in which well-being affects educational outcomes. Using an ecological approach, the book defines what we mean by well-being and resilience in education and how this relates to policy and children and young people's rights. The book considers strategies utilised by the education, health, voluntary and private sectors which promote well-being and resilience for children and young people from the early years to adulthood. This book also explores societal factors such as poverty and family well-being.

Childhood Well-being and Resilience goes on to provide examples of practice interventions inside and outside the classroom. It represents a sea change in professional approaches to well-being and resilience as protective factors against poor mental health. It includes chapters on key topics such as:

- The concept of child well-being, resilience and the rights of the child
- Peer interaction and well-being
- Social media and mental health
- Well-being and outdoor learning
- Mindfulness for young children
- International policy and child well-being

This book supports professionals to increase their knowledge, establish a skill set and build their confidence which can enable children and young people to develop good levels of well-being and to improve their resilience. Including reflective questions and case studies, *Childhood Well-being and Resilience* is essential reading for undergraduate students studying Early Childhood Studies, Education Studies, Teaching Awards and Family and Community Studies.

Zeta Williams-Brown is a Reader in Education for Social Justice at the University of Wolverhampton. She is leader of the Childhood, Youth and Families Research and Scholarship group for the Education Observatory. She is an executive member and currently Chair of the British Education Studies Association (BESA).

Sarah Mander is a Staff Tutor and Lecturer for The Open University. She has 20 years of practice experience in working with children, young people and their families across private, statutory and voluntary sectors. Sarah is currently studying for her Doctoral award and is researching Early Help workforce competencies.

CHILDHOOD WELL-BEING AND RESILIENCE

Influences on Educational Outcomes

Edited by
Zeta Williams-Brown
and Sarah Mander

LONDON AND NEW YORK

First published 2021
by Routledge
2 Park Square, Milton Park, Abingdon, Oxon OX14 4RN

and by Routledge
52 Vanderbilt Avenue, New York, NY 10017

Routledge is an imprint of the Taylor & Francis Group, an informa business

British Library Cataloguing-in-Publication Data
A catalogue record for this book is available from the British Library

Library of Congress Cataloging-in-Publication Data
A catalog record has been requested for this book

ISBN: 978-0-367-34242-5 (hbk)
ISBN: 978-0-367-34243-2 (pbk)
ISBN: 978-0-429-32463-5 (ebk)

Typeset in News Gothic
by codeMantra

Zeta Williams-Brown
For my amazing children: Mia, Damie and Fin
And my very supportive parents: Sue and John

Sarah Mander
This book is written in honour of and respect for all children,
to promote positive well-being and build resilience
which can improve happiness levels.
It has been made possible by learning valuable lessons
from my own children, Sean and Daniel; thank you

Contents

Abbreviations

The following abbreviations are used in the text:

BPS	British Psychological Society
CBT	Cognitive Behavioural Therapy
CYPMHWT	Children and Young People's Mental Health and Well-being Taskforce
DfE	Department for Education
ECEC	Early Childhood Education and Care
EMHP	Education Mental Health Practitioner
EYFS	Early Years Foundation Stage
GDPR	General Data Protection Regulation
LAC	Looked-After Children
MHFA	Mental Health First Aid training
NCB	National Children's Bureau
NICE	National Institute for Health and Care Excellence
NSPCC	National Society for the Prevention of Cruelty to Children
OECD	Organisation for Economic Co-operation and Development
ONS	Office for National Statistics
PSHE	Personal, Social, Health Education curriculum
PISA	Programme for International Student Assessment
SEND	Special Educational Needs and Disabilities
SENDCoP	Special Educational Needs and Disabilities Code of Practice
SFSS	Schools Families Support Service
UK	United Kingdom
UNCRC	United Nations Convention on the Rights of the Child

Contributors

Dylan Adams is a Senior Lecturer in Primary Education Studies at Cardiff Metropolitan University. His research interests include music, outdoor education, holistic education and creativity. Before working in higher education, he worked as a primary school teacher and as an educational consultant. He is a Fellow of the RSA and a member of the Executive committee of the British Education Studies Association.

Andrew Aston is a Research Assistant based at the University of Wolverhampton and is involved as a key researcher in the Headstart evaluation and Against the Odds research project. Andy plays a vital role in participant research engagement with schools, children and young people. At present, he conducts extensive primary research with schools and communities across England.

Gary Beauchamp is a Professor of Education and Associate Dean Research in the Cardiff School of Education and Social Policy at Cardiff Metropolitan University. He was a primary teacher for many years, before moving into higher education as a lecturer at Swansea University, before moving to Cardiff Metropolitan University where he currently oversees research, including supervising PhD students (mostly examining the uses of ICT in educational settings in the UK and internationally). He has published widely in books, academic journals and research reports, including for the Welsh Government.

Elisabetta Biffi is an Associate Professor at the "Riccardo Massa" Department of Human Sciences and Education – University of Milano-Bicocca, where she teaches "Narrative Theory and Practice" as part of the Master's Degree Course in Education. She participates in Italian and European research projects on the topics of childhood protection and children's rights; educator and teacher professional development; pedagogical documentation; narrative methods and arts-based methods for educational research.

Jayne Daly is a Senior Lecturer at the University of Wolverhampton teaching on a range of courses including the BA in Early Childhood Studies. Her early career in early childhood and education began over 30 years ago. Throughout her professional career, she worked within the public care, health and education sectors. She is currently engaged in doctoral research for her PhD in Education. Her research interests include childhood resilience, quality early years leadership, children's creative development and the impact of higher education on the life of the mature female learner. She is a Senior Fellow of Higher Education Academy.

Maria Dardanou is an Associate Professor at the Arctic University of Norway, Campus Tromsø and teaches pedagogy at Early Childhood Teacher Education department. Maria has 15 years of experience as a preschool teacher. Her research interests focuses on digital technology in early years, kindergarten and museum and multicultural education. Maria is a co-governor of the Special Interest Group *'Digital Childhoods, STEM and Multimodality'* of the European Early Childhood Research Association (EECERA).

Susan Davis is a Senior Lecturer in the school of Education and Social Policy at Cardiff Metropolitan University. She teaches on the PGCE primary programme, is a module leader, lecturer and dissertation supervisor on the MA in Education and is the Pathway Leader for the Professional Doctorate in Education (EdD) within the school. Previously, she was a primary school teacher, specialising in Foundation Phase pedagogy. Susan is a senior fellow of the Higher Education Academy (SFHEA). She is currently carrying out research into children's well-being, looking at the implementation of an emotional literacy programme on quiet, shy and anxious children in the Foundation Phase setting.

Sandra Dumitrescu is a Senior Lecturer in Early Childhood Studies with a particular interest in the professionalisation of Early Years practitioners and play for children who have profound and complex needs. She has previously worked as a registered health play specialist in a range of health care settings, within a play context.

Kathryn Ecclestone is a visiting Professor of Education at University of Sheffield. Kathryn began her education career in 1979 as a 'life and social skills' instructor on government employment schemes for 16–19 year olds. She worked on pre-vocational, vocational and Access to Higher Education Programmes before moving to post-16 teacher professional development in 1992. She has published widely in academic and mainstream media outlets and her research explores the educational and social implications of a perceived mental health 'crisis'. Kathryn is currently co-investigator in a 5-year research network on university students' mental health, funded by Research Innovation UK.

Cheryl Ellis is a Principal Lecturer at Cardiff Metropolitan University. She is a member of the university's outdoor learning team and regularly works with children and students within Forest School. Her key areas of research interest include outdoor learning and play, inclusion and additional learning needs. Having previously worked as a primary school teacher, Cheryl has experienced the 'practical realities' of classroom life.

Maria Benedetta Gambacorti-Passerini, PhD, is actually a researcher in Education and a lecturer of *Pedagogical Consultancy in Educational Discomfort* at the University of Milano-Bicocca, Department of Human Sciences and Education Riccardo Massa. Her studies concern the possible link between educational and health sciences, and the educational professionals' training.

Eirin Gamst-Nergård works as an Assistant Professor at UiT the Arctic University of Norway. Gamst-Nergård teaches pedagogy at Early Childhood teacher education, Department of Education. Her master's degree is in Educational Psychology. Gamst-Nergård has extensive teaching experience form kindergarten and elementary school system. She also has extensive experience as a school psychologist at BUP, Center for Child and Adolescent Psychiatry, and at Barnehabiliteringen, Center for Child Habilitation, both at the University Hospital in Northern-Norway, UNN. Gamst-Nergård's research interest is within the field of cultural psychology and early education programs.

Chantelle Haughton is a Senior Lecturer in Early Childhood Studies, Early Years Education and Professional Practice at Cardiff Metropolitan University and a Senior HEA Fellow. She is a Forest School Leader and trainer responsible for the development of an on campus Outdoor Learning Centre, which now uses an ancient strip of woodland and concrete patches on the university campus in a range of approaches. Chantelle was awarded Student Led Teaching Fellowship Award (2013) and Vice Chancellors Staff Award for Excellence (2011), HEA CATE finalist (2017) awards were related to the live, playful, innovative community engagement projects that involve students, local children and practitioners and other organisations as partners.

Dean-David Holyoake has done a lot of social science research and worked at a number of UK Universities including the Centre for Life Long Learning – University of Birmingham, University of Central England, Newman University College, University of Warwick and University of Wolverhampton. He would describe himself as a performance ethnographer and research fabricator (a fabnographer) with a particular interest in exploring mundane culture and seedy interactions. He has written books and professional articles on a variety of issues including Child and Adolescent Mental Health Services, philosophy and custard pies.

Michael Jopling is Professor of Education and Director of the Education Observatory at University of Wolverhampton. He has written widely on a range of areas including school collaboration, education policy, and social justice.

Zenna Kingdon is an Early Childhood Senior Lecturer at the University of Wolverhampton and a Reader at Birmingham City University.

Alyson Lewis is a Senior Lecturer and an award leader for the BA (Hons) Early Childhood Studies at Bath Spa University. She also delivers modules to students in China studying a dual programme. Her PhD examined the concept and practices of well-being in the early years' curriculum. She has co-authored 'An Introduction to the Foundation Phase in Wales' and published papers relating to well-being and children's rights. Her research interests include professional development, playful pedagogies and inclusive practice.

Caroline Lewis is a Senior Lecturer and Assistant Academic Director for the Discipline of Childhood and Education within University of Wales Trinity St David in Swansea. She has several years' experience within the higher education sector, is currently Programme Manager for the MA Education Studies and the post 16 PGCE (PCET) courses. Her research interests lie in the field of education policy, particularly that of Wales as well as the impact of poverty on children and young people as well as student experience and enhancement. She has been an executive member of the British Education Studies Association since 2013 and additionally is a member of the End Child Poverty (Wales).

Lydia Lewis is a Research Fellow in the Institute of Education, Faculty of Education, Health and Wellbeing, University of Wolverhampton. There, she leads the Education and Mental Health Research Group. She has also previously co-founded and co-convened the British Educational Research Association Mental Health, Wellbeing and Education Special Interest Group and the British Sociological Association Sociology of Mental Health Study Group. Her research work has focused on theoretically informed, applied sociological inquiry and knowledge exchange with the third sector. She has developed a programme of research on education and mental health, with a particular focus on adult community learning (ACL).

Chris Ludlow has taught over the last two decades across the primary age range in both urban and rural schools in the West Midlands. During this time, Chris has fulfilled a range of leadership roles, most recently as a deputy head of an infant school. Having experienced the benefits of his own meditation practice over a number of years, Chris developed the ThoughtBubbles mindfulness programme for children and families. The programme grew out of research conducted as part of his study for a Master's in Education. Following his time as a primary school teacher, Chris has been promoted; his new role is Programme Leader in Initial Teacher Training at University College Birmingham.

Helen Lyndon is currently the postgraduate programme lead for the Centre for Research in Early Childhood (CREC), in Birmingham, England. She taught across the primary age range before specialising in Early Childhood and achieving her Master's degree in Education. Helen then moved into Higher Education and has taught both undergraduate and postgraduate courses in early childhood and initial teacher education. Her doctoral research focuses on the development of listening practices through pedagogic mediation. Helen is the UK country coordinator for the European Early Childhood Research Association.

Sarah Mander is currently a Staff Tutor for the School of Education, Childhood, Youth and Sports with the Open University. She has previously worked in Higher Education Institutions across the Midlands region in Course Leader and Senior Lecturer roles. Sarah's practice experience has been gained in the statutory, voluntary and private sectors where her focus is mainly within early intervention and preventative work for children, young people and their families. Research interests include children and young people's well-being, mental health and safeguarding and she is currently studying for her Doctorate in Education.

Bill Myers is a Senior Lecturer and the Pathway Leader for ITT in Psychology and Social Sciences at the University of Wolverhampton and has been involved in research on; perceptions of self-harm in secondary schools; locus of control and its role in trainee teacher professional development and cyberbullying. Prior to his current post he trained at the Institute of Education, London and taught in secondary schools in London, Leicestershire and Birmingham and held numerous roles including head of Psychology and Health & Social Care, Head of Year and Head of Mentoring.

Emma Ormerod is an independent mental health researcher who uses her own lived experience of mental distress to inform her work. Emma has worked as a Research Manager for the National Survivor User Network (NSUN), a service user-led network for people with experience of mental health issues. Her research interests include survivor-led research, arts and well-being, trauma-informed approaches and co-production in mental health policy and practice. Emma is also the co-founder and Artistic Director/CEO of Underground Lights, a community theatre company that is run by and for people experiencing homelessness and/or mental distress.

John Owen is a Senior Lecturer in the Faculty of Education, Health and Wellbeing at the University of Wolverhampton. His background is in secondary education where he held a range of promoted posts at schools in the West Midlands, before joining the National Strategies with Walsall Local Authority and Later leading the ICT Curriculum support team, chairing the WMNet teaching and Learning Group and sitting on the WMNet Management Board. John has now moved into teacher training with both post-graduate and undergraduate students. He has done a significant amount of work related to online behaviour and safety among young people.

Cristina Palmieri is a Full Professor in General and Social Pedagogy and lectures of *Basis of Pedagogical Counseling* and *Pedagogy of Inclusion* in the Department of Human Sciences for Education 'Riccardo Massa' – University of Milano-Bicocca. Her research is about care in educational contexts, educational discomfort, practices and methodologies of educational work. She is author of many articles and books in the educational field, and she took parts in international and national funded projects.

Gavin Rhoades is a Principal Lecturer in the Faculty of Education, Health and Wellbeing at the University of Wolverhampton. His background is in secondary education and he was an Assistant Head Teacher at schools in Staffordshire and Cumbria, before moving into teacher training and then undergraduate Education Studies. He is currently studying for a Professional Doctorate and his thesis is a Q-methodology study looking at the complex views of higher education students around the concept of 'student satisfaction' and its use as a measure of quality in higher education.

Sian Sarwar is a Senior Lecturer in Early Childhood Studies and Programme Director for Education Studies and Social Policy. She has taught on the BA Secondary Music and PGCE and Early Childhood Studies BA Programmes. Her research interests in learner voice and education are central to her PhD research for which she is exploring the contexts and processes adopted by young people when participating in music.

Jacky Tyrie is a Lecturer in Early Childhood Studies in the School of Education, Swansea University. She has been a lecturer and researcher within higher education for the last 15 years and explores early childhood from sociological and geographical perspective focusing on research on children's rights within early childhood education and care. Jacky is a national leader in children's rights and co-ordinates the Children's Rights in Early Years Network (CREYN). Jacky is currently researching ways of examining young children's 'lived' experiences of human rights.

Sharon Vincent is a Reader in Child Welfare at Northumbria University. Her publications relate to child protection and safeguarding. She has a particular interest in multi-agency approaches to support vulnerable children and families and prevent abuse and neglect.

Zeta Williams-Brown is a Reader in Education for Social Justice at the University of Wolverhampton. She is leader of the Childhood, Youth and Families Research and Scholarship group for the Education Observatory. She is an executive member and currently Chair of the British Education Studies Association (BESA). Her technical research expertise specialises in qualitative methods, including Q-methodology.

Alison Wren is a Senior Lecturer in Education Studies at the University of Wolverhampton. Having completed her PhD at the University of the West of England in 2016, focusing on the lived experiences of pupils with SEN in relation to their TA support, Alison has continued to carry out research related to vulnerable groups within education. Her most recent study explores current provision for students with mental health needs.

Introduction

Zeta Williams-Brown and Sarah Mander

Our main aim for this book was to provide students with a resource that brings together theory on childhood well-being and resilience and relates it to current practice. The terms 'well-being' and 'resilience' have become buzzwords in education. Policy makers and Organisational Leaders now recognise what is termed as an emerging mental health crisis that has supported increasing levels of political emphasis on improving the mental health of our children and young people. The emphasis on building and developing effective well-being and resilience to guard against poor mental health is publically endorsed at the highest level by the Royal family, and also celebrities who are held by children and young people in high esteem. This represents a sea change in the professional approach to well-being and resilience, and places greater importance on these concepts than historically conceived.

However, there is a common theme evident throughout the book that details the complexity on defining and supporting childhood well-being and resilience. This is especially evident in the first section of the book. For instance, Lewis in Chapter 1 focuses on understanding the concept of childhood well-being and determines that its inherent complexity makes it difficult to reach a simple definition. In Chapter 2, Lewis, Ormerod and Ecclestone detail the similar difficulties in defining childhood resilience. Resilience in this chapter is seen as 'fluid, context dependent, socially situated and influenced by diverse environmental factors' (Ungar, 2008, in Chapter 1; Mohaupt, 2008).

The role of the child or young person, from birth to the age of 25 years, in developing and supporting their own well-being and resilience is evident throughout the book. Section 2 of the book is also dedicated to this focus. There is a real sense that the competency, capacity and capabilities of children are celebrated. This is evident in many of the book's chapters, including Lyndon in Chapter 4, who details the active role children play in the construction of their own knowledge and the need to listen to children, regarding them as experts and meaning-makers. Chapter 5 by Williams-Brown, Daly, Jopling and Aston evidences what resilience means to children. The chapter includes real examples of challenging situations and circumstances when children believe they have been resilient. It evidences that some children have been able to use or develop resilience to overcome their adversity. However, this is dependent on the child's experience, their resilience and the other forms of adversity that the child is experiencing at the same time. Contributors in this book have been careful not to focus solely on the child/young person and their well-being and resilience. It is important to thoroughly consider environmental influences and, where appropriate, that change occurs to ensure supporting childhood well-being and resilience is of paramount importance in our practice. An example of such change is evident in Chapter 10 by Jopling and Vincent who detail the need for collaborative working between Education and Social Work to support vulnerable families.

The book is structured in four parts. The first part is policy driven and focused on defining well-being and resilience in education. For example, Mander in Chapter 3 concentrates on the shifting policy context of student well-being within higher education. Section 2 focuses on children and young people's role in their own well-being and resilience. For instance, Rhoades, Owen and Myers in Chapter 7 consider issues around online social media usage and young people's mental health. The third section provides examples of practice interventions currently used to support children's well-being and resilience. These include the role of mindfulness detailed in Ludlow, Chapter 9. The final section of the book considers societal and cultural influences on children's and young people's well-being and resilience. Chapter in this section include Lewis, Chapter 13, who details the innovative Welsh approach to enhancing well-being.

The book has been written to support the learning of Levels 4 and 5 (years one and two) for undergraduate students studying relevant degrees including Early Years, Primary and Secondary Education Awards, Education Studies, Childhood, Family and Community Studies, Disability Studies and Special Needs/Inclusion Studies degrees. It is also highly relevant for practising teachers, practitioners, tutors and students in primary, secondary FE and HE teacher training, as well as current and future practitioners working across the private, voluntary and statutory sectors. The structure of each chapter has been designed to provide readers with the opportunity to critically develop their thinking about childhood well-being and resilience, by providing moments of reflection. Contributors have illustrated broad theories and concepts with individual and group tasks, case studies, discussion questions and recommended reading. In Chapter 8, Beauchamp et al. provide a case study carried out in an ancient Welsh woodland where a new teacher-led curriculum is being developed to examine key pedagogic theories, including the concept of risk, Grit theory and mindfulness. Holyoake, in Chapter 11, details Solution-Focused Resilience, evidencing his own professional practice in this field and uses 1-minute reflective questions to ask the reader to further consider their concept of resilience.

Overall, this book has uniquely brought together contributors, including noted and international academics, who have either practically experienced and/or researched childhood well-being and resilience practice in differing contexts and places. Examples of chapters that include international comparisons to the system in England include Chapter 14 by Biffi, Palmieri and Gambacorti-Passerini on practice in Italy and Chapter 15 by Dardanou and Gamst-Nergard on the case of Norway. It is an interesting exercise to consider the overall well-being of children across developed countries through the lens of UNICEF's 2013 report, and to reflect upon both the similarities and variations in practices described in this book. This provides opportunity for readers to reflect upon how well-being in educational practice can be developed. It is important to note that interventions detailed in this book are carried out by trained professionals. They are detailed to show the reader a variety of examples of what is currently experienced in practice, which should only be undertaken with specialist training. A bank of support organisations is available at the end of the book for reference, in the event that signposting and possibly access to specialist support is required. Therefore, the book enables the reader to identify potential professional development opportunities whilst also nourishing our own well-being. Examples of chapters that provide findings from a recent study include Chapter 6 by Wren on the importance of peer interaction and Chapter 12 by Kingdon on the need to consider the well-being of practitioners and how they can be supported to flourish. By bringing all contributing individuals together in one book, readers are encouraged to consider chapters in relation to one another and critically question the practical implementation of supporting childhood well-being and resilience.

Individual/group task

Before and after task – consider how you define well-being and resilience and how much you think we can support children and young people to maintain and develop their well-being and resilience in a variety of settings, for instance the early years, primary education, secondary schools, further education and/or higher education. Once you have read the relevant chapters reflect back on your original comments. Has your perception changed?

Whilst reading the book – critically consider questions such as:

What does well-being and resilience mean?

At present – are we (as professionals) successively supporting children and young people's well-being and resilience?

Reference

UNICEF (2013) *Child well-being in economically rich countries: changes in the first decade of the 21st century,* Innocenti Working Papers 2013-02, www.unicefirc.org/publications/pdf/iwp_2013_2.pdf [Accessed 30 January 2020].

Section 1

Defining well-being and resilience in education

1 Understanding the concept of child well-being

Domains, dimensions and discourses

Alyson Lewis

Introduction

This chapter examines the complex concept of well-being and aims to broaden and extend your understanding of this concept. Developing your knowledge and understanding of well-being is important particularly when there is a fast growing interest in education (McLaughlin, 2008). Mayr and Ulich (1999, p. 230) claim that well-being is "a complex physical and psychological state and disposition". Whereas Chambers (2014; cited in White and Abeyasekera, 2014, p. xi) suggests that "what people seek and value as wellbeing is subjective and varies by person, gender, age, relationships, status, place, culture and more". Morrow and Mayall (2009) suggest that well-being is the new term that politicians and educationalists use instead of children's 'welfare'. They also hypothesise that well-being shares the same meaning as 'welfare' across countries (Morrow and Mayall, 2009). Statham and Chase (2010, p. 6) argue that in general "there is still limited agreement on what the constituent components of child wellbeing are, or how they should be weighted in terms of importance or priority". This chapter demonstrates that well-being is understood and communicated in various ways, which can lead to confusion and uncertainty about its nature (Coleman, 2009). Therefore, the chapter is organised by first, explaining the complexity in defining well-being; second, exploring the various domains (also known as types of well-being); third, discussing the subjective and objective dimensions and, finally, explaining well-being discourses which are rooted in disciplines such as philosophy, psychology and economics.

This chapter aims to provide clarity about the nature of well-being and explores a claim by Raghavan and Alexandrova (2015) who state that a theory of child well-being does not currently exist because long-standing discourses, such as those within philosophy, were not originally written with children in mind. Ultimately, the chapter encourages you to think about whether a theory of child well-being is needed.

The complexity in defining well-being

Many different interpretations of well-being exist and La Placa et al. (2013) state that due to its inherent complexity, it is difficult to reach a simple definition. Mayr and Ulich (1999) suggest that well-being is difficult to define because there are numerous domains (types of well-being) that inter-relate. Similarly, Statham and Chase (2010) claim that well-being is difficult to narrow down to one simple definition because there are subjective and objective ways of understanding the concept.

Nonetheless, the New Economics Foundation (2009, p. 7) defines well-being as a concept that emerges in relation to "a dynamic interaction of different factors". Dodge et al., draw upon Reber's (1995) definition from psychology and explain in more detail that well-being is a state of being stable. They suggest that

> Stable wellbeing is when individuals have the psychological, social and physical resources they need to meet a particular psychological, social and/or physical challenge. When individuals have more challenges than resources, the see-saw dips, along with their well-being and vice-versa.
>
> (Dodge et al., 2012, p. 230)

Arguably, well-being is difficult to define because it is often conflated (mixed or merged together) with other concepts, such as 'happiness', 'life satisfaction', 'quality of life', 'emotional literacy', 'emotional intelligence' and 'positive mental health' to name but a few (Pollard and Lee, 2003; McLaughlin, 2008; Statham and Chase, 2010; Mashford-Scott et al., 2012). However, Coleman (2009, p. 283) asserts, "well-being is not quite the same as happiness". According to Morrow and Mayall (2009, p. 221), defining well-being is 'conceptually muddy' because it is conflated with other concepts.

The argument that well-being is conflated with other concepts and used synonymously supports Ereaut and Whiting's (2008) claim that well-being is socially and culturally constructed and does not have a fixed meaning. Also, this argument highlights that the concept is vague and ambiguous and can have many different meanings. Coleman (2009) suggests that when there are differences between how well-being is understood, it is very difficult to measure and operationalise. Therefore, it can be problematic, particularly for schools, to show that well-being has improved or changed.

Another complexity associated with defining well-being is a grammatical and semantic one. Well-being is considered a noun, but there are many different types of nouns, for example, there are common nouns, abstract nouns, concrete nouns, collective nouns and so on. As you read the following sections about domains and dimensions, you should start to notice that grammar and semantics play an important role in the meaning of well-being. I have chosen to present well-being with the hyphen for the main reason that I see *well* and *being* as representing my understanding of the concept. For example, *well* relates to a range of domains and *being* relates to existence and focuses on the philosophical aspect of the concept which is often neglected in discussions about well-being. You will notice in this chapter that *wellbeing* is sometimes written without the hyphen and this reflects the original quotes. Ereaut and Whiting (2008) state that wellbeing will become the norm as e-mail became email.

Individual/group task

Consider what well-being means to you?
How would you define well-being?
Does well-being have the same meaning for different age groups?

Well-being domains

Various well-being domains also known as types are used to describe well-being, which help to provide some clarity about its meaning. For example, adjectives are often used, such as 'emotional' well-being, 'social' well-being, 'physical' well-being, 'economic' well-being to name but a few. In 2003, Pollard and Lee (2003) conducted a systematic review of well-being and identified five domains, namely

- physical,
- psychological,
- cognitive,
- social and
- economic well-being.

In 2009, Fauth and Thompson (2009) identified four domains, namely

- physical well-being,
- mental health,
- emotional and social well-being,
- cognitive and language development and school performance, and
- beliefs.

Then in 2010, Statham and Chase (2010) identified three domains, namely

- emotional,
- physical and
- social well-being.

The Office for National Statistics (ONS) devised a framework for measuring well-being, which includes ten domains applicable to all age groups (ONS, 2015), but it highlights that measurement tools vary for the age groups (ONS, 2014). Therefore, many domains exist and there is no consensus.

In terms of well-being domains and policy which relate to children and young people, there is usually more focus on emotional and physical well-being and mental health and well-being. As a nation, Wales is interesting because it has recently introduced two well-being Acts, namely the Social Services and Well-being (Wales) Act 2014 and the Well-being of Future Generations (Wales) Act 2015. Both Acts focus on people having a say about what matters to them, and they focus on the present and future lives of all citizens. However, on closer scrutiny of policy documents in Wales that relate to children and young people, social well-being is often omitted. This omission is important because the nature of social well-being incorporates a range of social skills but specifically pro-social behaviour (Fauth and Thompson, 2009). According to Eisenberg (2003), pro-social behaviour is an important aspect of positive development, and if social well-being is not explicitly communicated in policy this suggests that a widespread negative view towards children may still exist (Haworth and Hart, 2007). Therefore, it is paramount that adults listen authentically to children and young people and value their contributions despite implicit messages in policy.

A dominant health and well-being and physical well-being focus in education-related policy supports Clack's (2012) argument that schools are being targeted to tackle health inequalities and various other societal ills. Others explain that the emotional domain is usually privileged in education-related policy because there are "powerful links in the human mind between emotion and cognition" (Whitebread, 2012, p. 28). Moreover, Craft et al. (2008) claim that "positive emotional states are necessary for most transferable learning, playfulness, discovery and invention" (p. 127).

Individual/group task

Are certain domains more dominant than others in your setting or placement? What domains are evident in the following policy documents relating to children and young people within the United Kingdom?

(1) Department for Education. 2019. *Keeping children safe in education: statutory guidance for schools and colleges.* London: Department for Education.
(2) Department for Education. 2018. *Working together to safeguard children: a guide to inter-agency working to safeguard and promote the welfare of children.* London: Department for Education.
(3) Department for Education. 2018. *Mental health and wellbeing provision in schools Review of published policies and information.* London: Department for Education.
(4) Department of Health. 2017. *Co-operating to safeguard children and young people in Northern Ireland.* Northern Ireland: Department of Health.
(5) Scottish Government. 2017. *Getting it right for every child (GIRFEC).* Scotland: Scottish Government.
(6) Welsh Government. 2013. *Building a brighter future: early years and childcare plan.* Cardiff: Welsh Government.

Subjective and objective dimensions of well-being

The two overarching dimensions of well-being, which are commonly associated with the concept, are the subjective and objective kind. For example, the subjective dimension perceives well-being as an *abstract* noun, whereas the objective dimension perceives well-being as a *concrete* noun, as in something you can see or hear. The subjective dimension tends to have an unfixed meaning and thought to be difficult to measure, whereas the objective dimension tends to have a fixed meaning and thought to be measurable (Ereaut and Whiting, 2008). Gasper (2010) suggests that nouns (in this case well-being) are typically reified which means making an abstract concept more concrete. He further argues that well-being is not a "definite single thing, or just two things – 'subjective well-being' and 'objective well-being' – or any number of things" (p. 352).

Since 2005, The Children's Society has been researching young people's subjective well-being and describe subjective well-being "as a positive state of mind in which a person feels good about life as a whole and its constituent parts, such as their relationships with others, the environments that they inhabit and how they see themselves" (The Children's Society, 2018, p. 9). UNICEF also

Table 1.1   The similarities and differences between the two most commonly reported dimensions of well-being

Differences Between subjective and objective well-being	
Subjective dimension	*Objective dimension*
Difficult/impossible to define	Can be defined
Unfixed definition	Fixed definition
Abstract noun	Concrete noun
Difficult to quantify/not measurable	Can be quantified/is measurable
Interpretivist stance	Positivist stance
Similarities Between subjective and objective well-being	
Complex	
Fluctuates and changes	
Based on people's values	

reports on subjective and objective well-being and use objective indicators such as poverty rates, infant mortality rates, low birth weight, immunisation rates, the Programme for International Student Assessment (PISA) results and the number of children enrolled in pre-school to report on well-being (UNICEF, 2013). These measures are known as proxy indicators and are used when you cannot measure exactly what you want or need. For example, when you cannot measure someone's subjective well-being, proxy indicators can be helpful. The aim should be to include objective and subjective data, which provide a comprehensive picture of well-being (McLellan and Steward, 2015).

According to Mashford-Scott et al. (2012), professionals working with younger children acknowledge both dimensions. Although they suggest the objective dimension is a more dominant perspective because "it serves to quantify wellbeing; making it more measurable" (Mashford-Scott et al., 2012, p. 239). The objective dimension is associated with a child demonstrating positive and negative behaviours, various skills and achievements. What is noteworthy is that the differences between the two dimensions are more often communicated. Table 1.1 shows that both dimensions share similarities and differences and therefore one should not be more dominant than the other.

Individual/group task

Is well-being reified in order to make it more measurable?
What are the implications of reifying well-being?

Leading discourses of well-being

Discourses can be described as "more-or-less coherent, systematically-organised ways of talking or writing, each underpinned by a set of beliefs, assumptions and values" (Ereaut and Whiting, 2008, p. 10). Well-being discourses are traditionally rooted in disciplines such as philosophy, psychology and economics. Philosophical discourses of well-being are associated with Greek Philosophers such as Aristippus of Cyrene, Plato and Aristotle and have been around for centuries (Ryan and Deci, 2001; Raghavan and Alexandrova, 2015). Generally, there are four different ways of understanding well-being within philosophy and these are known as:

(1) hedonism/mental states discourse,
(2) eudaimonism/flourishing discourse,
(3) needs-based/objectivist discourse and
(4) desire-based/preference satisfaction discourse.

The first two discourses generally relate to feelings and functioning whereas the last two relate to factors that contribute to well-being. Hedonism/mental states discourse is about feelings of happiness and pleasure (Ryan and Deci, 2001), whereas the eudaimonism/flourishing discourse is about fulfilment and leading a purposeful and meaningful life. Ryan and Deci (2001) cite the work of Waterman (1993) and claim "eudaimonia occurs when people's life activities are most congruent or meshing with deeply held values and are holistically or fully engaged. Under such circumstances people would feel intensely alive and authentic, existing as who they really are" (p. 146).

Proponents of the needs-based/objectivist discourse believe there are numerous underlying, necessary conditions for well-being to develop. Prerequisites such as, "health, income, education, freedom and so on" (Thompson and Marks, 2006, p. 9) are considered to be contributors to well-being.

The following explanation of well-being contains at least three different discourses, the hedonic/mental states discourse*, the eudaimonic/flourishing discourse** and the needs-based/objectivist discourse***:

> *well-being is a positive, social and mental state; it is not just the absence of pain, discomfort and incapacity. It requires that basic needs are met, **that individuals have a sense of purpose, that they feel able to achieve important personal goals and participate in society. ***It is enhanced by conditions that include supportive personal relationships, strong and inclusive communities, good health, financial and personal security, rewarding employment and a healthy and attractive environment.
>
> (Welsh Government, 2011, p. 46)

The desire-based/preference satisfaction discourse is understood by people satisfying their wants and desires. It broadly means that the more someone does something that makes them feel good, the more their well-being will increase (Thompson and Marks, 2006).

Psychology is another leading discipline that helps to further understand the concept of well-being. Even though 'humanistic' psychologists such as Rogers and Maslow and leaders of the 'positive' psychology movement Csikszentmihalyi and Seligman support the eudaimonic discourse (McLellan and Steward, 2015), it is thought that the positive psychology movement is more associated with developments in understanding well-being (Dodge et al., 2012). Around the 1960s, psychologists became very interested in measuring well-being and started investigating correlates of happiness in adults. This led to subjective well-being and happiness being used interchangeably (McLellan and Steward, 2015). Many psychologists support the view that subjective well-being encompasses two different discourses. First, the affect discourse which is about positive and negative emotions and feelings (McLellan and Steward, 2015). Second, the life satisfaction discourse where a person reflects on aspects of their life and makes a cognitive evaluation of their experience. This second discourse of subjective well-being is also referred to as an evaluation-based discourse (Thompson and Marks, 2006).

In the last decade or so McLellan and Steward (2015) suggest that the discipline of economics has been "championing the importance of well-being...by identifying well-being as a key indicator of the state of the nation" (p. 308). The success of a country was and still is traditionally measured using "standard macro-economic statistics" (Organisation for Economic Co-operation and Development [OECD], 2011, p. 14) such as Gross Domestic Product (GDP). However, GDP is an objective measure of economic growth and only provides part of a picture and it was being repeatedly used as a standard measure for people's well-being, life satisfaction and quality of life. But economists, Sen and Stiglitz, recognised that another discipline was needed to gain a better understanding of someone's well-being and looked to psychology. Some believe that economists turned to psychology because it is a discipline that focuses on "the scientific study of human mind and behaviour" (McLellan and Steward, 2015, p. 308) and is more associated with the measurement of concepts. Clack (2012) suggests that dismissing philosophy may ignore "the complex and often messy reality of being human" (Clack, 2012, p. 507).

Even though there are different understandings of well-being within philosophy, psychology and economics, Axford (2009) states that in order to gain a clearer picture of its nature, we should consider adopting more than one discourse of well-being.

Individual/group task

How beneficial do you think it is to adopt more than one discourse of well-being?

From reading the chapter so far, to what extent has your understanding of well-being changed or been extended and/or challenged?

Exploring child well-being discourses

As discussed above, well-being discourses are traditionally rooted in disciplines such as philosophy, psychology and economics. However, there is a weak theoretical underpinning associated with child well-being and a lack of research into understanding the conceptual nature of well-being (Pollard and Lee, 2003; McLaughlin, 2008; Statham and Chase, 2010; Mashford-Scott et al., 2012; Raghavan and Alexandrova, 2015). It could be argued that Amerijckx and Humblet (2014) and Raghavan and Alexandrova (2015) have made significant contributions in understanding child well-being.

In 2014, Amerijckx and Humblet (2014) conducted a study to gain some consensus about the concept of child well-being. They reviewed 209 papers in total from five databases and identified five discourses with contrasting aspects. Some of these aspects were dominant and some were under-represented (see Figure 1.1). Their work demonstrates the complex and multi-dimensional nature of well-being. In 2015, Raghavan and Alexandrova (2015) set out to theorise child well-being and developed the *two sources* theory focusing on the *present* and the *future* but in essence it resembles discourse three in Figure 1.1.

Child well-being discourses	
Under-represented aspects	Dominant aspects
Discourse one	
Positive	Negative
(e.g. strengths, capabilities, rights holders, agents of change)	(e.g. deficit view, difficulties, weaknesses, protection, vulnerable)
Discourse two	
Subjective	Objective
(e.g. feelings, thoughts, opinions)	(e.g. indicators, outcomes, statistics)
Discourse three	
State	Process
(e.g. present, here and now, active citizens, hedonic)	(e.g. future, long term, future adults, eudaimonic)
Discourse four	
Spiritual	Material
(e.g. non-material, psychological resources)	(e.g. physical resources, financial)
Discourse five	
Community	Individual
(e.g. larger groups, classroom, collective)	(e.g. individual child & personal circumstances)

Figure 1.1   Five child well-being discourses (adapted from Amerijckx and Humblet, 2014).

Amerijckx and Humblet (2014) found that aspects in the right-hand column (in Figure 1.1) such as *negative, objective, process, material and individual* were more dominant and aspects in the left-hand column, such as *positive, subjective, state, spiritual and collective* were under-represented aspects. Mashford-Scott et al. (2012) argue that when the objective aspect is more dominant, this "limits our ability to understand, measure and promote children's well-being in ways that are meaningful to children and their day-to-day lives" (p. 239). They also suggest that a more dominant focus on the objective aspect of well-being is closely linked to a specific image or perception of the child. They suggest an image that is "immature…lacking insight…and incapable of acting or speaking on their own behalf" (Mashford-Scott et al., 2012, p. 240). Therefore, the subjective aspect might be under-represented because some people take-it-for-granted that children "lack the capacity to contribute to their own well-being or do not have a valid and valuable contribution to make" (Lansdown, 2001, p. 93).

Arguably, there is a general feeling that children are incapable, and not sufficiently expert in communicating a personal view of themselves, and their world around them. Therefore, an alternative view would involve drawing upon the new sociology of childhood where children and young people are perceived as agents of change and are provided with the opportunity to act upon their world, where they are viewed as demonstrating "extraordinary competence from birth" (Waller, 2009, p. 7). The new sociology of childhood also advocates that children and young people are experts in their own lives; this concept is explored more in Chapter 3.

Individual/group task

What do you think is needed in order for professionals to pay more attention to the under-represented aspects in Figure 1.1?

Linking knowledge and understanding of child development and well-being theory

It is important to note that traditional discourses of well-being were constructed at a time in history when childhood was not viewed as a distinct life phase, and limited understanding existed about the concept of childhood. It was around the end of the fifteenth century that a more contemporary understanding of childhood started to emerge (Brockliss and Montgomery, 2013). This explains why Raghavan and Alexandrova (2015) claim that it is unlikely that philosophical discourses of well-being will not straightforwardly extend to children because they were not written with them in mind. Even though this is a reasonable claim the following discussion shows how existing knowledge and understanding of child development relates to some of the leading discourses of well-being.

In relation to the hedonic/mental states discourse within philosophy, babies as young as 2 months show emotions including happiness and pleasure through facial gestures (Neaum, 2010). Also from around the age of 12 months, young children start to "recognise other people's emotions and moods and express their own" (Neaum, 2010, p. 56). Whitebread (2012) carefully points out that research "probably under-estimates the level of understanding of young children about others' psychological states and characteristics" (p. 46). At around the age of 4 years, children usually reflect and communicate their feelings in various ways (Neaum, 2010). As children develop and gain more life experience they are more capable of understanding and expressing their emotions and are able to "think about themselves in more complex ways...they can also experience more than one feeling at a time" (Levine and Munsch, 2016, p. 428). Therefore, it could be argued that hedonic perspectives relate to children in some way.

In relation to the eudaimonic/flourishing discourse within philosophy, there is evidence to suggest that this discourse also relates to children. However, this discourse is not always considered applicable to children because it encompasses concepts such as living authentically, being true to yourself, realisation of potential and self-acceptance which are abstract ideas that very young children would find difficult to understand (Dodge et al., 2012). Nonetheless, 5-year olds "have a good sense of the past, present and future" (Neaum, 2010, p. 49), and many child development textbooks state that from around the age of 7 to 8 years, children start to think in the abstract (Neaum, 2010). The Children's Society (2018) describe eudaimonic well-being as living a worthwhile life and typically report the eudaimonic well-being of those aged between 8 and 15 years.

In terms of the needs-based/objectivist discourse situated within the discipline of philosophy Raghavan and Alexandrova (2015) claim this is the closest in nature to child well-being. They explain that in order for children to thrive and make progress they require underlying conditions or prerequisites that allow them to do this. An example of this can be found in the Australian early years learning framework for 0- to 5-year olds which states sound wellbeing results from the satisfaction of basic needs - the need for tenderness and affection; security and clarity; social recognition; to feel competent; physical needs and for meaning in life.

(Adapted from Laevers 1994) (Australian Government, 2009, p. 48)

It is widely accepted that forming attachments and positive relationships are essential for healthy learning and development (Page et al., 2013), which explains why many believe the needs-based/objectivist discourse is closest in nature to child well-being.

The two discourses within psychology, namely affect and life satisfaction, also relate to children. As previously mentioned, young children are very capable of communicating positive and negative emotions in a variety of ways – verbal, non-verbal such as through paint, collage, role-play to name but a few. However, making a judgement about life satisfaction which involves making a cognitive evaluation of aspects of their life might be difficult for younger children, particularly when they have less experience to draw upon and have a tendency to live in the here and now. However, as previously mentioned, by 5 years of age, children have the ability to understand and report on the past, present and future so it is possible for children to make cognitive evaluations of aspects that matter to them and their life.

Studies that report children's subjective well-being usually focus on around 8-year olds and above. The Growing up in Scotland (GUS) study state "little is known about the importance of relationships, material and other influences on subjective well-being in children younger than ten years old" (Parkes et al., 2014, p. 4). Therefore, for the purpose of the GUS study, Parkes et al. (2014) adapted Huebner's multi-dimensional Life Satisfaction Scale for 7-year olds.

This discussion shows that many of the leading discourses of well-being within philosophy and psychology relate to children and young people in some way which raises the question whether a theory of child-well-being is needed.

Individual/group task

Do we need a theory for child well-being if existing knowledge and understanding of child development relates to a range of well-being explanations? If yes, how would this be useful for professionals working with children and young people?

Conclusion

Well-being is a complex concept and is understood and communicated in different ways. It is also difficult to define as many factors inter-relate but the chapter provides an in-depth discussion and helps you to consider the meaning of well-being. In order to understand the concept, it is useful to think about well-being in terms of the various domains, its dimensions (subjective and objective) and discourses. Its disciplinary origins are rooted in philosophy, psychology and economics and therefore many discourses exist. The chapter shows how one explanation of well-being can include at least three discourses from different disciplines, which explains why there might be confusion and uncertainty about the concept.

Many argue there is a weak theoretical underpinning associated with child well-being, and Raghavan and Alexandrova (2015) state that a theory of child well-being does not currently exist because long-standing discourses, such as those within philosophy, were not originally written with children in mind. However, this chapter demonstrates that existing knowledge and understanding of child development relates to long-standing well-being discourses within psychology and psychology, particularly when framed within a positive development lens where children and young people are viewed as competent and able. Therefore, this chapter concludes that a theory of child well-being is not needed for the time being. This conclusion raises the question about what is needed in terms of child well-being. The author proposes that developments are needed in understanding children's subjective well-being, particularly for younger children. In terms of older children and young people, their voices need to be further acknowledged and acted upon.

Summary points

- A vast amount of well-being domains (also known as types of well-being) are in use. Therefore, in order to clarify the meaning, adjectives should be used to describe the type of well-being.
- The two dimensions most commonly associated with well-being are the subjective and objective kind. The differences between the two dimensions are more often communicated but they also share many similarities which need to be acknowledged.
- Well-being is understood in many different ways and theoretical explanations are rooted in disciplines such as psychology, philosophy and economics.
- Amerijckx and Humblet (2014) and Raghavan and Alexandrova (2015) have contributed to understanding and developing a discourse of child well-being.
- Long-standing explanations of well-being relate to children and young people when viewed with a positive child development lens.

Recommended reading

Lewis, A. 2019. Examining the concept of well-being and early childhood: adopting multi-disciplinary perspectives. *Journal of Early Childhood Research.* https://doi.org/10.1177%2F1476718X19860553.

Morris, I. 2009. *Teaching happiness and well-being in schools.* London: Continuum International Publishing Group.

Roberts, R. 2010. *Wellbeing from Birth.* London: SAGE Publications Ltd.

Watson, D., Emery, C., Bayliss, P., Boushel, M. and McInnes, K. 2012. *Children's social and emotional wellbeing in school.* Bristol: The Policy Press.

References

Amerijckx, P. and Humblet, G. 2014. Child well-being: what does it mean? *Children & Society* 28(5), pp. 404–415.

Australian Government. 2009. *Belonging, being and becoming.* Australia: Australian Government Department of Education, Employment and Workplace.

Axford, N. 2009. Child well-being through different lenses: why concept matters. *Child and Family Social Work* 14(3), pp. 372–383.

Brockliss, L. and Montgomery, H. 2013. Childhood: a historical approach. In: Kehily, J. (ed.), *Understanding childhood: a cross-disciplinary approach.* Bristol: The Policy Press. pp. 53–98.

The Children's Society. 2018. https://www.childrenssociety.org.uk/sites/default/files/the_good_childhood_report_full_2018.pdf [Accessed on 12 July 2019].

Clack, B. 2012. What difference does it make? Philosophical perspectives on the nature of well-being and the role of educational practice. *Research Paper in Education* 27(4), pp. 497–512.

Coleman, J. 2009. Well-being in schools: empirical measure, or politicians' dream? *Oxford Review of Education* 35(3), pp. 281–292.

Craft, A., Cremin, T. and Burnard, P. 2008. *Creative learning 3–11 and how we document it.* Stoke on Trent: Trentham Books.

Dodge, R., Daly, A., Huyton, J. and Sanders, L. 2012. The challenge of defining wellbeing. *International Journal of Wellbeing* 2(3), pp. 222–235.

Eisenberg, N. 2003. Prosocial behavior, empathy and sympathy. In: Bornstein, M., Davidson, L., Keyes, C., and Moore, K. (eds.), *Well-being: positive development across the life course.* London: Lawrence Erlbaum Associates Publishers. pp. 253–265.

Ereaut, G. and Whiting, R. 2008. *What do we mean by wellbeing and why might it matter?* London: DCSF.

Fauth, B. and Thompson, M. 2009. *Young children's well-being: indicators and domains of development.* London: National Children's Bureau. Highlight no. 252.

Gasper, D. 2010. Understanding the diversity of conceptions of well-being and quality of life. *The Journal of Socio-Economics* 39(3), pp. 351–360.

Haworth, J. and Hart, G. 2007. *Well-being: individual, community and social perspectives.* Hampshire: Palgrave Macmillan.

Lansdown, G. 2001. Children's welfare and children's rights. In: Foley, P., Roche, J. and Tucker, S. (eds.), *Children in society: contemporary theory, policy and practice.* Hampshire: Palgrave Macmillan. pp. 87–99.

La Placa, V., McNaught, A. and Knight, A. 2013. Discourse of wellbeing in research and practice. *International Journal of Wellbeing* 3(1), pp. 116–125.

Laevers, F. 1994. *Defining and assessing quality in Early Childhood education.* Studia Paedagogica. Leuven: Leuven University Press.

Levine, L. and Munsch, J. 2016. *Child development from infancy to adolescence.* London: SAGE Publications Ltd.

Mashford-Scott, A., Church, A. and Tayler, C. 2012. Seeking children's perspectives on their wellbeing in early childhood settings. *International Journal of Early Childhood* 44(3), pp. 231–247.

Mayr, T. and Ulich, M. 1999. Children's well-being in day care centres: an exploratory study. *International Journal of Early Years Education* 7(3), pp. 229–239.

McLaughlin, C. 2008. Emotional well-being and its relationship to schools and classrooms: a critical reflection. *British Journal of Guidance and Counselling* 36(4), pp. 353–366.

McLellan, R. and Steward, S. 2015. Measuring children and young people's wellbeing in the school context. *Cambridge Journal of Education* 45(3), pp. 307–332.

Morrow, V. and Mayall, B. 2009. What is wrong with children's well-being in the UK? Questions of meaning and measurement. *Journal of Social Welfare and Family Law* 31(3), pp. 217–229.

Neaum, S. 2010. *Childhood studies for early childhood studies.* Exeter: Learning Matters Ltd.

New Economics Foundation. 2009. *A guide to measuring children's well-being.* London: New Economics Foundation.

OECD. 2011. *How's life? Measuring well-being.* Paris: OECD Publishing.

ONS. 2014. Measuring national wellbeing – exploring the wellbeing of Children in the UK. Newport: ONS.

ONS. 2015. http://www.neighbourhood.statistics.gov.uk/HTMLDocs/dvc146/wrapper.html [Accessed on 21 December 2015].

Page, J., Clare, A. and Nutbrown, C. 2013. *Working with babies and children.* London: SAGE Publications Ltd.

Parkes, A., Sweeting, H. and Wright, D. 2014. *Growing up in Scotland.* Edinburgh: Scottish Government.

Pollard, E. and Lee, P. 2003. Child well-being: a systematic review of the literature. *Social Indicators Research* 61(1), pp. 59–78.

Raghavan, R. and Alexandrova, A. 2015. Toward a theory of child well-being. *Social Indicators Research* 121(3), pp. 887–902.

Reber, A. 1995. *Dictionary of psychology.* 2nd ed. Harmonsworth: Penguin.

Ryan, R. and Deci, E. 2001. On happiness and human potentials: a review of research on hedonic and eudaimonic well-being. *Annual Review Psychology* 52(1), pp. 141–166.

Statham, J. and Chase, E. 2010. *Childhood wellbeing: a brief overview.* United Kingdom: Childhood Wellbeing Research Centre.

Thompson, S. and Marks, N. 2006. *Measuring well-being in policy: issues and applications.* London: New Economics Foundation.

UNICEF. 2013. *Child well-being in rich countries: a comparative overview.* Italy: UNICEF.

Waller, T. 2009. *An introduction to early childhood.* London: SAGE Publications Ltd.

Waterman, A.S. 1993. Two conceptions of happiness: contrasts of personal expressiveness (eudaimonia) and hedonic enjoyment. *Journal of Personality & Social Psycholgy* 64(4), pp. 678–691.

Welsh Government. 2011. *Children and young people's wellbeing monitor for Wales.* Cardiff: Welsh Government.

White, S. and Abeyasekera, A. 2014. *Wellbeing and quality of life assessment: a practical guide.* Warwickshire: Practical Action Publishing Ltd.

Whitebread, D. 2012. *Developmental psychology & early childhood education.* London: SAGE Publications Ltd.

2 The concept of resilience and implications for interventions in schools

Lydia Lewis, Emma Ormerod and Kathryn Ecclestone

Introduction

As part of wider interest in well-being, the concept of resilience has become popular in many policy and practitioner discourses and across diverse policy areas. In the social policy arena, it has become especially popular in education and mental health (Ecclestone and Lewis, 2014). In these areas, in the UK context, the idea of enhancing children's resilience has grown since the late 1990s, legitimised by a series of policy-sponsored psycho-emotional interventions targeted at all children and young people. This trend is also prevalent in many other European countries, the USA and Australia.

Amidst growing social and political concern about children and young people's mental health, claims to build or enhance resilience are highly appealing. Yet, as we show in this chapter, the ubiquity and ever-widening scope of the concept of resilience in policy and everyday conversation belies its contested meanings. We describe how these meanings have important moral and practical implications in educational and other social policy settings. Our critique of the policy discourse of resilience and of school-based interventions claimed to build resilience highlights their potential educational and wider social consequences. We conclude by outlining alternative approaches to supporting the well-being of children and young people in schools that may be considered more educationally and socially progressive. We locate our discussion in the context of UK, and particularly English, government policy on mental health and well-being in schools.

The policy context

The concept of 'resilience' has become increasingly popular in diverse social policy and practitioner discourses (e.g. Chandler 2014). In the UK, it is especially prevalent in the areas of mental health and education (see Ecclestone and Lewis, 2014; Lewis et al., 2015). The election of the New Labour government in 1997 led to enthusiastic claims for 'evidence-based practice' and 'What Works' initiatives to improve social, educational and health outcomes. Influenced by diverse psychological approaches and ideas including cognitive behavioural therapy (CBT), person-centred counselling, mindfulness and positive psychology, a series of policy-sponsored interventions emerged in social, educational and community settings from the early 2000s onwards (Ecclestone and Hayes, 2009a; Ecclestone and Lewis, 2014). Chapters 8 and 9 explore some of these approaches in further detail.

An increasing educational focus on resilience has been part of a wider agenda to promote young people's social and emotional 'well-being' (National Institute for Health and Care

Excellence [NICE], 2009). In part, this was a response to "reports of high levels of mental health problems in children and young people and the linking of this to poor educational outcomes" (Lewis et al., 2015, p. 38, citing Coleman, 2009). In both primary and secondary schools, interventions adopting an organisation-wide approach to developing social and emotional skills for all pupils (universal interventions) have been implemented, alongside targeted ones, such as nurture groups, for those experiencing specific difficulties, including mental health problems (see Rawdin 2016; Brown, 2018; Goldberg et al., 2019). Within these, resilience often features alongside other aspects of well-being such as confidence, self-esteem, problem-solving, attentiveness and good relationships with others (e.g. NICE, 2009), and is constructed, variously, as a skill, attribute, mindset or capability that can be taught and transferred to different life situations.

Since the late 1990s, English policy and academic discourses in this area have fluctuated hugely between 'social and emotional learning', 'emotional well-being', 'character' and, in the past 5 years, with the introduction of the Special Educational Need and Disabilities (SEND) Code of Practice (DfE & DoH, 2015) and the Green Paper discussed below, 'mental health' (see Ecclestone, 2012). Policy discourses in the last decade have privileged resilience as a key trait or attribute in character education, with this considered a way of addressing social disadvantage and social problems (e.g. DfE, 2019; see also NatCen Social Research & the National Children's Bureau Research and Policy Team, 2017, p. 3). In this shifting discursive and practice terrain, notions of 'resilience building' are invariably accompanied by concerns about psycho-emotional vulnerability.

The development of resilience in educational settings parallels its rise in mental health policy contexts where it has featured alongside the allied (and extensively critiqued) concept of 'recovery' (Harper and Speed, 2012).In the *Future in Mind* report (Children and Young People's Mental Health and Wellbeing Taskforce [CYPMHWT], 2015), schools are urged to develop universal 'whole school approaches' that develop resilience. In *The Five Year Forward View for Mental Health* (Mental Health Taskforce, 2016, p. 23), the approach set out in this report is endorsed as "a model for wider system reform" involving local authorities and social policy and voluntary sectors, working together to build resilience, promote mental health and enable access to mental health services for children and young people. A national concordat to take a prevention-focused approach to improving the public's mental health was subsequently developed (Public Health England, 2017).

In the last few years, escalating public, media and political concerns about children and young people's mental health have been fuelled by reports suggesting rapid and big increases in emotional distress and mental health problems among this population (e.g. The Children's Society, 2019; Hazell, 2019; Young 2019; compare Sadler et al., 2019; for a critique of claims that mental illness has been increasing in societies like Britain, see Busfield, 2012). In 2017, the DfE and Department of Health (DoH) issued a Green Paper on Children and Young People's Mental Health. This proposed to establish designated Senior Leads for mental health in all schools and colleges, new Mental Health Support Teams to work in schools, supervised by NHS Child and Adolescent Mental Health Services (CAMHS) staff, and to pilot a four-week waiting time for CAMHS. Schools and colleges are encouraged "to develop practice in building resilience and supporting pupils with mental health issues as part of their work in removing barriers to social mobility" (p. 28).

In 2018, the Government committed to take forward all proposals in the Green Paper. One outcome is the piloting of university-based courses for new Education Mental Health Practitioner (EMHP) roles that incorporate teaching in cognitive-behavioural techniques for self-help and self-management. The Government also requires mental health to be part of the compulsory Personal,

Social and Health Education (PSHE) curriculum. The proposals are being delivered through joint work between the DfE and the DoH (now called the Department of Health and Social Care), whose 2019 *NHS Long Term Plan* defines priorities for CAMHS, centred on improving access to services within a broader prevention agenda (see NHS England, 2019, p. 51).

Individual/group task

What understandings of resilience seem to emerge in policy discourses and initiatives such as those summarised above?

What might be the pros and cons of those understandings in educational settings?

Defining resilience

In social research, resilience has generally been understood as a process involving positive adaptation in the face of adversity (Luthar and Cicchetti, 2000; Ungar, 2015). More specifically, Windle (2011, p. 152) defines it as "the process of negotiating, managing and adapting to significant sources of stress or trauma". Definitions therefore involve an input perspective (exposure to adversity or risk, where environmental and experiential factors have included poverty, domestic violence, child abuse or neglect, and loss of a parent) and an outcome perspective that considers "whether coping mechanisms lead to outcomes within or above the expected range" (Mohaupt, 2009, p. 65). Such outcomes may include educational achievement, social competence and emotional or behavioural adjustment. 'Positive adaptation' is defined in relation to demonstration of these or by the "absence of emotional or behavioural maladjustment" (Luthar and Cicchetti, 2000, p. 858). Longer-term educational, occupational, health (including mental health) and social (relationship) outcomes are also sometimes considered. If an individual or group achieves positive outcomes despite adversity, resilience is inferred.

From this perspective, resilience is "a process rather than a static concept or an individual characteristic", psychological attribute or trait (Mohaupt, 2009, p. 65). Within a social ecological framework, generating resilience involves transactions between an individual and their environment (Ungar, 2015). Here, resilience exists in this transactional space rather than being a property of individuals. This dynamic view avoids regarding resilience as a fixed personal characteristic or individual attribute. Instead, resilience is seen as fluid, context-dependent, socially situated and influenced by diverse environmental factors (Ungar, 2008; Mohaupt, 2009). This means that both resilience and risk alter as children's circumstances change (Rutter, 1990) and "across the life course, the experience of resilience will vary" (Windle, 2011, p. 152).

A social understanding, then, sees resilience as generated within and through "children's interactions with multiple reciprocating systems", such as schools and families (Ungar et al., 2013, p. 349). Researchers often refer to 'protective factors' – supportive aspects of children's lives that, despite adversity, help them cope and achieve good outcomes despite adversity. These protective factors operate at multiple, interacting levels. They include the individual (internal factors such as social or intellectual skills and orientations); the immediate environment, including the family (e.g. relationships with parents and other care-givers); the wider social environment, including external institutions such as the school, and the community; and national social institutions for education, health and welfare (Burchardt and Huerta, 2008; Mohaupt, 2009). As Windle (2011, p. 152) explains "assets and resources within the individual, their life and environment facilitate the capacity for adaptation and 'bouncing back' in the face of adversity". External institutional protective factors include "the strength of social support networks and the ability to extend these networks, having positive school experiences and opportunities to engage in social life" (Mohaupt, 2009, p. 65).

Individual/group task

Reflection

Consider what changing circumstances are likely to influence resilience for children and young people.

Conceptual questions

What do you understand by a policy or professional 'discourse'?

What might be some ethical and political implications of different ways of understanding 'resilience'?

Considering that meanings of resilience are contested, what questions surround the idea of 'evidence-based' interventions in this area?

What are the political and practice implications of locating concern about resilience in a wider context of public panic about mental health?

Critical evaluation of resilience in policy and professional discourses and research

As the discussion above indicates, there are political, moral and ethical dimensions and ramifications of different definitions of resilience. A key criticism is that although the concept of resilience is ostensibly positive and helpful in focusing on children's strengths, it depoliticises social problems by turning them into individual ones. In particular, the popularity of 'resilience' can be understood within the political ideology of 'neoliberalism' which has grown since the 1980s to dominate policy perspectives in Western countries. Within this ideology, the state withdraws from collective welfare and social provision and, instead, promotes free markets and competition, and social and political life becomes 'economized' - viewed in economic terms (Brown, 2016). The idea of resilience may be easily co-opted into associated political discourses in which people are diverted out of public health care systems by encouraging self-regulation and self-reliance (Bottrell, 2009; Howell and Voronka, 2012) and people become construed in terms of human capital (Brown, 2016) – how they can serve the market through their knowledge, skills, competencies and other attributes (Westphalen, 1999). Structural inequalities are reframed within individualizing discourses of 'choice', 'empowerment', 'resilience' and so forth that "mask wider societal issues of class, gender and race" (Royle, 2017, p. 63) and shift responsibility for social problems from the state onto individuals (see Boynden and Cooper, 2007; Harrison, 2012; Howell and Voronka, 2012). Encouraging people to look inward for resilience also discourages collective political action to confront social injustice (Howell and Voronka, 2012). These processes are sometimes referred to in terms of the shaping of the neo-liberal subject or citizen (e.g. Aranda et al., 2012; McLeod, 2012).

In this neoliberal context, Spohrer and Bailey (2018: online) link the discourses of character and resilience in English education policy to a logic of human capital enhancement and an "intensification of the demand for self-government and self-investment", especially for those from disadvantaged backgrounds (see also Garrett, 2017). For example the DfE (2019, p. 5) views developing aspects of character and resilience as helping the most disadvantaged compete in the labour market. At the same time, however, the ideological effects of resilience described above are partly achieved through its widespread use in social policy discourse as something everyone needs to develop, rather than restricting its use to the context of serious adversity (see Ecclestone and Lewis, 2014). For example, in the consultation document cited above, the DfE (2019, p. 5) defines resilience as "being able to bounce back from the knocks that life inevitably brings to all of us". This inclusive framing of resilience sounds progressive. Yet, it overlooks the social and economic context and the forms of adversity and hardship which give rise to the need for resilience (British Psychological Society [BPS], 2019), painting matters of social inequality and social injustice out of the picture.

Research on resilience has similarly been criticised for its reductionist individual-level focus, which includes claims that resilience is a trait that can be trained and transferred to different contexts, thereby producing a distorted perspective that overlooks or downplays the complexities and social constraints of children's lives (Bottrell, 2009; Mohaupt, 2009; Royle, 2017). There is some research on resilience at a communal and community level (e.g. Barnes and Morris, 2007; Ungar et al., 2008; Mguni and Bacon, 2010; Norman, 2012), but this tends to be under-represented in the academic literature (Mohaupt, 2008; Royle, 2017). And while, as discussed above, resilience research has theorised the concept in multi-level terms, in practice the wider influences and power inequalities are often reduced to the psychological level, for example through ideas of self-efficacy or sense of control (Harper and Speed, 2012). Again, then, there is an incumbent 'responsibilising' of individuals rather than the state (Boyden and Cooper, 2007; Harper and Speed, 2012; Howell and Voronka, 2012).

Therefore, another dimension of critique relates to the moralising embedded in requiring people to demonstrate resilience as a matter of personal responsibility, "especially when resilience is mistaken as a personal trait rather than a process" (Mohaupt, 2008, p. 67). As Olchawski (2018: online) states, "For children living in poverty and abuse, trying to make them 'resilient' can unfairly place the onus on them to deal with something that should not be happening to them". The discourse of resilience may consequently have pernicious effects on vulnerable citizens with little power. These include burdening individual children and young people with the weight of social problems by encouraging them to intern-alise risk and responsibility (Collin, 2018). Potentially, then, the resilience discourse blames the victim, not only for problems they experience but also for not being resilient.

A resilience perspective is often predicated on "a pre-existing understanding of 'risk' and 'posi-tive' outcomes or adaptation which involve value judgements and assumptions" (Mohaupt, 2009, p. 66). This may be important to counteract moral relativism arising from sensitivity about defining what are desirable or undesirable conditions, behaviours or practices affecting children. However, in judging what constitutes risk or adversity there are dangers of socially pathologising the lives of children and young people, as 'disadvantaged' or 'lacking' in certain respects. Indeed, instead of an 'assets/strengths' model in which children are viewed "in terms of existing capability and the structural inequalities that limit choices and possibilities", resilience perspectives are often "driven by notions of risk, vulnerability and dysfunction" (Royle, 2017, p. 55, citing Ecclestone and Lewis, 2014) and belie a persistent deficit model (Harper and Speed, 2012).

Individualised understandings of resilience, bolstered by a policy perspective that sees it as an aspect of character that children experiencing social disadvantage must develop, can end up "putting the problem in the child" (BPS, 2019). The discourse of resilience suggests that children, rather than educational approaches, institutions or regimes, or wider educational and social systems, are problematic and need to change. Furthermore, approaches to building resilience for children and young people "may ignore the social situations from which behaviours manifest" (Royle, 2017, p. 55). In this manner, resilience discourse helps to ensure maintenance of the schooling status quo and the wider social order – it is inherently conservative (see Garrett, 2017, p. 151).

Following these arguments, expectations about what policy-makers and professionals regard as positive outcomes, and the pathways to achieving these, are highly normative. Their power to define resilience, and the related one of 'recovery' in relation to mental health problems, operates within a moral framework of what constitutes being 'mentally healthy' or 'well adjusted,' with this being the only valued state (see Howell and Voronka, 2012). In the context of emotional distress, the resourcefulness and creativity of certain behaviours for dealing with unliveable situations may be overlooked or pathologised as symptoms of 'mental illness'. There may also be a failure to realise that 'successful' outcomes could come from ostensibly maladaptive or resistant behaviour (Mohaupt, 2009) and from a refusal to conform to or accept existing social arrangements and expectations. This may be understood as 'resistant resilience' associated with challenging the status quo (Bottrell, 2009; Aranda et al., 2012).

Illuminating the culturally bound, moral and political nature of ideas about resilience highlights political struggle and collective action for progressive social change as one way of generating 'resilience'. More broadly, it indicates that understandings of resilience should encompass agency – opportunities to act on and shape our social worlds, and not just be confined to coping with or adapting to these (Edwards, 2007). These ideas are given further consideration below.

Individual/group task: concepts and ethical reflection

What is meant by moral relativism?

How does this relate to the idea of cultural relativism?

Can you think of a social problem where these ways of thinking have been a barrier to effective policy action? How would the problem be viewed differently from a human rights perspective?

How are critiques of moral and cultural relativism relevant to understanding a resilience perspective in social research and social policy?

Interventions that aim to build resilience

Widespread government support for universal approaches to promoting positive mental health and well-being has led to numerous and diverse types of school-based intervention in which resilience is a key strand. Some programmes present their aims explicitly in terms of developing resilience as a mechanism for social and emotional well-being and to prevent mental health problems. Some are rooted in positive psychology (see Seligman et al., 2009) and a cognitive-behavioural, skills-based approach. Here, resilience is depicted as one of "a set of psychological constructs (a slippery mix of attitude, disposition, skill, behaviour and capability)" that comprise emotional well-being and that are "perceived to be teachable and measurable" (Lewis et al., 2015, p. 37). These include "stoicism, emotional literacy (self-awareness, empathy, emotional regulation and management), optimism, altruism and self-esteem" (Lewis et al., 2015, p. 37). Some programmes focus on emotional regulation through step-wise strategies for dealing with upsetting experiences and social problem-solving. Examples in the UK include the UK Resilience Programme, which is derived from the American Penn Resilience Programme (see Challen et al., 2011) and SUMO (Stop, Understand, Move On) (see Royle, 2017; SUMO4Schools, 2019).

Such interventions have associated evidence claims about protective factors which support resilience and are sometimes used as part of whole-school approaches and wider programmes which include community and family-level supports (e.g. Royle, 2017). Nevertheless, claims that the interventions build resilience, and their targeting of individual skills or competencies, can be criticised for over-simplification, with the approach lacking ecological relevance for young people, i.e. integration into the reality of their lives and their cultural contexts (Luthar and Cicchetti, 2000). We would argue that even if the interventions teach useful socio-emotional skills, they offer a very narrow, individualised way of understanding resilience and cannot build it according to the transactional, multi-level understandings discussed earlier.

Consequently, it has been argued that resilience interventions are too 'actor-centred' (Mohaupt, 2009) and fail to take action on environmental influences. Edwards (2007, pp. 257, 259) points out they "rarely recognise the interplay between context and individual, central to even interactionist accounts of development"; "efforts at enhancing resilience at an individual level need to be accompanied by parallel attempts at configuring social practices of support across settings", including the school, family and in the community. She also suggests developing children's agency as an aspect of resilience, for example through employing democratic principles in schools, so children are afforded an active role in constructing the school environment through developing shared values and goals and being involved in decision-making at a range of levels.

From this perspective, active listening and agency-enhancement are integral to student well-being in schools. This is highlighted by criticism of the ways in which the imposition of individually focused resilience interventions position children and young people in ambivalent terms and risk doing vulnerable children a further injustice. As described by Collin (2018, pp. 2–3):

> agentic subjects are … called to action at the same time as they are constrained and have their agency denied. Children and young people must become more resilient, but they are routinely excluded from the processes and institutions which largely define the terms of their relationships to the world.

Seen in the light of agency, some resilience interventions can be viewed as simply behaviour modification and management programmes, involving "prosocialisation to the norm of schooling" (Royle, 2017, p. 59). Well-being interventions have also been theorised as forms of 'therapeutic governance' – a mode of social control concerned with social risk management (Pupavac, 2001) in which governance is exercised through therapeutic discourse and pedagogies that shape people's subjectivities and forms of agency; here, for example, by encouraging children and young people to monitor their own well-being and that of their peers. Crucially, therapeutic governance both encourages and sometimes requires people to see themselves as psychologically vulnerable and to be regarded that way by professionals. One outcome is that therapeutic ideas, assumptions and practices are now normalised in people's everyday lives, organisational cultures and educational settings (see Ecclestone and Hayes, 2009a; Ecclestone and Lewis, 2014) and in educational movements framed by notions of social justice (Ecclestone and Brunila, 2015).

From these critical standpoints, then, and despite the well-meaning intentions of intervention advocates, all kinds of individually focused interventions to promote well-being and resilience are associated with an unhelpful "preoccupation with people's psycho-emotional vulnerability" (Lewis, 2014, p. 359, citing Ecclestone, 2004). Following this argument, therapeutic introspection diminishes possibilities for agency and human potential by detracting from an outward-facing, more potentially liberating focus on subject-based knowledge and learning where people can view the world through a wider social and political lens (Ecclestone, 2007; Ecclestone and Hayes, 2009b).

In light of these concerns, some authors have argued that we should resist the policy discourse of resilience in the context of mental health and well-being (Harper and Speed, 2012) and child development and poverty (Boynden and Cooper, 2007). In a similar vein, many think we should resist the rising use of well-being interventions in schools and challenge the ways in which alarm about mental health is shaping education (Ecclestone, 2007; Ecclestone and Hayes, 2009a; Ecclestone and Rawdin, 2016).

Individual/group task: conceptual questions

What is the meaning of the term 'ideology'?

Do you think that resilience can be a helpful term to support the development of children and young people, or should it be avoided due to its potentially negative ideological effects?

Do you think resilience can and should be developed in schools?

Alternative educational approaches to well-being

In this chapter, we have questioned both the underlying meanings of resilience in educational policy and the claims associated with school-based interventions that promote positive thinking and socio-emotional skills. In particular, we have highlighted questions about the ecological relevance of these interventions and their wider social effects. In this final section, we argue that psycho-behavioural approaches should not be the dominant policy or professional approach to supporting young people's well-being. Instead, the focus needs to be on constructing the environmental conditions for good mental health (Billington et al., 2019).

The aim of a contextual approach is to expand the freedom and opportunities of children and young people through the affordances of their environment, which in schools include the curriculum and educational ethos. As noted earlier, democratic principles may be advocated as part of such a contextual approach. However, different long-running political and philosophical traditions offer competing ideas about how curriculum content, teaching and institutional cultures should be shaped to foster well-being, and about whether education should be explicitly framed by well-being at all.

One approach is a liberal holistic and person-centred standpoint which counters the psychological and behavioural training approaches currently prevalent in schools. Embedded in the educational environment, integrated into the curriculum and humanistic in ethos, this approach emphasises agency development by offering choice and opportunity, providing recognition (value, respect and full humanity), and helping children and young people to generate life resources, including cultural capital (knowledge and learning) and social capital (relationships, networks and community trust) (Lewis, 2014). Here, the onus is on supporting students to access and develop a range of inter-related resources which can help them to navigate difficulties in their lives and to carve out "a path to a life that they value" (Edwards, 2007; Royle, 2017, p. 58). Hence, instead of being a direct, stand-alone educational outcome and aspiration or goal, well-being and resilience are viewed in the context of "objectives concerned with the development of knowledge, understanding, autonomy and values that will enable those being educated to construct and participate in communities that promote and reinforce [human] flourishing" (Hyland, 2009, p. 124).

A person-centred humanistic pedagogy contrasts with a technocratic approach that imposes 'evidence-based' psycho-behavioural training. It involves listening actively to children and young people and taking their concerns seriously (Hobbs et al., 2000). Advocates argue that this is crucial for children and young people dealing with stress or adversity because a sense of social alienation often accompanies experiences of distress (Lewis, 2014). The approach also avoids damage done by interventions that lack relevance for young people and reinforce feelings that others, especially adults, do not understand their feelings and experiences.

Some advocates suggest that developing well-being in schools could draw on the social purpose tradition of adult education (see Caldwell, 2013). Here, a humanistic, or person/student-centred approach is combined with a liberatory (or critical pedagogical) tradition to start from the experiences of children and young people and then to build on these in order to illuminate personal experiences in wider social perspective (Lewis, 2014). A student-centred, liberatory curriculum to support well-being would take learners' particular context as a foundation and "incorporate the causes of inequality, well-being, risk and community development as subject matter" (Royle, 2017, p. 64). From this perspective, learning in areas such as the arts, humanities and social sciences can help students appreciate the social embed-dedness of their own experiences, as related to matters of mental health and well-being, and provide a basis for reflexive engagement with the world around them (see Lewis, 2014).

Other educators favour a holistic, rich curriculum-related understanding of well-being in place of universal psycho-behavioural interventions. Here, a strong subject foundation across disciplines helps children and young people to relate their lives to a past, present and future world. Yet, crucially, well-being and resilience are not explicit topics or intended outcomes, nor is the purpose of learning to help students explore their own experiences or feelings (Ecclestone and Rawdin, 2016). Instead, subject knowledge and extra-curricular activities have an intrinsic value and an external focus; the crucial point here is that they should not be an instrumental vehicle for well-being or resilience (see Ecclestone and Hayes, 2009a, 2009b).

Conclusion

This chapter has raised important critical questions about understandings of resilience in the context of social policy concerned with the education and welfare of children and young people and associated interventions used in schools. In turn, this raises educational questions about whether and how goals concerning resilience and well-being should relate to the broader curriculum. Finally, the arguments set out suggest the need for caution on the part of educators about endorsing what has become a large, publicly funded, lucrative commercial market for well-being interventions, and caution about evaluations of effectiveness that are also carried out in this market.

Individual/group task: critical evaluation

Evaluate the different approaches to well-being in schools set out in this chapter.
What benefits and drawbacks can you identify for each?
Would you support any of them?
In light of the arguments in this chapter, what advice would you give a school thinking of introducing a resilience intervention?

Summary points

- The seemingly progressive sounding idea that schools and other educational settings should develop people's resilience as part of well-being needs to be subjected to critical scrutiny.
- Policy-led discourses of resilience tend to be overwhelmingly psychologically rooted and offer behavioural interventions that claim to teach resilience as a skill, mindset or attribute.
- Social research offers a strong context-based alternative to reductionist psycho-behavioural understandings of resilience.
- Long-running educational traditions – behavioural, liberal-humanistic and critical-liberatory – offer different understandings of the role of curriculum subjects and teaching and learning processes in developing resilience.
- For those involved in the education and welfare of children and young people, important questions concern what resilience is, how it can best be developed, and whether the development of resilience should be an explicit educational aim.

Acknowledgements

We thank our colleague, Andy Aston for contributing his ideas towards this chapter.

Recommended reading

Bache, I. and Reardon, L. (2016), *The Politics and Policy of Wellbeing: Understanding the Rise and Significance of a New Agenda*, Cheltenham: Edward Elgar Publishing.
Spratt, J. (2017), *Wellbeing, Equity and Education. A Critical Analysis of Discourses of Wellbeing in Schools*, New York: Springer.
Suissa, J., Winstanley, C. and Marples, R. (eds.) (2014), *Education, Philosophy and Wellbeing: New Perspectives on the Work of John White*, London and New York: Routledge.

References

Aranda, K., Zeeman, L., Scholes, J. and Morales, A. (2012), The resilient subject: Exploring subjectivity, identity and the body in narratives of resilience, *Health An Inter-disciplinary Journal for the Social Study of Health, Illness and Medicine*, 16(5): 548–563.
Barnes, M. and Morris, K. (2007), Networks, connectedness and resilience: Learning from the children's fund in context, *Social Policy and Society*, 6: 193–97.
Billington, T., Gibson, S., Lahmar, J. and Fogg, P. (2019), Mental health interventions in schools: Clinical discourse and the denial of affect. Paper presented to the British Educational Research Association Annual Conference, Manchester, September.

Bottrell, W. (2009), Understanding 'Marginal' Perspectives: Towards a Social Theory of Resilience, *Qualitative Social Work*, 8(3): 321–39.

Boyden, J. and Cooper, E. (2007), Questioning the power of resilience: Are children up to the task of disrupting the transmission of poverty? *CPRC Working Paper 73*, Chronic Poverty Research Centre, Oxford.

BPS (2019), (Department for Education) Character and resilience: A call for evidence (web site). https://www.bps.org.uk/news-and-policy/department-education-character-and-resilience-call-evidence Accessed 29 January 2020.

Brown, R. (2018), Mental Health and Wellbeing Provision in Schools. Review of published policies and information. Research report. DfE and Government Social Research, Oct. https://assets.publishing.service.gov.uk/government/uploads/system/uploads/attachment_data/file/747709/Mental_health_and_wellbeing_provision_in_schools.pdf

Brown, W. (2016), Sacrificial Citizenship: Neoliberalism, Human Capital, and Austerity Politics, *Constellations*, 23(1): 3–14.

Burchardt, T. and Huerta, M. (2008), Introduction: Resilience and social exclusion, *Social Policy and Society*, 8(1): 59–61.

Caldwell, P. (2013), Recreating social purpose adult education, *Adults Learning*, 25(4): 39–41.

Challen, A., Noden, P., West, A. and Machin, S. (2011), *UK Resilience Programme Evaluation: Final Report*. London: London School of Economics and Political Science, for the Department for Education.

Chandler, D. (2014), *Resilience: The Governance of Complexity – Critical Issues in Global Politics*, London: Routledge.

The Children's Society (2019), *The Good Childhood Report 2019*, London: The Children's Society.

Coleman, J. (2009), Well-being in schools: Empirical measure, or politician's dream? *Oxford Review of Education*, 35(3): 281–292.

Collin, P. (2018), Thinking in common about resilience: Introduction. In David Rowe, Reena Dobson and Helen Barcham (Eds.), *The Occasional Papers, Institute for Culture and Society (tOPICS)* Western Sydney University, *Resilience*, 9(1): 2–4.

CYPMHWT (2015), *Future in Mind: Promoting, Protecting and Improving Our Children and Young People's Mental Health and Wellbeing*, London: Department of Health and NHS England.

DfE (2019), *Character and Resilience: A Call for Evidence*, London: DfE, 27 May. https://consult.education.gov.uk/character-citizenship-cadets-team/character-and-resilience-a-call-for-evidence/supporting_documents/Character%20and%20Resilience%20Call%20for%20Evidence.pdf. Accessed 29 January 2020.

DfE and DoH (2015), *Special educational needs and disability code of practice: 0 to 25 years*, London: Department for Education and Department of Health.

DfE and DoH (2017), *Transforming Children and Young People's Mental Health Provision: A Green Paper*, London: Department for Education and Department of Health.

Ecclestone, K. (2004), Developing Self-esteem and Emotional Well-being – Inclusion or Intrusion?, *Adults Learning*, 16(3): 11–13.

Ecclestone, K. (2007), Resisting images of the "diminished self": The implications of emotional well-being and emotional engagement in education policy, *Journal of Education Policy*, 22(4): 455–470.

Ecclestone, K. (2012), Emotional well-being in education policy and practice: The need for interdisciplinary perspectives and a sociological imagination, *Research papers in Education*, 27(4): 383–387.

Ecclestone, K. and Brunila, K. (2015), Governing emotionally vulnerable subjects and "therapisation" of social justice, *Pedagogy, Culture & Society*, 23(4): 485–506.

Ecclestone, K. and Hayes, D. (2009a), *The Dangerous Rise of Therapeutic Education*, London: Routledge.

Ecclestone, K., and Hayes, D. (2009b), Changing the subject: The educational implications of emotional well-being, *Oxford Review of Education*, 35(3): 371–389.

Ecclestone, K. and Lewis, L. (2014), Interventions for resilience in educational settings: challenging policy discourses of risk and vulnerability, *Journal of Education Policy*, 29(2): 195–216.

Ecclestone, K. and Rawdin, C. (2016), Reinforcing the "diminished" subject? The implications of the "vulnerability zeitgeist" for well-being in educational settings, *Cambridge Journal of Education*, 46(3): 377–393.

Edwards, A. (2007), Working collaboratively to build resilience: A CHAT approach, *Social Policy and Society*, 6: 255–264.

Garrett, P. (2017), Resilience. In P. Garrett, *Welfare Words: Critical Social Work and Social Policy*, London: Sage. 133–153.

Goldberg, J., Sklad, M., Elfrink, T., Schreurs, K., Bohlmeijer, E. and Clarke, A. (2019), Effectiveness of interventions adopting a whole school approach to enhancing social and emotional development: A meta-analysis, *European Journal of Psychology of Education*, 34(4): 755–782.

Harper, D., and Speed, E. (2012), Uncovering recovery: The resistible rise of recovery and resilience, *Studies in Social Justice*, 6(1): 9–25.

Harrison, E. (2012), Bouncing back? Recession, resilience and everyday lives, *Critical Social Policy*, 33(1): 97–113.

Hazell, W. (2019), Exclusive: Schools' mental health crisis "out of control". TES 9 May. https://www.tes.com/news/exclusive-schools-mental-health-crisis-out-control. Accessed 16 September 2019.

Hobbs, C., Todd, L. and Taylor, J. (2000), Consulting with children and young people: Enabling educational psychologists to work collaboratively, *Educational and Child Psychology*, 17(4): 107–116.

Howell, A. and Voronka, J. (2012), Introduction: The politics of resilience and recovery in mental health care, *Studies in Social Justice*, 6(1): 1–7.

Hyland, T. (2009), Mindfulness and the therapeutic function of education, *Journal of Philosophy in Education*, 43(1): 119–131.

Lewis, L. (2014), Responding to the mental health and wellbeing agenda in adult community learning, *Journal of Research in Post-Compulsory Education*, 19(4): 357–377.

Lewis, L., Ecclestone, K. and Lund, P. (2015), Can a rules-based model illuminate resilience mechanisms? *Pedagogy in Practice*, 1(2): 36–65.

Luthar, S. and Cicchetti, D. (2000), The construct of resilience: Implications for interventions and social policies, *Development and Psychopathology*, 12: 857–85.

McLeod, J. (2012), Vulnerability and the neo-liberal youth citizen: A view from Australia, *Comparative Education*, 48(1): 11–26.

Mental Health Taskforce (2016), *The Five Year Forward for Mental Health*. https://www.england.nhs.uk/wp-content/uploads/2016/02/Mental-Health-Taskforce-FYFV-final.pdf. Accessed 29 January 2020.

Mguni, N. and Bacon, N. (2010), *Taking the Temperature of Local Communities, The Wellbeing and Resilience Measure (WaRM)*, London, The Young Foundation Local Wellbeing Project.

Mohaupt, S. (2009), Review article: Resilience and social exclusion, *Social Policy and Society*, 8(1): 63–71.

NatCen Social Research & the National Children's Bureau Research and Policy Team (2017), *Developing Character Skills in Schools, Summary Report*, London: DfE and Government Social Research.

NHS England (2019), *The NHS Long Term Plan*, Leeds and London: NHS England.

NICE (2009), *Promoting Young People's Social and Emotional Well-being in Secondary Education: Consultation on the Evidence*, London: NICE.

Norman, W. (2012), *Adapting to Change, the Role of Community Resilience*, London: The Young Foundation. https://www.barrowcadbury.org.uk/wp-content/uploads/2012/10/Adapting_Change.pdf. Accessed 29 January 2020.

Olchawski, J. (2018), The resilience narrative obscures the wider causes and solutions for children's mental health, *Mental Health Today*. 29 October. https://www.mentalhealthtoday.co.uk/blog/children/the-resilience-narrative-obscures-the-wider-causes-and-solutions-for-childrens-mental-health. Accessed 5 August 2019.

Public Health England (2017), *Prevention Concordat for Better Mental Health*. https://www.gov.uk/government/publications/prevention-concordat-for-better-mental-health-consensus-statement/prevention-concordat-for-better-mental-health. Accessed 16 September 2019.

Pupavac, V. (2001), Therapeutic governance: Psycho-social intervention and trauma risk management, *Disasters*, 25(4): 358–372.

Rawdin, C. (2016), *Professional subjectivities in a therapeutically-orientated education system*, Unpublished PhD thesis, University of Birmingham.

Royle, K. (2017), Resilience programmes and their place in education, a critical review with reference to interventions in Wolverhampton, *Journal of Education and Human Development*, 6(1): 53–65.

Rutter, M. (1990), Psychosocial resilience and protective mechanisms, in J. Rolf, A. Masten, D. Cicchetti, K. Neuchterlein and S. Weintraub (Eds.), *Risk and Protective Factors in the Development of Psychopathology*, New York: Cambridge University Press. 181–214.

Sadler, K., Visard, T., Ford, T. et al. (2019), *Mental Health of Children and Young People in England, 2017. Summary of Key Findings*, Nov. Leeds: NHS Digital. https://files.digital.nhs.uk/A6/EA7D58/MHCYP%202017%20Summary.pdf. Accessed 29 January 2020.

Seligman, M., Ernst, R., Gillham, J., Reivich, K. and Linkins, M. (2009), Positive education: Positive psychology and classroom interventions, *Oxford Review of Education*, 35(3): 293–311.

Spohrer, K. and Bailey, P. (2018), Character and resilience in English education policy: social mobility, self-governance and biopolitics, *Critical Studies in Education*, Published Online 29th Oct.

SUMO4Schools (2019), https://www.sumo4schools.com. Accessed 16 September 2019.

Ungar, M. (2008), Resilience across Cultures. *British Journal of Social Work*, 38(2): 218–235.

Ungar, M. (2015), Practitioner review: Diagnosing childhood resilience, *Journal of Child Psychology and Psychiatry*, 56(1): 4–17.

Ungar,M., Brown, M.,Liebenberg,L.,Cheung,M. & Levine,K. (2008), Distinguishing Pathways to Resilience Amongst Canadian Youth, *Canadian Journal of Community Mental Health,* 27(1): 1–13.

Ungar, M., Ghazinour, M. and Richter, J. (2013), Annual research review: What is resilience within the social ecology of human development? *The Journal of Child Psychology and Psychiatry*, 54(4): 348–366.

Westphalen, S. (1999), Reporting on Human Capital: Objectives and Trends, Paper presented to the *Measuring and Reporting Intellectual Capital: Experience, Issues, and Prospects* International Symposium, Amsterdam, 9–10 June. https://www.oecd.org/sti/ind/1948014.pdf

Windle, G. (2011), The resilience network: What is resilience? A systematic review and concept analysis, *Reviews in Clinical Gerontology*, 21: 152–169.

Young, S. (2019), Two thirds of parents and grandparents think childhoods are getting worse, study finds, *Independent.* https://www.independent.co.uk/life-style/health-and-families/childhood-uk-parents-action-children-survey-government-cuts-a8995551.html. Accessed 16 September 2019.

3 Well-being, mental health and the student population

Sarah Mander

Introduction

This chapter focuses on university student well-being, explaining why this subject area is an essential inclusion within this book. It concentrates on the shifting policy context of student well-being within higher education. The importance of policy is highlighted in the first University Mental Health Charter which reflects upon the significance of listening to one another's experiences of mental health in "the simple and radical act of sitting together to listen…and share ideas about how we could prevent students from experiencing difficulties…" (Hughes and Spencer, 2019, p. 4). The chapter introduces the policy and legislative frameworks which underpin delivery of quality, sustainable well-being and mental health delivery in UK higher education institutions. Analysis of the current mental health strategy is provided with translation of policy to practice provided in examples and independent study tasks. Challenge is made regarding the efficacy of the strategy. The theory of stigma surrounding mental health is explained. The chapter also discusses the most tragic outcome of poor mental health, that is suicide. Crucially, it considers the relationship and importance of promoting well-being as a strategy to prevent escalation of poor mental health.

Essentially, the book would have been incomplete without considering the mental health and well-being of our student population because universities are fundamentally connected to the development of this book. The various chapters have been authored by Academics who routinely engage with and support students emanating from diverse backgrounds and abilities, who are of a wide age range and socio-economic background and who participate in undergraduate or postgraduate study. It is anticipated that the book's readership will comprise of mostly undergraduate students whose well-being should be protected, nurtured and sustained. Therefore, this chapter aims to improve knowledge and understanding of student well-being amongst our target readership through psychoeducation and self-help tools. It also sets out to raise awareness of student well-being amongst both professional communities and families in order to highlight the potential vulnerabilities of student well-being and secure improved understanding of both their good and poor mental health.

The current policy and legislative context

The Future in Mind (2015) policy launched a five-year vision to promote, protect and improve the mental health and well-being of children and young people aged 0–25 across the four nations of the

UK (Department for Health, 2015). The case for action stated there was a compelling moral, social and economic rationale for a change in culture in the way we support children and young people's emotional well-being and mental health. National recognition was afforded to the requirement to make significant improvements in mental health services because of escalating needs and subsequent failure of services to meet these needs. Its main aims are to promote resilience, prevention and provide early intervention; improve access to effective support; care for the most vulnerable; provide accountability and transparency; and to develop a workforce competent in delivering these aims (Department for Health, 2015).

Individual task

Research the ways in which Future in Mind (2015) has impacted upon university students' well-being since its inception. Utilising the university webpages, review: the range of services that currently promote well-being within universities in which professionals are involved in delivering these services.

In response, Universities UK launched a new framework in 2017 to aid universities in improving student mental health and well-being. The policy, #stepchange, aligns with the publication of the School's Green Paper, Transforming children and young people's mental health provision (HMGOV, 2017a). It provides a continuum of the same public message and strategy that mental health and well-being has been under-focussed, under-resourced and misunderstood for the 0–25 age range. #stepchange bridges the gap for the 19–25 age range in respect of policy and practice in mental health and well-being. It is consistent with the extended age range of the 2015 Special Educational Needs and Disability Code of Practice (SENDCoP), which currently supports young people up to the age of 25 and also contributes to the SENDCoP legislative responsibilities (Department of Education and Department for Health, 2015).

In cases where mental health conditions result in significant impairment, which has a long-term effect on students' abilities to carry out day-to-day duties, students might select to classify themselves as disabled and therefore be eligible for reasonable adjustments to aid their studies, as determined by provisions of the SENDCoP (Department of Education and Department for Health, 2015). The factors informing self-classification of disability are enshrined within the Equality Act 2010 (HMGOV, 2010) and therefore form a legislative duty for organisations in the UK, including universities. The changes in disability classification arising from the Equality Act 2010, combined with actual increase in mental health conditions, have resulted in an increasing proportion of all disability disclosed by first-year students attributable to mental health conditions; 17% in 2015/16 compared to 5% in 2006/07 (Thorley, 2017). It should be noted that not all students are under the age of 25, and that mature students beyond this age are also supported by the Equality Act 2010 if they feel their mental health should be categorised as a disability. This support enables Universities to satisfy their legal obligations to protect all stakeholders – students, staff, volunteers and visitors – from harassment, victimisation and discrimination.

The #stepchange strategy has been re-branded in 2020 and will be identified as Universities UK Mentally Healthy Universities Strategic Framework. It intends, as promised in the 2017 policy, to provide a self-improvement tool for universities to evaluate the progress of their well-being and mental health work. Student Minds have published the first University Mental Health Charter which illustrates a good practice model for improving well-being and mental health outcomes in universities. It is a collaborative approach from a range of university communities and stakeholders to formulate a quality improvement scheme which recognises and rewards universities who can demonstrate the application of good practice. The charter, which distinguishes the process as "a marathon and not a sprint" (Hughes and Spencer, 2019, p. 4), is piloted by the University of Derby in 2020.

The case for action

Both #stepchange and the school's Green Paper (as it is referred to within education settings) communicate that significant changes in attitudes towards mental health and well-being are required in order to reverse the trend of poor mental health in the UK. Amongst Higher Education students, levels of poor mental health and low well-being continue to increase, and are disproportionately high compared to the remainder of the UK adult population (Thorley, 2017). For the first time, there is an emphasis on the strategic responsibilities of educational institutions to address mental health issues and to improve well-being. The policies present opportunities for educational institutions, such as schools and universities, to prioritise mental health and well-being to a breadth and depth previously unexpected or consistently applied. It is also in universities' interest to promote positive well-being. Research that informed the #stepchange agenda revealed stress, anxiety, depression, grief, sleeping difficulties and relationship problems negatively affect higher education attainment. Students who experience these issues also report a lower sense of belonging and engagement with their university; these factors are strongly linked with higher retention and lower dropout rates (Thorley, 2017).

The #stepchange initiative aims to provide a more comprehensive approach for the whole student community to thrive and succeed, in addition to meeting the needs of students who experience mental health illness. The profile of well-being has been raised through publication of this framework and is part of a wider programme of work to meet the increase in mental health needs within the UK.

Students who experience poor mental health

Almost three-quarters of adults who experience mental health symptoms do so before the age of 25 (IPPR, 2017) which means universities are required to be responsive to students who embark on their Higher Education journey with existing mental health conditions or develop mental illness whilst they are studying. Additionally, more students are disclosing poor mental health to their Universities; the Institute for Public Policy Research (2017) reported a fivefold increase. Whilst an actual growth in mental health illness, diagnosable as mental health conditions using the Diagnostic and Statistical Manual of Mental Disorders fifth edition (DSM-5), has undoubtedly occurred, there are other, wider factors affecting this increase. These include a concerted effort by people and organisations who are in positions of influence, such as soap and TV drama storylines, actors and reality TV stars, celebrities, the sporting community, the Royal family, social media, politicians and many more, to reduce the stigma surrounding disclosure of poor mental health. Stigma relates to the negative impact or barriers which people experience because they do not fit in with society. It is characterised as a process based upon the social construction of identity, where a *spoiled identity* is created because stigmatised people cannot fulfil their social, cultural and moral obligations within society. For example, a student experiencing poor well-being might feel unable to attend lectures or socialise with peers, and therefore might become an outsider with discreditable social status. Stigma therefore affects what is most important to us and impacts upon how others perceive us (Goffman, 1963).

Public mental health campaigns have been launched to reduce stigma around mental health and promote well-being and encourage society to talk openly and freely about their emotions. For example, recently the 2019 collaborative Young Minds and ITV mental wellness campaign, Britain Get Talking, acknowledges that building good relationships with family, friends and our wider community is positive for our well-being. It highlights the difficulties children and young people experience in talking openly about their mental health and how strong relationships can support them in sharing feelings and knowing they are understood. The activity of paused screenings in high rating shows encourages parents and carers to initiate regular conversations with their children, taking a moment to put down their mobile phones and ask how they are feeling (Young Minds, 2019). Promotions such as this have resulted in feelings of low well-being and potential poor mental health being more understood through improved knowledge and acceptance, and society – including students – feeling more empowered and confident to share concerns about their mental health. It provides opportunities to remove stigma associated with mental health difficulties as they become more commonplace; more normalised. While demand for young people's mental health services has increased, support organisations have become more available both is quantity and specialisms. Even though there are significant challenges in accessing services due to long-term waiting lists, assessment thresholds and geographical isolation, the improved perceived availability of support can subsequently encourage disclosure.

Individual/group task

Reflective question: Before you continue reading, reflect on your current perceptions of student mental health.

What do you think influences student well-being?

The #stepchange framework (Universities UK, 2017)

The framework consists of eight strands, which constitute the direction and nature of travel required.

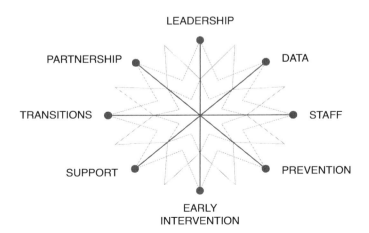

Figure 3.1   The #stepchange framework (Universities UK, 2017).

Leadership

The requisite cultural and structural changes to improve emotional well-being and mental health within higher education command a *whole university* approach. This includes staff at all levels, led by the Vice-Chancellor and Governors, to embed #stepchange within strategy, policies, processes, procedures and guidance documents. Leaders are required to cultivate and nurture engagement from all staff to motivate and ensure participation, and to assist in identifying potential difficulties. This can be achieved through creating a vision that engages stakeholders to identify with change by valuing the associated outcomes; the necessary changing of hearts and minds can be achieved through experiencing the benefits of change (Fullen, 2006). Through effective communication, the vision can be implemented with action planning, creativity and innovation. Resources to enable this development should ensure financial sustainability and evaluation of progress must consider students' views on a regular basis. It is important to highlight that significant knowledge and understanding of how best to promote positive well-being whilst also appreciating the complexity of mental health conditions is required in order to formulate such vision. Students may accelerate and reverse along the continuum which ranges from being mentally well to mentally ill throughout their higher education lifecycle and their changing needs should be supported. This is best achieved through a collaborative approach, where specialist advice and guidance is encouraged and embraced to fully inform the #stepchange strategy. It is also crucial that a *one size fits all* approach is discouraged. This is because of the diversity in student profile across higher education institutions where the demographic, the characteristics of student communities, vary according to age, gender, ethnicity, family background, socio-economic circumstances, geographical location and employability opportunities. The strategy to widen participation in higher education which encourages students from more disadvantaged backgrounds and under-represented groups, such as Traveller communities and Looked After Children, to study at university has been strengthened in the Higher Education and Research Act (HMGOV, 2017b) (Department for Education, 2018). This means that in order to promote inclusive educational practice, universities are required to remove barriers, such as those which arise with poor mental health, in order to secure retention and progression of students. The #stepchange vision is therefore understandably complex and requires much consideration.

Prevention and early intervention

The #stepchange agenda focuses upon promoting universal well-being for all students, and making available appropriate interventions at an early stage in circumstances of declining student mental health. Strategies to promote well-being should aim to enhance a sense of belonging and enable students to develop their social identity which can improve retention and academic success, thus impacting positively on overall student well-being (Thomas, 2012). Some of these strategies are already firmly embedded in university cultures; for example, projects which build resilience such as participating in clubs and societies and also enhanced support at points of transition through induction and succession planning. Peer mentoring, developed in many universities as a core practice, is reciprocally beneficial for the mentor and the mentee. Research suggests it can be an empowering experience for all involved because it improves self-confidence, reduces isolation, increases self-esteem, promotes acceptance and reduces stigma surrounding mental health, generates understanding and as a consequence cultivates a culture of empathy rather than judgement (Pettigrew and Tropp, 2006; Reavley et al., 2012). Adequate training and support is required for mentors in order to equip them with the necessary skills and also to protect their own well-being. Mentors additionally benefit from enhanced personal development and employability skills which contribute to their well-being (Gulliver and Byrom, 2014). As well-being becomes more *in vogue,* it is also good practice to integrate well-being and mental health into pedagogical practice; for example, to develop core modules for first-year students to introduce positive mental health strategies and serve as a tool for transparency in culture and ethos to promote universal well-being. Digital communication, including the use of social media, is a routine mechanism to inform students about well-being support, thus extending universal support to a wider audience in the student community.

As with everyone, students' well-being is not a static state; it fluctuates across their university lifecycle. The main objective of early intervention is to restrict escalation of need as it arises to prevent further complexity or crisis. Students are able to identify specific challenges which might cause escalation of need, and which are therefore priority areas for universities to focus their support services. These challenges include financial difficulties, employment opportunities, social media and risk of sexual exploitation. It is also known that there are increased risks of poor well-being and rising mental health needs amongst under-represented groups, including students emanating from low socio-economic backgrounds, high achievers, carers and minority gender and sexual identity groups (Brown, 2016). Enhanced mental health support for students with protected characteristics determined by the Equality Act 2010, should be made available. Hidden harms, a phrase first used to describe the detrimental effect substance misusing parents can have on their children (HMGOV, 2011), are also prolific causal factors for declining mental health amongst the student population. The definition of a hidden harm relates to problems that are personally experienced but not necessarily known to others which render the harm discreet, and as a consequence, unreachable to those who might be in a position to help. In addition to substance misuse, hidden harms affecting students extend to include other addictions such as gambling; domestic abuse; covert bullying and harassment; and undisclosed disability. Through creating a culture of safe disclosure, where university counselling services are a referral option, early intervention can occur in both recognised and unidentified mental health concerns.

In situations where prevention and/or early intervention are unsuccessful, the threshold might be crossed where crisis situations may occur. Accountability lies with universities to develop strategies that manage associated risks. Universities have a legal duty to safeguard their students, and other members of the higher education community such as staff and volunteers. The #stepchange strategy advocates the creation of crisis plans which provide a named person who takes responsibility for providing responsive support (Universities UK, 2017). Examples of crisis situations include occurrence of hate crime, sexual misconduct and harassment, and suicide/suicide prevention. Although there has been an escalation in the number and frequency of student suicides in the UK, it can be increasingly difficult to identify students who are at risk of suicide; a relatively low proportion, around a quarter, have disclosed their intentions to professionals (HEFCE, 2015). Universities are challenged to generate accurate and current data around student depression, alcohol or drug use, personality and mood disorders and self-harm which can be indicators of potential suicidal tendencies as many students who need help are not necessarily accessing it (HEFCE, 2015). Therefore, initiatives such as the award-winning Three Minutes to Save a Life, a suicide mitigation programme formulated by Clare Dickens of the University of Wolverhampton which advocates a whole university approach and attempts to remove stigma associated with poor mental health are crucial (Dickens, 2017).

Group task

Watch the film, Three Minutes to Save a Life, at https://www.youtube.com/watch?v=2Augsl9fizA. In particular, consider how well-being can be utilised to help de-escalate mental health needs. Formulate a well-being plan of safety for a (fictional) student experiencing poor mental health.

Partnerships, support, transition

First, it is essential to acknowledge that partnerships begin with the student, their families, and their transitional education establishments. This is because they are the key stakeholders and understand the needs of students the most effectively. In Listening to Children, Lyndon emphasises the most effective outcomes are secured through applying a participatory approach with children because they are "experts in their own lives" (Langsted, 1994, p. 29; Clark and Moss, 2011, p. 10). She commands us to listen, to seek children's opinions and to ensure professionals act upon them to improve their well-being. The same principle should be applied for students in higher education. A range of models are currently utilised in universities to secure feedback from students, such as National Student Surveys (Office for Students, 2019), which gathers opinion about their student experience. More recently, the new buzzword in higher education, *co-creation*, is considered good practice (Piper and Emmanuel, 2019). The University Mental Health Charter advises that "creating a culture that supports good well-being" (Hughes and Spanner, 2019, p. 67) is most readily achieved where students are partners in the development of university well-being strategy. We can therefore be hopeful that students will be listened to and empowered to be equal partners in order to improve well-being, although historical attempts to achieve this might indicate otherwise.

When considering professional partnerships, in order to provide an integrated service model of student well-being universities are required to collaborate effectively with a range of partners. This is to provide a seamless transition across the thresholds described above to meet the continuum of need and extend provision of services if well-being declines and mental health needs escalate (Universities UK, 2017). Whilst universities have provided counselling services free of charge for students since the 1950s (Byrom and Murphy, 2018), this support is not designed as a single model response due to limited capacity and a distinct skill set. Partnership working is fundamental in achieving this as it ensures an appropriate range of specialist support is available for students. It is important to remember that the primary function of universities is as providers of education which they should remain expert in. They are not expected to become specialists in mental health but are required to promote positive student well-being and address emerging mental health needs. Therefore, partnership working can be the most effective and efficient method of fulfilling these obligations. It also contributes to community cohesion and promotes the reputation of the university, both of which are major contributors to sustainability (Universities UK, 2017).

Partnerships and support services can be categorised in three ways: the statutory sector, the voluntary sector and virtual support. The statutory sector comprises the NHS including GP's, and mental health teams; the Police who are responsible for crime and disorder including responding to situations such as those where domestic abuse or perhaps forced marriage and honour-based violence are prevalent; and social care who have a legal duty to assist vulnerable adults, such as students who experience disability, and also to support care leavers and students with caring responsibilities. The #stepchange agenda acknowledges that partnerships are essential, particularly with the NHS, and encourages links with local communities (Universities UK, 2017).

The voluntary sector are well-established providers of services that enhance mainstream statutory sector delivery, and at times are commissioned to provide services which the statutory sector cannot, potentially because of lack of specialism, or capacity or due to financial efficiency. We do know that the voluntary sector plays an increasingly crucial and valued role in delivering children and young people's services (Mander in Brown, 2017). Future in Mind (Department for Health, 2015) urges that we look to the voluntary sector to provide children and young people's mental health services to help breakdown the stigma of mental health within society because this shifts perceptions away from the more clinical aspect of mainstream health services. Universities collaborate with a range of providers so that students can access the right support at the right time. This includes faith groups, the Samaritans, financial support groups, domestic abuse outreach, addiction support groups, bereavement counsellors and many more. Perhaps, the most important consideration is to ensure that the well-being support offer is updated to ensure currency and associated ability to meet emergent need.

Virtual support, whether on-line or by '"phone, offers accessible, viable and discreet support for students. Community forums and blogs are increasing and provide a more personalised, less formal approach. The restrictions and concerns regarding non-professional support mechanisms accessed online are outlined in Chapter 7 which discusses mental health and digital lives; the same concerns apply in higher education. The mission of Student Minds, the leading student online mental health charity, is to empower university communities to self-care for their well-being and mental health and provide support for others. Their blog offers opportunities for students to both write and read about challenges to their well-being and mental health and proffer guidance and advice through stories of personal experience (Student Minds, 2019). Blogs such as this one extend psychoeducational learning to students who might most benefit from them, but who are traditionally least likely to engage in support. One example is discreet support for male students amongst whom there have been increases in suicide in recent years; around three-quarters of all suicides are committed by males (ONS, 2019).

However, the trials and tribulations of working in partnership are well documented across time (Cameron et al., 2000; Siraj-Blatchford et al., 2007; Hussain, 2014). In an earlier publication, writing about inter-professional working between education and health sectors, I explored the challenges of partnership working. Specifically, the differences between organisational disciplines, training, methods of working, goals and priorities can restrict partnership working. Working cultures particularly impact upon the success of partnership working because appreciation of individual structures and practices may not be understood (Mander and Sturge, 2015). Chapter 10 further explores the challenges of partnership working between education and social care and it is fair to conclude these challenges are highly relevant today. For the #stepchange agenda, these challenges can result in failure to progress support services and a consequent escalation of student mental health needs.

Individual task

Access the Student Minds blog at https://www.studentmindsblog.co.uk/p/explore-blog.html.
  Review the range of topics discussed.
  Write your own blog which reflects upon your learning about student well-being, and how this can best be promoted in universities.
  Decide whether to publish your blog, or keep for your own reference.

Data

Data analysis is required to measure needs and recognise at risk groups. It can assist in detecting changes in students' behaviours, for example poor attendance at lectures and/or decline in academic grades, which might indicate increased risk of low well-being, and to target support appropriately. When collating data, universities are compelled to consider wider influences such as living environments and relationships in order to provide a more holistic perspective of student well-being (Universities UK, 2017).

Subsequent evaluation of data enables Universities to map existing services and identify gaps in provision, and of course to assess institutional progress for the #stepchange agenda. However, following the strengthening of data protection with the implementation of General Data Protection Regulation (GDPR) in 2019, students have the freedom to request erasure of data which can potentially under-report on this progress. Conversely, with consent, GDPR (2018) can support the sharing of information with key partners at points of transition, which are known to hold potential for increasing vulnerability to poor well-being. This information sharing subsequently enables continuity of care for those with existing mental health conditions.

The relationship between data and suicide

Recent changes to some university admissions procedures request students consent to sharing information relating to their mental health and well-being with parents/carers; it is important to note that GDPR (2018) restricts disclosures of this nature without consent. The Higher Education Policy Institute Student Academic Survey (2019) specifically researched whether students felt it might be appropriate to share personal data relating to their mental health with parents, particularly when extreme circumstances such a failed suicide attempt, had been made. Around 82% of students were in agreement that sharing of such personal data would be expected and/or encouraged, although this was marginally less welcomed by the more independent over 26 age range (HEPI, 2019). It is the first time a research question of this nature was included within the annual survey and is undoubtedly influenced by vigorous campaigning from family members such as Iain Thacker following the tragic suicide of his daughter, Ceara, aged 19, in 2018. Ceara's previous suicide attempt had not been shared with her family, as information sharing consent had not been provided, although her father feels strongly that family support might have prevented a subsequent fatal attempt (BBC News, 2019). Suicide is, of course, the ultimate tragedy of mental health and impacts severely upon the whole university community. Whilst it might appear distasteful to discuss, negative outcomes of mental health, and particularly suicide, have damaging repercussions for the reputation of the institution which is most unhelpful for all involved, particularly students who experience poor mental health.

Staff

The #stepchange agenda recognises that both staff and students are valuable for universities because human capital is the essence of its delivery arm. The agenda is explicit that University staff are key to promoting improved well-being and good mental health, and that they should be appropriately supported to achieve this (Universities UK, 2017). This support includes professional development such as Mental Health First Aid (MHFA) training. MHFA courses equip staff with practical skills and knowledge to identify triggers and signs of mental health issues, the confidence to act in a timely, relevant and sensitive manner to provide reassurance and support utilising enhanced interpersonal skills such as active listening, empathy and congruence. Training should initially focus upon staff who have regular contact with students. Academic staff are naturally at the forefront of this group, and the strategy determines that well-being and mental health support delivery time is to be incorporated into workload allocation for academics (Universities UK, 2017). This means that in order to build capacity for academic staff, dedicated hours should be specified within their individual timetables. Inevitably, this is time which would have previously been utilised for other tasks including delivering lectures and therefore presents challenges for universities in respect of staff availability, effective resource management and their obligation to engage with the #stepchange agenda.

In respect of university staff, the #stepchange agenda is clear that student and staff mental health should be aligned, hence the formal adjustment required to workload allocations (Universities UK, 2017) in attempts to avoid over-burdening staff. However, interviews with senior higher education institution staff refer to the current academic role as the fourth emergency service for stressed students (Financial Times, 2019) with associated negative impact on academics who may already feel isolated at work with little support for their own well-being and self-care. Some staff members may feel unable and/or unwilling to upskill in the discipline of mental health; for example, if they have personal or familial experience of poor mental health it might reduce their own sense of well-being and blur their professional boundaries (Hughes et al., 2018). However, there is well-established evidence that MHFA training improves knowledge which might serve as psychoeducation and therefore has the potential to impact positively upon trainees (Morgan et al., 2018). It also has the potential to reduce stigma and help stimulate conversations about well-being. Nonetheless, further research is also required regarding the efficacy of MHFA to improve well-being outcomes for recipients. A recent study conducted in Australia, where MHFA training began in 2000, examined MHFA undertaken by parents to support their adolescent children. The impact of the training proved beneficial for parents, in that their mental health literacy improved, and they reported the experience was positive. However, it was not possible to detect changes in their children's mental health (Morgan et al., 2019). Various factors might have influenced reporting, including misreporting and underdisclosure which is commonplace in research of discreet and sensitive health issues. Crucially, the power dynamics of family relationships are likely to have influenced data generated, but it is notable that a similar relationship of power imbalance exists between academics and students. Therefore, it is possible the academic task of mental health outreach and support for students can be compromised and restricted by the primary function of their relationship.

Individual/group task

Academic staff are not the only group who can outreach positive well-being and mental health support in universities.

Select a university and make a virtual visit through their website to identify the range of staff who might enable positive well-being.

Consider what needs to happen to ensure these staff are sufficiently equipped to deliver the #stepchange agenda.

Conclusion

It is evident that the vision of #stepchange is well researched and carefully constructed, although publishing of a strategy to promote positive student well-being and mental health was long overdue. Its implementation, however, requires further clarity and perhaps leaves more questions than it provides answers. Despite the agenda being active for a number of years, a standardised evaluative toolkit has not yet been published and therefore outcomes of the substantial investment afforded for this strategy have yet to be identified and shared. Whilst a toolkit is promised, declining well-being amongst the student population has continued and for some students this has resulted in a poor student experience. The absence of evaluation which is nationally competitive restricts universities' opportunity to market their student well-being initiatives with sufficient rigour. As the student experience is considered the most important and prestigious measure of a university's success and has a major influence on its sustainability, the #stepchange agenda has created a public gap which would appear to detract from the student experience even where universities have developed excellent practice for student well-being.

Finally, whilst the focus for this chapter centred around policy it is important to acknowledge the many aspects of student well-being which are not discussed. There are some exceptional initiatives delivered in universities which are innovative, engaging and successful. Additionally, there are many university staff who deliver high-quality well-being support on a daily basis who are not mentioned within this book but who are highly valued because of their vital roles of creating and sustaining student well-being.

Summary points

- Current policy initiatives focus on early intervention and prevention to promote student well-being.
- Students' academic success is influenced by their well-being.
- The #stepchange agenda provides a detailed framework for higher education reform to promote student well-being and support mental health but proves challenging to implement in practice.
- The core purpose of universities remains to educate; delivery of well-being and mental health agendas must be balanced appropriately but sufficiently.
- A national evaluative framework is long overdue and essential for the longevity and quality outcome of this strategy.

Recommended reading (taken from The University Mental Health Charter)

Barden, N. and Caleb, R. (2019) *Student mental health and wellbeing in higher education. A practical guide.* London: Sage.

Houghton, A.M. and Anderson, J. (2017) *Embedding mental wellbeing in the curriculum: Maximising success in higher education.* York: Higher Education Academy.

For academics:- Hughes, G., Panjwani, M., Tulcidas, P., Byrom, N. (2018) For student minds. *Student Mental Health the Role and Experiences of Academics.* http://www.studentminds.org.uk/uploads/3/7/8/4/3784584/180129_student_mental_health__the_role_and_experience_of_academics__student_minds_pdf.pdf [accessed 20 January 2020].

Also, there are a range of published case studies available on-line which exemplify how universities have implemented the #stepchange agenda. Please access these to view the policy in action.

References

BBC News (2019) *Ceara Thacker: Dead student's father hits out at university* [online]. https://www.bbc.co.uk/news/uk-england-merseyside-49715394 [accessed 14 January 2020].

Brown, P. (2016) *The invisible problem? Improving students' mental health.* Oxford: Higher Educational Policy Institute.

Byrom, N. C. and Murphy, R. A. (2018) Individual differences are more than a gene × environment interaction: The role of learning. *Journal of Experimental Psychology: Animal Learning and Cognition.* Vol. **44**(1) pp. 36–55.

Cameron, A., Lart, R., Harrison, L., MacDonald, G. and Smith, R. (2000) *Factors promoting and obstacles hindering joint working: A systematic review.* School for policy studies, Bristol: University of Bristol.

Clark, A. and Moss, P. (2011) *Listening to young children: The mosaic approach.* London: National Children's Bureau.

Department for Education (2018) *Access and participation secretary of state for education guidance for the office of students* [online]. https://www.officeforstudents.org.uk/media/1112/access-and-participation-guidance.pdf [accessed 14 January 2020].

Department for Education and Department of Health (2015) *Special educational needs and disability code of practice: 0 to 25 years* [online]. https://www.gov.uk/government/publications/send-code-of-practice-0-to-25 [accessed 13 January 2020].

Department of Health (2015) *Future in mind: Promoting, protecting and improving our children and young people's mental health and wellbeing* [online]. https://assets.publishing.service.gov.uk/government/uploads/system/uploads/attachment_data/file/414024/Childrens_Mental_Health.pdf [accessed 19 December 2019].

Dickens, C. for University of Wolverhampton (2017) *Three minutes to save a life* [online]. http://www.nspa.org.uk/wp-content/uploads/2019/02/Suicide-Mitigation-Aiming-to-Combine-Compassion-and-Governance-in-a-HE-setting-.pdf [accessed 10 January 2020].

Financial Times (2019) *Academics forced to act as 'fourth emergency service' for stressed students* [online]. https://www.ft.com/content/381c6c7e-d947-11e9-9c26-419d783e10e8 [accessed 2 January 2020].

Fullen, M. with Hill, P. and Crevola, C. (2006) *Breakthrough.* London: SAGE.

General Data Protection Regulation (GDPR). (2018). *General data protection regulation (GDPR)* [online]. https://gdpr-info.eu/ [accessed 14 January 2020].

Goffman, E. (1963). *Stigma: Notes on the management of spoiled identity.* New York: Prentice-Hall.

Gulliver, E. and Byrom, N. (2014) *Peer support for student mental health* [online]. https://www.studentminds.org.uk/uploads/3/7/8/4/3784584/peer_support_for_student_mental_health.pdf [accessed 2 January 2020].

Higher Education Funding Council for England (2015) *Understanding provision for students with mental health problems and intensive support needs* [online]. http://www.studentminds.org.uk/uploads/3/7/8/4/3784584/summary_of_the_hefce_report.pdf [accessed 13 January 2020].

Higher Education Policy Institute (2019) *Student academic experience survey 2019* [online]. https://www.hepi.ac.uk/wp-content/uploads/2019/06/Student-Academic-Experience-Survey-2019.pdf [accessed 14 January 2020].

HMGOV (2010) *The equality act.* London: The Stationery Office.

HMGOV (2011) *Advisory council on the misuse of drugs [ACMD] (2003). Hidden harm: Responding to the needs of children of problem drug users. The report of an inquiry by the ACMD* [online]. https://assets.publishing.

service.gov.uk/government/uploads/system/uploads/attachment_data/file/120620/hidden-harm-full.pdf [accessed 17 January 2020].

HMGOV (2017a) Transforming children and young people's mental health provision: A Green paper [online]. https://assets.publishing.service.gov.uk/government/uploads/system/uploads/attachment_data/file/664855/Transforming_children_and_young_people_s_mental_health_provision.pdf [accessed 20 January 2020].

HMGOV (2017b) *Higher education and research act.* London: The Stationery Office.

Hughes, G., Panjwani, M., Tulcidas, P. and Byrom, N. (2018) For student minds. *Student Mental Health the Role and Experiences of Academics* [online]. http://www.studentminds.org.uk/uploads/3/7/8/4/3784584/180129_student_mental_health__the_role_and_experience_of_academics__student_minds_pdf.pdf [accessed 20 January 2020].

Hughes, G. and Spanner, L. (2019) *The university mental health charter.* Leeds: Student Minds.

Hussain, D. (2014) Skills and knowledge for effective practice. In Brownhill, S. (ed.) *Empowering the children's and young people's workforce. Practice based knowledge, skills and understanding.* Oxon: Routledge. pp. 121–139.

Langsted, O. (1994) Looking at quality from the child's perspective, pp. 28–42. In Moss, P. and Pence, A. (eds.) *Valuing quality in early childhood services.* London: Paul Chapman Publishing.

Mander, S. (2017) How big is our society? In, Brown, Z. (ed.), *Children, families and communities: Contemporary influences and challenges.* Abingdon: Routledge. pp. 103–114.

Mander, S. and Sturge, S. (2015) Early help mechanisms – A mere fad or ground breaking reformation to child protection systems? The importance of interprofessional working; the educational and health perspective. *Pedagogy in Practice, University of Wolverhampton.* Vol. 1(2), pp. 1–8.

Morgan, A.J., Ross, A. and Reavley, N.J. (2018) Systematic review and meta-analysis of mental health first aid training: Effects on knowledge, stigma, and helping behaviour. *PLoS One.* Vol. **13**(5), pp. 1–20.

Morgan, A.J., Fischer, J.A., Hart, L. M. Kelly, C.M., Kitchener, B.A., Reavley, N.J, Yap, M.B.H., Cvetkovski, S. and Jorm, A.J. (2019) Does mental health first aid training improve the mental health of aid recipients? The training for parents of teenagers randomised controlled trial. *BMC Psychiatry.* Vol. **19**(99), pp. 1–14.

Office for National Statistics (2019) Suicides in the UK: 2018 registrations [online]. https://www.ons.gov.uk/peoplepopulationandcommunity/birthsdeathsandmarriages/deaths/bulletins/suicidesintheunitedkingdom/2018registrations [accessed 19 January 2020].

Office for Students (2019) *The national student survey* [online]. https://www.thestudentsurvey.com [accessed 20 January 2020].

Pettigrew, T.F. and Tropp, L.R. (2006) A meta-analytic test of intergroup contact theory. *Journal of Personality and Social Psychology.* Vol. **90**(5), p. 751.

Piper, R. and Emmanuel, T. (2019). *Co-producing mental health strategies with students: A guide for the higher education sector.* Leeds: Student Minds [online]. https://www.studentminds.org.uk/uploads/3/7/8/4/3784584/cpdn_document_artwork.pdf [accessed 4 January 2020].

Reavley, N.J., McCann, T.V. and Jorm, A.F. (2012) Mental health literacy in higher education students. *Early Intervention in Psychiatry.* Vol. **6**(1), pp. 45–52.

Siraj-Blatchford, I., Clarke, K. and Needham, M. (2007) *Team around the child.* Stoke on Trent: Trentham Publishing.

Student Minds (2019) *Student minds blog* [online]. https://www.studentmindsblog.co.uk/p/explore-blog.html [accessed 19 December 2019].

Thomas, L. (2012) *Building student engagement and belonging in higher education at a time of change* [online]. https://www.heacademy.ac.uk/system/files/what_works_final_report.pdf [accessed 7 January 2020].

Thorley, C. (2017) *Not by degrees: Improving student mental health in the UK's universities.* London: Institute for Public Policy Research.

Universities UK (2015) *Student mental well-being in higher education a good practice guide* [online] https://www.universitiesuk.ac.uk/policy-and-analysis/reports/Documents/2015/student-mental-wellbeing-in-he.pdf [accessed 20 December 2019].

Universities UK (2017) *#stepchange mental health in higher education* [online]. http://www.universitiesuk.ac.uk/policy-and-analysis/stepchange/Pages/default.aspx [accessed 10 January 2020].

Young Minds (2019) *Get Britain talking* [online]. https://youngminds.org.uk/get-involved/campaign-with-us/britain-get-talking/ [accessed 17 January 2020].

4   Listening to children
The rights of the child

Helen Lyndon

This chapter explores a drive to listen to children and will explore how a participatory approach to children's services can support children's health and well-being. Through first considering the changing context of childhood, children are presented as active participants and 'experts in their own lives' (Langstead, 1994, p. 29; Clark and Moss, 2011, p. 10). The complexity of defining a listening approach is then discussed and placed within the context of English practice in both early years and the statutory school sector. The chapter explores approaches which have sought to better listen and evaluates the practicalities of such an approach. The chapter closes on my own professional and academic experiences of listening to children and considers the benefits for children's well-being of such a participatory approach.

Individual/group task

Before we begin, consider your view of childhood; how does this view compare to that of your parents' generation? How does the view of childhood change over time?

A view of childhood

Each child's individual experience of childhood is different and situated within a complex web of societal influence. Childhood is indicative of the time and context within which it unfolds and the relationship between childhood and adulthood continually evolves (Jenks, 2005). There is a growing body of scholarly materials around the new sociology of childhood that considers the way in which society views the child and how diverse this can be; the social class of the family and their geographical location, along with many other contextual factors, will impact on how childhood unfolds. Children's lives are regulated by the adults around them. Historically, children have been viewed as adults-in-waiting and treated accordingly. Isabella was the child bride of Richard II and married at 6 years of age to form political alliance between England and France in the fourteenth century. Children routinely worked through the industrial revolution and even had their right to work enshrined in the Geneva Declaration on the Rights of the Child (United Nations, 1924). The current view of childhood is that children have vulnerabilities and are in need of adult protection (James and James, 2004); this need for protection manifests itself in public policy and legislation. Such policy and legislation then governs adult behaviour and so influences our ongoing understanding of childhood (Prout and

James, 2015). An example of this is the Children Act (1989), which outlines parental responsibility and places children's safeguarding and welfare as the responsibility of the family, local authorities, courts and other agencies. The largely western, protectionist view of childhood has resulted in children being objects of care and services rather than active participants. With time and reflection, this view has been challenged and subsequently influenced the development of a children's rights perspective, discussed in the following section, as well as influencing research and policy that seek to listen to children and ensure they have voice in matters which relate to them such as their care, education and health. Young children are now increasingly viewed a 'meaning-makers' (Clark, 2017, p. 22) and 'experts in their own lives' (Langstead, 1994, p. 29; Clark and Moss, 2011, p. 10). This view emphasises the child or young person as active in the construction of their own knowledge and influential in terms of policy and practice development.

What is 'listening to children'?

Listening to children can be considered as listening to the opinions and wishes of children and acting upon such wishes; the phrase children's voices can be used interchangeably (Brooks and Murray, 2018). Despite there now being a selection of research focusing on children's voices, there is some disparity in how the concept is defined. More than ten years ago, Tangen (2008) discussed the multi-layered concept of listening to children that was both a method of consultation as well as the phenomena of children's views. The interaction required, when listening to children, was central to Tangen's (2008) discussion and essential to this was the reciprocal relationship required to listen; it is an active process between two or more people.

The interaction involved in listening was also central to the National Childcare Bureau's definition of listening as part of its 'Listening as a way of life' funded programme (Rich, 2011). In this programme, listening to children was said to be an active process which involves both the interpretation of the recipient as well as their response. It is not enough simply to listen, there needs to be acknowledgement and action to follow. This definition also acknowledges how listening to children in the early years will be multifaceted and include all the senses; this is also pertinent to those with additional needs. Preverbal children should also be considered as 'tuning into babies' enables interpretation of the youngest children's experiences (Rich, 2011, p. 1). This broader definition of listening was also applied in later government-funded research by Coleyshaw et al. (2012) which highlighted that listening was an interactive process not limited to spoken language. This is indicative of the seminal work of Loris Malaguzzi, founder of Reggio Emeilia's educational philosophy and author of the famous poem which outlines the 100 languages of children (see Edwards, Gandini and Foreman, 2011). This influential educational philosophy highlights the many ways in which children can communicate and the interplay between this and children as active participants learning in a social context.

Individual/group task

How do you listen to the children in your care? How can you listen to their actions and thoughts as well as their speech?

As well as listening as an active process in which children's views and experiences are sought, listening is also considered in light of the democratic principles which are embedded in the action required as a result. Bath (2013) described listening to children as a democratic care practice and stressed the importance of seeking the views of everyone involved in children's care and education; she stated that listening needed to be embedded within practice and opportunities should be provided for decision making within daily routines as well as one off consultancy for specific events. This democratic element to defining 'listening to children' is also apparent in Brooker's (2011) discussions around taking children seriously. She believes that letting children and young people have their say is preferable as it highlights the responsive element needed; by having their say children's views are used to shape new developments. Brooker (2011) also discussed the mediated element of listening; all listening is interpreted by the mind of the listener and this element cannot be forgotten as listening which is tokenistic or non-responsive will not have impact or lead to improved outcomes for children.

Non-responsive or tokenistic listening (Hart, 1992; Brooker, 2011) would be received by children in a similar way to not listening at all. By not listening to the voices of children, their perspective on process and potential outcomes is not sought and this can have a detrimental impact on well-being. Decisions that are made without children, in which they are treated as passive recipients, will result in reduced independence and ownership. An illustration of this would be an educational review in which only the voices of teachers and parents or carers contributed to an educational plan. Whilst they might consider the child's *best interest* (see section below on rights), without seeking the child's view more directly, decisions might be made which could negatively impact on the well-being of the child, for example moving a child to an alternative provision would remove their social relationships and familiar support mechanisms.

A child's right to be heard

The rights of children are enshrined in law after coming to the attention of the world largely during the late nineteenth and early twentieth century (Boylan and Dalrymple, 2009). The United Nations Convention on the Rights of the Child (UNICEF, 1989) was the culmination of this work and the treaty outlines children's economic, political, cultural, social and civic rights in 54 articles. Whilst the treaty supports children's well-being generally, there are two articles that specifically relate to listening to children: articles 3 and 12. Article 3 ensures that the best interests of the child are a primary consideration in all matters of welfare and law i.e. those making decisions should do so with the children's best interests at the fore. Article 12 ensures that children have the right to express their own viewpoint and that such views should be given due weight in accordance with the age and maturity of the child (UNICEF, 1989).

These two articles might appear, on the surface, to be aligned in their support of children's voice. The reality however is a tension between best interests and the right to a viewpoint which centres on the power that adults have to make decisions over children. Adults and children will not always agree on the best course of action and do not always have priorities which are aligned. This power imbalance is reflective of the protectionist view of childhood offered earlier in the chapter by James and James (2004) and reflects the current societal view of childhood. An illustration of this tension between best interests and the right to a viewpoint can be seen when exploring the well-being of children placed within the care of the local authority. Decisions here are the responsibility of those professionals within the local authority and will be based on their breadth of professional experience. Here, it takes the professional time and effort to ensure the child is listened to, and due consideration given to their wishes. The decision to remove a child from their family is never one taken lightly and can be at odds with the view of the child.

Individual/group task

Consider situations where a child's positive well-being is at risk, for example through experiencing bullying, when presenting with additional needs, when their welfare and security is at risk and when their health is at risk.

In these situations, how might the professional's opinion of the best course of action differ from the view of the child? How might such tensions be reconciled?

Listening within the curriculum

The Early Years Foundation Stage (EYFS) (DfE, 2017), which guides practice in England, places following children's interests as a central aim and this provides flexibility for listening cultures to develop in settings. Many settings operate a child-centred approach which enables the children's own interests to inform activities. Whilst there is no single agreed definition of child centred, it follows the assumption of the child being the centre of learning and schooling and able to direct their own learning (Chung and Walsh, 2010); it is known to contrast with a more formal and didactic educational approach which is often experienced by children as they progress from early years to statutory schooling (Jones and Lyndon, 2018). In early childhood, the enabling environment supports children in following these interests and the role of the adult is to support through this continued provision as well as adult-led activities. Whilst my own professional experience saw a flexibility within the EYFS to provide a listening approach, the statutory framework falls short of advocating this specifically (DfE, 2017). There is no provision within the statutory framework to involve children in decisions which affect their learning and development or their care. This is in direct contrast with the Special Educational Needs and Disability (SEND) framework (DfE, 2015, p. 20) which clearly states that 'children, their parents and young people are involved in discussions and decisions about their individual support and local provision'. The difference here being the age group covered by the SEND legislation (until 25 years of age) better fits the dominant view of age-related competency. In England, as children transition into the National Curriculum (DfE, 2013) between reception classes and year one, there is a shift in both the curriculum covered and the prevailing pedagogical style (Jones and Lyndon, 2018) resulting in a more formal curriculum delivery, not child centred, as discussed above. This National Curriculum (DfE, 2013) also falls short of directly advocating for children's voice but, through elements of citizenship, provides scope for this to be embedded in practice. It is through the citizenship curriculum and through a settings' pastoral care policy that well-being is directly addressed with the children, for example bullying and its consequences for both victims and perpetrators might be the subject of citizenship lessons.

Individual/group task

Consider your own practice and experience. When are children's ideas and opinions listened to? How do children's ideas influence practice development? Can you identify areas of practice which could make better use of children's views and opinions? How might these small steps impact on children's well-being?

Why listen to children?

Ensuring that children's views are incorporated into decisions which affect them provides an ethical approach which empowers children and supports positive well-being. Participatory pedagogy ensures children's views are central to the development of practice (Pascal and Bertram, 2009). It recognises the world view discussed above, that children are experts in their own lives (Langstead, 1994, p. 29; Clark and Moss, 2011, p. 10). Participatory pedagogy has democratic values (as defined by Dewey, 1916) and provides an empowering approach to education. It also recognises Freire's liberating approach to education (1996) and challenges a more traditional approach in which teachers are seen as owners of knowledge which is passed unreservedly to children. In promoting a more participatory pedagogy, children have the opportunity to develop across the vast breadth of knowledge rather than a prescribed and potentially narrow curriculum (Moss, 2017), which can only have a positive influence on their well-being as the child's interests drive their cognitive development.

Hart's ladder (1992) provides a helpful scale on which children's participation can be measured. The ladder provides eight segments, between rungs of the ladder, which range from full participation and shared decisions with adults at the top to manipulation as non-participation at the bottom of the ladder. What this illustrates well is the tokenism which exists in practice; the ladder places this under an umbrella of non-participation. Tokenism can be exemplified by adults who are seen to be seeking children's views when in fact decision making sits solely with the adults involved. Whilst Hart's ladder (1992) provides a useful mechanism to consider participation, it does not provide support for methods to actively engage participation. It does however provide a useful tool for reflection and self-evaluation when decision-making in the context of children's experience.

Individual/group task

Consider a recent change in the setting. To what extent were the children listened to? Where on Hart's ladder would your practice sit?

   How could practice at the bottom of Hart's ladder impact upon children's well-being?

   (Adapted from Hart, 1992, p. 8.)

How to listen to children?

One influential approach in early childhood is the Mosaic Approach which was first defined by Clark and Moss in 2001. This approach has been used extensively in early childhood research (Clark, Mcquail and Moss, 2003; Clark, Kjorholt and Moss 2005; Clark and Moss, 2005, 2011; Clark, 2017; Kingdon, 2019; Lyndon, 2019a) and has the capacity to be applied to work across the educational spectrum and provide specific application to those with additional needs or whose well-being may have been compromised. The Mosaic Approach has embraced the new sociology of childhood and responds to a previously adult-centred approach to education (Moss, 2019).

Children are not *objects* of education, they are *active participants* in their own learning through collaboration with adults and peers (Clark and Moss, 2011; Lyndon et al, 2019). The approach recognises that every child will have a unique world view. Children are seen as active participants in their own education and the Mosaic developed around one child will be very different from that of another (Clark and Moss, 2011). There are some basic assumptions which underpin the Mosaic Approach. First, children are experts in their own lives (Langstead, 1994, p. 29; Clark and Moss, 2011 p. 10); each child will offer a unique perspective on their own experiences (Clark and Moss, 2011, p. 5) and they create and develop their knowledge. This supports a social-constructivist view of knowledge similar to that of Vygotsky (1978) and Bruner (1990). The approach also recognises that children are competent and have many ways of communicating; the adult's role is to facilitate this communication through their own intervention and through a well-resourced, rich environment. Finally, the approach is underpinned by the rights-based agenda discussed earlier in this section and articles 12 and 13 of the United Nations Convention on the Rights of the Child (UNICEF, 1989), which state that children's views should be sought in matters which affect them.

This view of childhood, and the competency of children, then supports a 'framework for listening' (Clark and Moss, 2011, p. 5). The framework uses multiple methods as it recognises that children communicate in many verbal and non-verbal ways; as well as verbal communication through conferencing there is symbolic communication through the use of images. These methods then become a prompt for further reflection and discussion for children and practitioners (Lyndon, 2019b). This is a central element as active listening is emphasised; children participate in the interpretation of the evidence gathered as well as practitioners and parents. There is an acknowledgement that interpretations will vary; this discussion can be central in implementing change and improving practice. Clark and Moss (2011) highlight the importance of being open to the unexpected; using the children's priorities and concerns come to the fore. It was this adaptability and desire to develop practice that resulted in the research project which follows; a desire to both evaluate current practice and to embed a listening approach.

The Mosaic approach is broken down into steps. In the first instance, children and adults gather evidence through a variety of methods. Discussions take place with parents, carers, practitioners and children. The children also engage in photo elicitation, map making and are observed in daily routine (Lyndon, 2019a). The information from the different methods is pieced together and forms a prompt for dialogue, reflection and interpretation which then informs change (Clark and Moss, 2011; Clarke, 2017). The selection of methods helps to build up an overall picture of the child's interests, it represents their voice. By integrating verbal information from discussions as well as visual information such as pictures, a broad picture emerges from the child's experience. Patterns can be sought across the different methods and any differences discussed. The children then get the opportunity to reflect upon their own Mosaic and participate in the interpretation of evidence (Clarke, 2017). This is an important step; listening not just to hear what's been said but listening to inform change (Clark, Kjorholt and Moss, 2005).

The original Mosaic approach (Clark and Moss, 2011) reported by engaging in this process, the children became more confident in expressing their views. They also found that relationships, rather than specific activities, were particularly important to the children. This demonstrated that the children held very different priorities to the practitioners in the setting (Clark and Moss, 2011). The Mosaic approach was also used to reconsider the learning environment and make changes based on the children's views and preferences (Clark, Kjorholt and Moss, 2005). Moss (2017, p. 9) describes the Mosaic approach as 'the most influential and widely used method in service today' due to the influence it has had on early years research and practice.

One of the larger research projects which undertook Mosaic methodology was The Spaces to Play project (Clark and Moss, 2005); a key aim of the study was to demonstrate how young children could contribute to the development of spaces. Mosaics were built around observations, photo elicitation, book making, interviews, map making and tours with the children as well as range of methods to listen to the voices of parents and practitioners. This project resulted in reimagined outdoor spaces in which adults and children could sit together and which better facilitated free-flow play.

Whilst the Mosaic approach originally focused on early childhood, there are applications to older children, specifically when working with children with additional needs. The Mosaic explores children's experiences through 'talking, walking, making and reviewing' (Clarke, 2017, p. 19), and this flexibility and multi-modal process can accommodate children whose needs require specific consideration. The range of data collection methods, which do not all rely upon verbal responses, allow a composite picture of the experiences of the child to be built. Paige-Smith and Rix (2011) utilised the Mosaic approach (Clark and Moss, 2011) to build a better picture of the experiences of children with Downs Syndrome. Observations supported by photographs, followed by reflective discussions, allowed the researchers to develop a first-person narrative to illustrate the child's view. In this study, the first-person narratives which were developed supported the children's well-being by having a positive impact on the child's self-image and agency which was cultivated through the reflective sessions (Paige-Smith and Rix, 2011). Specifically, Paige-Smith and Rix (2011) saw shifts in parental understanding of their children's experiences and illustrate this with the example of throwing. Throwing was a behaviour that one parent was trying to discourage whereas the Mosaic and subsequent reflections enabled the parent to see how much enjoyment the child experienced when throwing.

The scope of the Mosaic approach to work with children with additional needs was also identified in 2004 by Beresford et al. who saw application when working with children on the autistic spectrum. This research demonstrated the multi-disciplinary aspects which could be incorporated into the Mosaic around each child; posters and social stories were included which were informed by professional practice. This research highlighted the importance of the role of the professional's voice within practice and the adaptability of the Mosaic approach to accommodate this.

The benefits of listening to children

Use has been made of the Mosaic approach in exploring children's perspectives on a variety of topics. Waller (2010) explored children's gender identity in outdoor play spaces and discovered that free flow play in the outdoor environment has the capacity to perpetuate gender difference. Tan and Gibson (2017) used Mosaic methodology to explore the arts-based experiences of children in both the home and setting environment and concluded that children relished the opportunity to create original artwork. The children also conveyed that, whilst they saw the process as one of learning, they saw their artwork as a finished product and mixed experiences were reported in the home setting; findings encouraged practitioners to review their pedagogical assumptions. Projects which have utilised Mosaic methodology discuss the importance of the participatory nature of the approach which ensures that children and young people have their views heard. This supports the development of agency and promotes positive well-being for those children.

My own professional and academic experience also supports the impact that a participatory approach, such as the Mosaic approach, can have on children of all ages and specifically those with additional needs. Having made use of such multiple methods and focused on the view of children (Lyndon, 2019a, 2019b; Lyndon et al., 2019), the importance of methods which are not reliant upon verbal responses became paramount. Photography is an accessible method for many children and can provide valuable insight into a child's preferences without the need for verbal competence. In my first research project (see also Lyndon, 2019a), a child who had presented with delayed speech and language, who was not specifically targeted by the research, had shown an interest in the camera and undertaking photography. This was in contrast to the expectation of the practitioners and his parents who all believed that he would not be interested in participating. He first exercised his right to participate and made use of the camera to document his interests in trains. He took a series of images of the tracks being built and his friends engaging in subsequent play. He then indicated his desire to create a photoboard of his interests by sitting down and selecting his printed photographs. Practitioners reconsidered their own assumptions as a result of this interaction and I believe photography offered this child an alternative language through which he could be heard, as per the work of Malaguzzi (Edwards, Gandini and Forman, 2011). All children who participated in this project exercised their right to be heard and relished the opportunity to participate. Practitioners reported increased levels of confidence in the children demonstrating a positive impact on their well-being.

In later research (Lyndon, 2019b; Lyndon et al., 2019), I explored the effectiveness of drawing as a mechanism for listening. Here, again the non-verbal nature of the task provided participation options for those who found verbal communication challenging and for those who were experiencing reduced well-being. Free drawing allowed children to respond to prompts without the need for discussion (Lyndon 2019b) and on one occasion a child expressed their emotions regarding transitions into the setting. Large black swirls of crayon were layered on top of one another as the child sought solitude away from other children. Eventually, she was ready to share that she felt unhappy and was missing her parents; this enabled practitioners to reconsider her current well-being and to reflect upon general transitional practice within the setting. The open-ended nature of drawing allows children to respond at their own developmental level, making it appropriate for a range of needs (Lyndon, 2019b). The child's voice is evident in both the process of drawing as well as the outcome adding to its versatility; researchers and practitioners can observe the process of drawing as well as analysing the outcome. Again, in this research, children demonstrated confidence in expressing their views and relished the opportunity to participate despite their level of verbal competence.

Listening to children, and valuing their voice, promotes agency and democratic values within our settings and so supports well-being and development. Children have the capacity to engage in those decisions which affect them, if we can adapt the way we listen to meet their needs. Adopting a participatory approach, such as this, demonstrates an ethical approach and one which can promote democracy to future generations.

Individual/group task

How could you develop better listening methods within your own professional context? Would the use of drawing or digital imagery better support a listening culture?

How might you trail such techniques within the setting? Given your knowledge of the children, what impact might this have on their overall well-being?

Summary points

- Children are increasingly viewed as active participants and experts of their own experience; a participatory approach to care and education supports this view and develops the child's agency and well-being.
- Definitions of children's voice and listening to children broadly agree that listening is an active process and children require acknowledgement and action as a result of such listening.
- The Mosaic approach (Clark and Moss, 2011) provides an effective multi-modal way of listening to children. This approach has specific application for the youngest children in our settings and those with additional needs due to the non-verbal methods which are available within the Mosaic.
- Drawing and photography are particularly effective in demonstrating the views of children for whom traditional dialogue or discussion may prove ineffective. These methods can facilitate improved well-being.

Recommended reading

Clark, A. (2017) *Listening to young children: a guide to understanding and using the mosaic approach, expanded third edition.* London: Jessica Kingsley.

References

Bath, C. (2013) Conceptualising listening to young children as an ethic of care in early childhood education and care. *Children and Society* **27** (5) pp. 361–371.

Beresford, B., Tozer, R., Rabiee, P. and Sloper, P. (2004) Developing an approach to involving children with autistic spectrum disorders in a social care research project. *British Journal of Learning Disabilities* **32** (4) pp. 180–185.

Boylan, J. and Dalrymple, J. (2009) *Understanding advocacy for children and young people.* Maidenhead: Open University Press.

Brooker, L. (2011) Taking children seriously: an alternative agenda for research? *Journal of Early Childhood Research* **9** (2) pp. 137–149.

Brooks, E. and Murray, J. (2018) Ready, steady, learn: school readiness and children's voices in English early childhood settings. *International Journal of Primary, Elementary and Early Years Education* **46** (2) pp. 143–156.

Bruner, J. (1990) *Acts of meaning.* Cambridge, MA: Harvard University Press.

Children Act (1989) http://www.legislation.gov.uk/ukpga/1989/41/introduction [last accessed 20 December 2019].

Chung, S. and Walsh, D. (2010) Unpacking child-centredness: a history of meanings. *Journal of Curriculum Studies* **32** (2) pp. 215–234.

Clark, A., Kjorholt, A. and Moss, P. (2005) *Beyond listening: children's perspectives on early childhood services.* Bristol: The Policy Press.

Clark, A., Mcquail, S. and Moss, P. (2003) *Exploring the field of listening to and consulting with young children.* Research Report RR445. Nottingham: DfES. https://dera.ioe.ac.uk/8367/1/RR445.pdf [last accessed 10 December 2019].

Clark, A. and Moss, P. (2005) *Spaces to play: more listening to young children using the mosaic approach.* London: NCB.

Clark, A. and Moss, P. (2011) *Listening to young children: the mosaic approach.* London: NCB

Clark, A. (2017) *Listening to young children: a guide to understanding and using the mosaic approach, expanded third edition.* London: Jessica Kingsley.

Coleyshaw, L., Whitmarsh, J., Jopling, M. and Hadfield, M. (2012) *Listening to children's perspectives: improving the quality of provision in early years settings.* Research Report DfE-RR239b. https://assets.publishing.service.gov.uk/government/uploads/system/uploads/attachment_data/file/183412/DfE-RR239b_report.pdf [last accessed 20 December 2019].

Dewey, J. (1916) *Democracy in education.* New York: Palgrave Macmillan reprinted 2004 New York: Dover.

DfE (2013) *The national curriculum in England: framework document.* https://assets.publishing.service.gov.uk/government/uploads/system/uploads/attachment_data/file/381344/Master_final_national_curriculum_28_Nov.pdf [last accessed 10 December 2019].

DfE (2015) *Special educational needs and disability code of practice.* https://assets.publishing.service.gov.uk/government/uploads/system/uploads/attachment_data/file/398815/SEND_Code_of_Practice_January_2015.pdf [last accessed 10 December 2019].

DfE (2017) *Statutory framework for the early years foundation stage.* https://assets.publishing.service.gov.uk/government/uploads/system/uploads/attachment_data/file/596629/EYFS_STATUTORY_FRAMEWORK_2017.pdf [last accessed 08 November 2019].

Edwards, C., Gandini, L. and Forman, G. (2011) *The hundred languages of children: third edition.* Oxford: Praeger.

Freire, P. (1996) *Pedagogy of the oppressed.* London: Penguin.

Hart, R. (1992) *Children's participation from tokenism to citizenship.* https://www.unicef-irc.org/publications/pdf/childrens_participation.pdf [last accessed 10 December 2019].

James, A. and James, A. (2004) *Constructing childhood: theory, policy and social practice.* Basingstoke: Palgrave Macmillan.

Jenks, C. (2005) *Childhood: second edition.* Abingdon: Routledge.

Jones, G. and Lyndon, H. (2018) The role of play in childhood pp. 32–42. In Brown, Z. and Ward, S. (eds.), *Contemporary issues in childhood: a bio-ecological approach.* Abingdon: Routledge.

Kingdon, Z. (2019) Using the mosaic approach as an ethnographic methodology pp. 109–123. In Brown, Z. and Perkins, H. (eds.), *Using innovative methods in early years research: beyond the conventional.* Abingdon: Routledge.

Langstead, O. (1994) Looking at quality from the child's perspective pp. 28–42. In Moss, P. and Pence, A. (eds.), *Valuing quality in early childhood services.* London: Paul Chapman Publishing.

Lyndon, H. (2019a) Mosaic: participatory research in early years pp. 103–113. In Lambert, M. (ed.), *Practical research methods in education.* Abingdon: Routledge.

Lyndon, H. (2019b) The use of drawing methods with young children in research pp. 63–76. In Brown, Z. and Perkins, H. (eds.), *Using innovative methods in early years research: beyond the conventional.* Abingdon: Routledge.

Lyndon, H., Bertram, T., Brown, Z. and Pascal, C. (2019) Pedagogically mediated listening practices; the development of pedagogy through the development of trust. *European Early Childhood Research Journal* **27** (3) pp. 360–370.

Moss, P. (2017) Power and resistance in early childhood education: from dominant discourse to democratic experimentalism. *Journal of Pedagogy* **8** (1) pp.11–32.

Moss, P. (2019) *Alternative narratives in early childhood: an introduction for students and practitioners.* Abingdon: Routledge.

Paige-Smith, A. and Rix, J. (2011) Researching early intervention and young children's perspectives – developing and using a 'listening to children' approach. *British Journal of Special Education* **38** (1) pp. 28–36.

Pascal, C. and Bertram, T. (2009) Listening to young citizens: the struggle to make real a participatory paradigm in research with young children. *European Early Childhood Education Research Journal* **17** (2) pp. 249–262.

Prout, A. and James, A. (2015) *Constructing and reconstructing childhood: contemporary issues in the sociological study of childhood.* Abingdon: Routledge.

Rich, D. (2011) *Listening as a way of life: listening to babies.* London: National Children's Bureau.

Tan, M. and Gibson, R. (2017) You feel like you're an artist. Like Leonardo da Vinci: capturing young children's voices and attitudes towards visual art. *International Journal of Education through Art* **13** (3) pp. 295–315.

Tangen, R. (2008) Listening to children's voices in educational research: some theoretical and methodological problems. *European Journal of Special Needs Education* **23** (2) pp. 157–166.

UNICEF, (1989) The united nations convention on the rights of the child. https://downloads.unicef.org.uk/wp-content/uploads/2010/05/UNCRC_united_nations_convention_on_the_rights_of_the_child.pdf?_ga=2.176675557.1356134371.1499802013-1656737017.1499802013 [last accessed 06 December 2019].

United Nations (1924). *Geneva declaration of the rights of the child.* www.un-documents.net/gdrc1924 [last accessed 10 December 2019].

Vygotsky, L. (1978) *Mind in society: the development of higher psychological processes.* Cambridge, MA: Harvard University Press.

Waller, T. (2010) 'Let's throw that big stick in the river': an exploration of gender in the construction of shared narratives around outdoor spaces. *European Early Childhood Research Journal* **18** (4) pp. 527–542.

Section 2

The role of children and young people in their own well-being and resilience

5 What does resilience mean to children?

Zeta Williams-Brown, Jayne Daly,
Michael Jopling and Andrew Aston

Children encounter a vast range of adverse experiences, ranging from poverty, lack of access to quality education or disability to family illness, addiction, prejudice or bereavement. For some children, these disadvantages seem to develop their resilience and encourage them to seek to change the course of their life. Others find it much more difficult to overcome them. We therefore need to question why are some children so resilient?

Today resilience is a fashionable word and you may encounter it frequently, particularly in texts that are concerned with children's well-being. The term resilience is a buzzword, seen in policy and used in practice. Programmes such as the UK Resilience Programme and Headstart have been developed in order to support childhood resilience. Yet, the term remains complex and multi-faceted.

In this chapter, we consider the complexity involved in defining the term resilience and identifying the need to consider and celebrate moments of resilience, whether they are in relation to minor or major adverse experiences for children. We also consider theory around whether children are born with inbuilt traits that support them being resilient and the influences of family and community on children's resilience. This chapter provides examples of childhood resilience in both minor and major circumstances of adversity.

We would like you to complete the below task before reading this chapter.

Individual/group task

Individually try to define *Resilience* in your own words.
Compare your definition to those of your peers.
How do they compare?
What similarities/differences are there in your interpretations?

The complexity of defining resilience

Masten (2014) explains how the term originated from the Latin word '*resilire*' which means *to rebound*. What does rebounding have to do with supporting well-being? We know all children suffer difficulties during their lives. This may be through extreme circumstances such as bereavement, violence, war, sexual exploitation, disability, illness and poverty or more local examples such as the break-up of families, racism, bullying or moving home. This list is not exhaustive and no listed 'category' here is deemed to be more of a threat to children and their well-being than any other, but it is important that you understand there is a vast range of circumstances that potentially could affect children. A resilient person is seen to be able to utilise their environmental resources to navigate adversity and thrive in the same way as others in less risky contexts (Ungar, 2004).

Although concerns have been expressed about its conceptual 'slipperiness' (Ecclestone and Lewis, 2014), many definitions of resilience focus on significant adversity that individuals have had to try and overcome. Luthar et al. (2000, p. 543) state that resilience refers to

> a dynamic process encompassing positive adaptations within the context of significant adversity. Implicit within this notion are two critical conditions: (1) exposure to significant threat or severe adversity; and (2) the achievement of positive adaptation despite major assaults on the developmental process.

In this definition, Luther refers specifically to 'significant or severe adversity', 'critical conditions', and 'major assaults'. How these conditions are measured is left open to individual interpretation. Terms such as 'bouncing back', 'adversity' and 'disadvantage' also appear frequently and consistently in definitions of resilience. For instance, Windle (2011, p. 163) states

> Resilience is the process of negotiating, managing and adapting to significant sources of stress or trauma. Assets and resources within the individual, their life and environment facilitate this capacity for adaptation and 'bouncing back' in the face of adversity. Across the life course, the experience of resilience will vary.

Southwick et al.'s (2014, p. 2) definition also includes the term 'bouncing back', but extends the scope of resilience away from focusing on 'significant sources of stress' to consider the minor and major *adverse* experiences children encounter where resilience can be identified and supported. It defines resilience in the main as "the ability to bend, but not break, bounce back and perhaps even grow in the face of adverse life experience".

In this section, we have evidenced that resilience is a complex, multi-faceted concept. It is therefore important that we clearly state how we have defined resilience in this chapter. Here, we utilise Southwick's definition to consider resilience in its broadest sense to include how children cope with the minor or major experiences of adversity they can encounter that require them to be resilient.

Do children possess traits that support their resilience?

Many question why some are able to *thrive* while others *purely survive* adversity (Southwick et al., 2014; Rose et al., 2016; Clanchy, 2019). There is a nature/nurture debate that surrounds childhood resilience. Are children born resilient or do they develop resilience during childhood? This chapter identifies the importance of both nature and nurture in the development of resilience.

Rutter's (1987) early work concluded that children can be born with traits that enable them to rebound from adversity. The resilient child is seen in this context to have extraordinary strengths, qualities and/or personality traits that allow them to thrive and develop in the face of adversity. Personality factors of those who are deemed resilient include a proactive approach to problem-solving, positive social relationships, including positive attention from family members, persistence and concentration, autonomy, independence and positive self-esteem and self-concept (Mayr and Ulich, 2009).

Dweck's (2012) research provides us with examples of how children respond differently to scenarios and how this can be influenced by their mindset. In one example, Dweck focuses on how children tackle a puzzle. Some see difficult puzzles as a challenge, whereas others are visibly nervous at the prospect of another task at which they might fail. Dweck suggested that children who were ready for that challenge had a *growth mindset*, and those affected by the pressure and the potential embarrassment of failure had a *fixed mindset*. Dweck's (2012) work is important in this context because it highlights the importance of mindset as a factor in their development and their responses to resilience. It helps us to consider the individual child, their mindset and the impact any experience can have on their mental health, future aspirations and life outcomes.

Resilience and 'grit' have become commonly aligned with many resources. Fite et al. (2016) investigated the individual traits of children who overcame adversity in their lives in comparison to other family members who were not. They suggested that being resilient is not about *bouncing back* at all, but about the inbuilt trait or 'grittiness' that occurs through self-regulation and *self-determined grit*. They believe that some of us have inbuilt traits and a natural ability to cope better with daily life pressures than our peers through positive self-control (Tedesqui and Young, 2018). In order to be able to self-regulate (the ability to cope or oversee oneself without need of external support), they found that individuals needed perseverance of effort with grit. However, they also added *contentiousness* and *self-control* as naturistic personal traits needed for successful resilience. Miller (in Fry, 2016) suggests that 'grittier' individuals are individuals who are positive and hopeful, having patience and good self-regulation to support themselves through adversity in their lives. As we have outlined, terms such as grit, toughness, ability to rebound and courage have been linked to resilience in a number of publications (Smith et al., 2008; Lucas et al., 2015; Middaugh, 2017; Arya and Lal, 2018). However, concerns have been expressed about the ease with which such approaches can be associated with discourses of 'character building' and performativity, as well as promoting individual, rather than social or communal, responses to adversity (Ecclestone, 2012; Ecclestone & Lewis, 2014; Royle, 2017). Further detail can be found in Chapter 2 of this book. This runs the risk of undermining or stigmatising children who are regarded as less resilient.

The impact of the environment on childhood resilience

Southwick et al. (2014, p. 2) state that there is "a host of biological, psychological, social and cultural factors that interact with one another to determine how one responds to stressful experiences". For instance, Masten (2014, p. 3) suggests that we develop resilience as some kind of *ordinary magic* that can be derived from 'ordinary resources and processes'. Early close supportive relationships with others (not necessarily family members) can help children overcome challenges, and close cultural encouragement and guidance are beneficial in supporting resilience. Petterson and Burke Albers (2003, cited in Owen 2018) suggest that if children are consistently exposed to adversity (e.g. poverty), much of their *natural resilience* becomes eroded. This would suggest that poverty has a constant impact on the child through adverse situations. Examples of this might include poor diet, living in inadequate quality housing or lacking opportunities to socialize. This therefore suggests that that home, family, friends and community are fundamental to a child's well-being and resilience so that they can flourish (Miller, cited Fry, 2016).

Research has identified the importance of close bonds between parents and their children in minimising stressors (Trevarthen, 2002; Berridge and Kringelbach, 2011). For example, Orbuch et al. (2005, p. 171) discuss the importance of parent-child links for childhood cancer survivors and focus on the resilience of families. In citing relevant research, they state:

> We argue that when children report having supportive and open relationships with their parents, they also report positive coping and recovery even under distressing circumstances. This argument is consistent with scholars (Peterson and Hann, 1999; Young, Miller, Norton and Hill, 1995) who proposed that parent-child relationships that are warm and supportive allow children to develop positive self-esteem and increased social competence and life satisfaction. The quality of parent-child relationships might be especially important for children when they are experiencing a stressful life event, such as a serious and chronic illness.

We need to be mindful that families are varied and diverse and include nuclear families, lone parents, same gender couples, adoptive families, families with guardianship and foster families. Research has told us that families build their own protective patterns of resilience. How effective they are in achieving this, according to Ungar (2015), depends on cultural influences and how readily available supportive resources are for them to access.

The move from focusing solely on family support to support from others is important. There is also an acceptance that supportive relationships can extend beyond the immediate family to relationships in other aspects of a child's life, including school and the community. Ungar (2011) emphasises the need for high-quality cultural encounters and interactions to support children's self-regulation. Communities and cultures can influence families by supportive behaviours that provide a nurturing environment in both positive and negative situations. When responding to disaster, communities can provide a lifeline to families. The consideration of community influence in this way brings to mind the African proverb *it takes a village to raise a child.* However, Masten (2014) warns this is not always straightforward. There can be difficulties between cultures and the wider community that can result in families becoming isolated, which makes it more difficult for them to access support and resources. Alternatively, cultural need can be misunderstood (Ungar, 2015). Conkbayir (2017) determines that as humans we often misinterpret the need of children with *'messy lives'* due to our own cultural norms, but we must be sensitive to the fact that many children remain at risk. An example of this may be the child whom we assume is living in a well-functioning family, but who in fact is being neglected by parents who are alcohol dependent and so quickly learns to care for themselves. This might be the cultural norm for this child and as a practitioner it is down to us to look for signs that all is not well. In this case, the 2-year old may happily pull up a chair to stand on to wash or help himself/herself to food, showing unusual independence.

There is also a concern in today's society that extended family and community are less cohesive and play much less of a role in children's lives than used to be the case. For instance, there are fewer children who play outside with their peers because of heightened safety concerns and neighbourhoods are no longer as connected as they were in past generations. There is a worry here, as Palmer (2006) noted, that we are now "physically containing the next generation of children" (Wright, 2015, p. 155). Not all children have experience of or access to community influences and support in today's society, which is likely to have an impact on their resilience.

Individual/group task

Consider your definition of resilience. How many of these terms formed part of your definition?
Grit/grittiness,
Toughness,
Ability to rebound/buoyancy
Courage
Trait
Self-determination
Self-regulation
If you did why do you think you chose these terms?
Did you also consider the need for children to use their initiative and be able to access support from family, friends, potentially a religion and/or the community?

The main difficulty with any definition of resilience is trying to generalise the characteristics and qualities of resilience for all children. Children are unique and will have varying levels of resilience depending on their predisposed characteristics, the experiences they have from birth, support groups throughout their childhood, and the adverse experiences they subsequently encounter.

Individual/group task

Reflect on your own childhood. You may consider yourself to have been a resilient child, but were there times in your childhood when you were more or less resilient in response to experiences you had?

Example of significant adversity and resilience in childhood

This section reviews the literature and research which examines the complex ways children can be resilient and the range of significant adversity they experience. Mayr and Ulich (2009) highlight longitudinal studies that have found children who have experienced high-risk adversity can show resilience and develop positively and successfully into adulthood. If you search for articles on resilience in childhood, you will find examples of resilience that portray a wide variety of experiences. They include individualised, case-specific experiences, for instance children who have experienced abuse and neglect, illness, bereavement and trauma. As Wright (2015 p.40) notes, some children literally have to *fight for their lives*.

It is important to note that the adversity children experience may only be known by the child's immediate family, friends or possibly local community members, such as a teacher. Examples of such adverse circumstances may include children's educational experiences. The two vignettes below are real-life scenarios that were detailed in a previous publication about childhood resilience (Brown and Daly, 2017). They provide detail of the complex, significant forms of adversity children can encounter. For confidentiality purposes, they have been anonymised.

Vignette 1

Joseph's Story

Joseph was an only child, a happy teenager who enjoyed school. His teachers noticed he had a close network of friends and a particularly close relationship with his mother and father. Joseph's mother had been recently diagnosed with multiple sclerosis and his father was her full-time carer. Joseph's extended family was limited, but his mother's sister (his aunt) helped out where possible.

While Joseph was sitting for his GCSE's, his teachers noticed a marked change in his behaviour. He was much quieter than normal and seemed to distance himself from his friends. One of the teachers asked Joseph to stay behind after school to discuss this. She learned that his father has just been diagnosed with terminal cancer and had only months to live. Joseph had been helping his mother whilst his father had been attending hospital for treatment, but now his father had discharged himself to support Joseph.

Joseph's father unfortunately passed away, but the request that his father left him with was that he needed to be strong as the 'man of the house'. With this in mind, Joseph went on to complete his exams. His mother was now cared for by his aunt when Joseph was at school, but Joseph took on the head of the household role. Joseph left school and went on to study business at college and then university. He and his mother remained close until her death when Joseph was in his 20s.

Today, Joseph is a happy, well-educated and successful self-employed businessman with a family.

Some adverse circumstances, such as serious and chronic illness of children and/or their family, are experienced by many children. It can be surmised that some children are likely to develop and demonstrate resilience for a diverse range of adverse experiences, for instance the experiences of looked-after children, children with special educational needs or disabilities, children living in poverty and children who are asylum seekers. Given the current war-torn circumstances in countries such as Syria, we have also included below a vignette focusing on the resilience of refugee children (Brown and Daly, 2017).

Vignette 2

Amiras' story

Amira is a 10-year-old girl who, until 2 years ago, was living happily with her family in a small Syrian village. The family were well-liked in the community and had many close contacts. Amira's family were farmers and she loves animals, but now this is all gone. War has meant that Amira witnessed her father's and her grandfather's murder at the farm as they protected their livestock and home. The farm and animals were destroyed.

The rest of the family which included Amira's mother, grandmother and her 6-year-old brother set up home in a derelict former school. Food was scarce and the family lived mainly on whatever they could forage or beg. Bellies were no longer full as they had been in the old days.

Amira's mother decided that things were now becoming too dangerous so Amira and her brother were sent on the long, arduous journey to Europe. Her mother, however, would not be going as she needed to stay behind to care for Amira's ailing grandmother.

Amira's and her brothers' journey was long and traumatic. During their journey, they saw people they had been travelling with die of disease, malnutrition, dehydration, drown and even be shot. Amira steadfastly protected her brother and together they arrived in Europe. She knew nothing of the new culture and could not speak the language when they arrived. Amira has lost contact with her mother and grandmother and does not know if they are still alive.

Individual/group task

Before you go on, we would like you to reflect on the complex range of significant adversity children can experience.

Please reflect personally on examples you may know about.

We would also encourage you to consider experiences of children across the world. For instance, when you watch the news consider the real life experiences for children including war and poverty.

The headstart programme evaluation: evidence of resilience

The co-authors of this chapter are currently involved in an evaluation project for Headstart Wolverhampton. Headstart is a long-term programme funded by the Big Lottery (2017–2021) trialling a broad range of initiatives for improving resilience and emotional well-being in 10- to 16-year olds in six locations in England. In Wolverhampton, it includes implementing the SUMO-based resilience programme in schools and a range of activities in the community including relax and craft, dance, active bodies…active minds, and flourishing families (Royle, 2017; Brown and Daly, 2019). The quantitative element of the evaluation, which used the Child and Youth Resilience Measure (Ungar and Liebenberg, 2011), revealed that children in Wolverhampton (surveyed in Years 6–8 so far) were more resilient than the norm overall but also suggested that their resilience declines as they move into and through secondary school. During the evaluation in 2018–2019, we asked children to provide us with examples of their resilience. Only 17% of the 76 children involved chose to identify life-changing examples of adversity that included loss, divorce, personal illness and illness of others. The quotations below provide further examples of significant adversity experienced by children and how they felt they had been resilient:

- My Mum and Dad divorced and I see my Dad every Thursday.
- I lost my cousin and had to say goodbye to him but I had to get through it both for my sake and my families.
- My boyfriend passed away.
- My Mum passed away just around last year and I bounced back stronger than ever. I've inspired people to be stronger and they've inspired me too.

Example of everyday adversity and resilience in childhood

The Headstart evaluation has produced interesting findings relating to children's perceptions of resilience and their everyday experiences of resilience. Almost half of the 77 children who completed a card sort data collection method called Q-methodology agreed that they were resilient people. Most of the children shared similar understanding of resilience as it related to them, and this was associated more with success through perseverance than endurance through mental toughness. 'Worrying about stuff' featured prominently among the participants and they tended to feel people did not listen to their problems. This was particularly the case at school where there was a strong consensus that they did not like it and felt unsupported.

However, despite negative perspectives on their experiences of school, 50% of the 76 children who provided examples of their resilience identified everyday examples of adversity from school or school-related activities. It can be debated whether in some of these examples children were highlighting their perseverance more than resilience. However, they detailed moments where they were encountering adversity and trying to overcome it. Some of the direct examples they provided included the following:

- I am resilient when I am at school because no matter what, I am always trying again.
- When I first started secondary school even though I didn't know my way around, I still really tried to make friends and get to class on time.
- When I did my mocks I just revised more because I wanted to do well and I know I could do better.
- I was getting ready for a test and I was getting frustrated at the fact that I was forgetting things I had already been taught. Fortunately, I ended up passing the test for my secondary school and my whole family and I were and still are very proud of my resilience.
- Someone was being rude to my best friend. I stood up to her even though I wasn't fighting. I told the teacher and didn't give up to help my best friend.

In total, 83% (including the school-related examples above) of the 76 children identified everyday examples of adversity and resilience. They were each asked to detail one example. Many of the examples they chose to identify could be considered ordinary, but not necessarily minor, experiences of adversity.

Some of the home-related examples included the following:

- When I was six, I wanted to ride my bike without help so I asked my Dad to take the extra wheels off. I kept falling but I did not give up.
- My Dad said that my cousin is better than me at English, then I said, "Ok but I will learn it too".
- My brother was hurt and I had a headache. I was in pain a lot and I still looked after him.
- I used to never be good at running but I kept trying every year and I got better.
- Trying to get into the dance company. I keep trying and trying but I still haven't got in yet, but I'm not going to give up.

Individual/group task

The vignettes and research examples do not present an exhaustive list.

Can you think of other significant and everyday experiences where children might demonstrate resilience?

Conclusion

This chapter has presented many examples of significant and everyday adversity that evidence the complex, individualised circumstances children face at home, at school and in their community. The definition of resilience utilised in this chapter (Southwick et al., 2014) is illustrated by these examples of moments where children were able to use their resilience to overcome adversity.

Rutter (2012) believes that the exposure of children to minimal stressors has the potential to support the development of resilience. Should children then experience some minimal stressors to support their resilience? It can be seen from the examples evidenced in this chapter that some children have been able to use or develop resilience to overcome their adversity. However, this is dependent on the child's experience, their resilience and the other forms of adversity that the child is experiencing at the same time. What we can say is that all of these examples should be seen as moments where children have been resilient (because they have persevered and/ or bounced back in the face of adversity) and they should be identified to these children and celebrated with them.

Summary points

- Resilience is complex, multi-faceted and difficult to define.
- Children can possess traits that support their resilience and also be influenced/ supported by their environment.
- Children can be resilient during experiences of significant and everyday adversity.
- Children benefit when moments of resilience (whether significant or every day) are identified and celebrated with them.

Recommended reading

Brown, Z., and Daly, J. (2017) The complexities of childhood resilience, in, Brown, Z. and Ward, S. (eds.) *Contemporary issues in childhood: A bio-ecological approach*. London: Routledge. pp. 43–55.

Brown, Z., and Daly, J. (2019) The 'resilient' child: Defining and supporting children's resilience in educational practice, in, Simon, C. and Ward, S. (eds.) *A student's guide to education studies*. London: Routledge.

Clanchy, K. (2019) *Some kids I taught and what they taught me*. London: Picador.

Masten, A.S. (2014) Global protectives on resilience in children and youth, *Journal of Child Development* **85**(1) pp. 6–20.

Southwick, S.M., Bonanno, G.A., Masten, A.S., Panter Brick, C., and Yehuda, R. (2014) Resilience definitions theory and challenge interdisciplinary perspectives. *European Journal of Psychotraumatology* **5**(Oct 2014) pp. 1–19.

References

Arya, B., and Lal, D.S. (2018) Grit and sense of coherence as predictors of well-being. *Indian Journal of Positive Psychology* **9**(1) pp. 169–172.

Berridge, K. C., and Kringelbach, M.L. (2011) Building a neuroscience of pleasure and well- being. *Journal of Psychology of Well-being* **1**(3) pp. 1–26.

Conkbayir M (2017) *Early childhood and neuroscience. Theory, research and implications for practice.* London: Bloomsbury. Dweck, C. (2012) *Mindset: Changing the way you think to fulfil your potential.* Great Britain: Robinson.

Ecclestone, K. (2012) From emotional well-being to 'Citizens of Character': Challenging behavioural interventions and new policy discourses. *Research Papers in Education* **27**(4) pp. 463–480.

Ecclestone, K., and Lewis, L. (2014) Interventions for resilience in educational settings: Challenging policy discourses of risk and vulnerability, *Journal of Education Policy* **29**(2) pp. 195–216.

Fite, R.E., Lindeman, M.I.H., Rogers A.P., Voyles, E., and Durik, A.M. (2016) Knowing oneself and long term goal pursuit: Relations among self-concept clarity, conscientiousness and grit personality and individual differences *Personality and individual difference.* **108**(2017) pp. 191–194.

Fry, M. (2016) *Miller C A: true 'Grit' leads to true greatness. Inspiring women in STEM conference* 2 December 2016). [online] www.njbiz.com Accessed 21 August 2017.

Lucas G.M., Gratch, J., Cheng, L., and Marcella, S. (2015) When the going gets tough: Grit predicts costly perseverance, *Journal of Research in Personality* **59** pp. 15–22.

Luthar, S., Cicchetti, D., and Becker, B. (2000) The construct of resilience: A critical evaluation and guidelines for future work. *Child Development* **71**(3) pp. 543–562.

Mayr, T., and Ulich, M. (2009) Social-emotional well-being and resilience of children in early childhood setting-PERIK: An empirically based observation scale for practitioners. *Early Years* **29**(1) pp. 45–57.

Middaugh, D.J. (2017) True grit, *Nursing Management* (September–October, 2017) **26**(5) pp. 347–348.

Orbuch, T., Parry, C., Chester, M., Fritz, J. and Repetto, P. (2005) Parent-Child relationships and quality of life: Resilience among childhood cancer survivors. *Family Relationships* **54**(2) pp. 171–183.

Owen, A. (2018) Child poverty and life chances, in, Brown, Z. and Ward, S. (Eds.) *Contemporary issues in childhood: a bio-ecological approach* (8, pp. 94–102). London: Routledge.

Palmer, S. (2006) *Toxic childhood: How the modern world is damaging our children and what we can do about it.* London: Orion Books.

Rose, J., Gilbert L., Richards, V. (2016) *Health and well being in early childhood.* London: SAGE.

Royle, K. (2017) Resilience programmes and their place in education: A critical review with reference to interventions in Wolverhampton, *Journal of Education and Human Development* **6**(1) pp. 53–65.

Rutter, M. (1987) Psychological resilience and protective mechanisms, *American Journal of Orthopsychiatry* **57** pp. 316–331.

Rutter, M. (2012) Resilience as a dynamic concept. *Development and Psychopathology* **24** pp. 335–344.

Smith, B.W., Dalen, J., Wiggins, K., Tooley, E., Christopher, P., and Bernard, J. (2008) The brief resilience scale: Assessing the ability to bounce back. *International Journal of Behavioural Medicine* **15** pp. 194–200.

Tedesqui, R.A.B., and Young, B.W. (2018) Comparing the contribution of consciousness, self-control, and grit to key criteria of sport expertise development. *Psychology of Sport and Exercise* **34** pp. 110–118.

Trevarthen, C. (2002) Learning in companionship: Education in the north. *The Journal of Scottish Education* **10** pp. 16–25.

Ungar, M. (2004) A constructionist discourse of resilience; Multiple contexts, multiple realities among at risk children and youth. *Youth and Society* **35**(3) pp. 341–365.

Ungar, M. (2011) The social ecology of resilience: Addressing contextual and cultural ambiguity of a nascent construct. *American Journal of Orthopsychiatry* **81** pp. 1–17.

Ungar, M. (2015) Varied patterns of family resilience in challenging contexts. *Journal of Marital and Family Therapy* **42**(1) pp. 19–31.

Ungar, M., and Liebenberg, L. (2011) Assessing resilience across cultures using mixed methods: Construction of the child and youth resilience measure, *Journal of Multiple Methods in Research* **5**(2) pp. 126–149.

Windle, G. (2011). What is resilience? A review and concept analysis. *Reviews in Clinical Gerontology* **21**(2) pp 152–169.

Wright, H.R. (2015) *Child in society.* London: SAGE.

6 The importance of positive peer relationships for child well-being and resilience

Alison Wren

Introduction

Human beings are social animals. We have an innate drive to belong and to build rewarding reciprocal bonds with other people. While children's earliest relationships are typically with parents and siblings, the relationships forged with peers differ in a number of crucial ways. First, unlike familial links, peer relationships are voluntary; children choose who to interact with and, more importantly, who to continue to interact with over time. Second, peer relationships are characterised by a more balanced power dynamic. Relationships with peers tend to be more equal with the peers chosen most often being of a similar age and, therefore, being at similar socio-cognitive, moral and/or developmental levels. Finally, peer relationships (unlike familial ties) are also far more prone to disruption and dissolution, the effects of which can reach into adult life.

This chapter starts by outlining the typical developmental trajectory of peer relationships from the early years through to adolescence. Following on from this, research highlighting the outcomes related to both positive and negative peer interactions is outlined, with specific focus on resilience and well-being throughout the life course. The chapter concludes with guidance for practitioners regarding how to support social development through positive pupil–peer interaction both in school and in other areas.

Glossary

Term	Definition
Peer interaction	Examples of children interacting with other children either verbally or non-verbally, most often measured quantitatively in research. Interactions can last for as little as a few seconds. Interaction is not necessarily indicative of friendship.
Peer relationships	Relationships between children and their peers. May be positive or negative. Relationships happen over time and involve action by more than one member of the relationship.
Friendship	No single definition. Broadly, friendship is a positive relationship and requires stability over time and reciprocity.
Social competence	The skills, knowledge and understanding needed to start, maintain and manage relationships with others. Sometimes called social skills.
Rejected children	Children who are not liked by peers and not chosen by peers for friendship.
Neglected children	Children who have low visibility in a group. They are neither liked nor disliked but are not chosen by peers as friends.
Popular children	Children who are well liked by peers and are regularly chosen by peers as friends. Popular children are also recorded as having stable friendships.

Individual/group task

Before you continue with the chapter, think about your own friendships and how they developed over your time at school. Put this into a timeline.

Can you remember when you first had a best friend? How did friends affect your experience at school?

The development of peer relationships

Children start making connections with other children at a much younger age than was at first thought. Even before they can speak, babies communicate non-verbally with other babies; mimicking behaviours and showing preferences for familiar peers over unfamiliar individuals. Studies have recorded examples of attempts at peer interaction in children as young as 6 months old (Meadows, 2009). *Friendship* is based upon location and access rather than individual behaviours or characteristics. Even at this early stage, those children with higher levels of social experience (multiple siblings, more opportunities to see peers, mothers with higher levels of social interaction) have been found to be more social with peers and more responsive to the actions of others (Hartup, 1983).

Through the Early Years Foundation Stage (EYFS), the focus shifts gradually from parents and family towards other children and those links to peers become increasingly important. Toddlers develop ingroups and outgroups, power hierarchies and start to identify *friends* who they show a preference for as playmates (Meadows, 2009). Belonging becomes increasingly more important and rejection a cause of distress. Friendships are based upon behaviours at this point, with positive attention, co-operation and gift-giving resulting in greater numbers of friends. Children who are aggressive or immature in their style of play have been shown to be subject to greater levels of peer rejection (Snyder and Patterson, 1995).

During primary school, friendships become more complex as children's social cognitive skills and communication skills develop. Making friends becomes more challenging, and friendships develop more gradually. A key factor in who children choose as friends at this point is proximity and access, and consequently networks of friends often change and shift with the pattern of the school year (Rubin, Bukowski and Parker, 2006). Children start to understand their peers' perspectives, and reciprocity of positive behaviours becomes more important. Children's friendships are based around the idea of fairness, and behaviour that is perceived to be unfair can result in friendships ending.

In secondary school, friendships become more intimate and mutual. Friends become the most important relationships for many children, and the people with whom secrets are shared and problems within their lives are resolved (Erwin, 1998). As children have learned how to compromise, friendships are less likely to end suddenly. Children over the age of 12 are also less possessive of peers, meaning that friendship networks may grow. As in adult relationships, the fundamental components of successful friendships at this stage are trust, emotional closeness, support and sustainability despite distance or time apart.

What do we mean by 'resilience' and 'well-being'?

The definition of resilience varies within the literature. Some authors feel that resilience involves some element of risk or challenge which must be overcome by an individual (Alvord and Grados, 2005). Others suggest that resilience is simply the skills and abilities needed to cope successfully with everyday life (Hill et al., 2007). What is clear across the literature is that resilient children are better able to adapt to changes in their lives; they can *bounce back*. This concept is explored further in Chapter 5.

Well-being is a concept that is also hard to quantify. Historically related to health and socio-economic situation, more recent definitions have defined well-being as being a multi-dimensional concept describing the overall quality of a person's life (Rees, Pople and Goswami, 2011). For children, this could include physical, social and emotional well-being, should consider their current and future prospects, and should also consider how well-being is culturally bound.

Taken together, these two concepts can be linked to a number of different factors which are directly linked to peer relationships in research including self-esteem, aspiration, aggression, problem solving, cooperation and group working, and adjustment during periods of transition. The following sections outline the challenges of causation, alongside research which suggests an adaptive value to peer relationships and negative effects related to the lack of friends.

Which came first, the friendships or the resilience?

Despite the challenges of research into pupil–peer relationships, a strong link between friendship and well-being/resilience has emerged from the literature. Many authors urge caution regarding the causative/correlative links between the two, with a lack of clarity remaining regarding the directionality of any effect recorded (Brendgen, 2012). A lack of longitudinal research, in particular, has made it difficult to clarify whether an individual's friendship status as a child results in the developmental, cognitive and social patterns observed in the literature. It is, of course, possible that an individual would have had the same outcomes and that their friendship status simply serves as an indicator or predictor of later outcomes.

While causation remains unclear, many authors argue that the myriad studies recording a pattern in relation to *friendlessness* and later negative outcomes suggest that strong stable friendships in childhood may be beneficial for building resilience in children (Ladd, Kochenderfer and Coleman, 1996; Parker and Asher, 1987). As such, friendship might act as a buffer against stress or against the potential negative effects of other factors even if it can't necessarily solve the underlying cause of the negative outcomes.

Discussion task

In teams, prepare arguments for either friendship as the foundations of resilience or vice versa. Use the evidence presented in the chapter alongside your own experience of peer relationships in school.

Resilience within the school environment

There is a range of evidence to suggest that children with fewer friends or those with poor quality friendships are less likely to succeed academically or to enjoy their time at school as compared to their popular peers, and that this may be related to their ability to adapt and cope with the changing school environment. Specifically, children with fewer friends have been found to be more likely to withdraw from education early and to have negative perceptions about their school experiences in general (Ladd, Kochenderfer and Coleman, 1996). Social competence has also been linked directly to cognitive ability and academic achievement and to levels of engagement in school activity (Li et al., 2011). So, what is it about having friends that makes school an easier place to navigate?

Cantor and Harlow (1994) suggest that friendships enable children to develop more flexibility in their approaches to tasks. By spending time with close friends, children learn that people have different ways of thinking about things and this, in turn, develops into a more adaptable or flexible way of thinking about a challenge or barrier that a child may face. Alongside this, because of the trust and closeness that is fundamental to successful friendship, children may feel able to ask for help from peers even when they are not confident to request this from adults.

Another factor that may explain the differences in educational experience and outcome for popular children as compared to their peers without stable friendships are findings from the literature that learning and school activity are more successful when children are able to work with their friends. Newcomb and Bagwell (1996) carried out a meta-analysis which found that children who are able to work with close friends had higher levels of on-task engagement and better outcomes than children working with *acquaintances*, children who they did not identify as either a friend or as someone they disliked. In part, the researchers suggested that this was related to the friends' ability to understand and articulate each other's strengths and weaknesses, which lead to more effective collaboration. Friends were also better able to resolve conflicts in order to meet the goal of the task. Interestingly, some research has suggested that this positive effect of working with a friend is only beneficial for tasks where the individual child could not succeed without the support offered (Azmitia and Montgomery, 1993).

A further explanation for the more positive school experiences of *friended* children is that the experience of having a friend develops, within the child, both a positive attitude to school and a desire to achieve academically. In contrast, friendless children were found to be more likely to be disruptive or have negative school perceptions (Li et al., 2011). Ladd, Kochenderfer and Coleman (1996) reported that the qualities of friendships had an impact on these effects, with friendships that included high levels of mutual validation and support found to be the most powerful in terms of positive early school adjustment. In contrast, the children who had experienced conflict rather than validation from peers were much more likely to avoid school or have lower levels of engagement in class activities.

Findings suggest that having friends equips the child with tools to be able to overcome challenges within the school environment. The friends, in effect, become more resilient through their support of one another.

Individual task

List three benefits of peer relationships for pupil's school experience.
   What would be the longer-term outcomes of these benefits?
   How could these children be at an advantage compared to peers in the future?

Resilience in school transitions

Transition between classes or between schools has been found to be a time of stress for many children that, if not handled carefully, can result in later negative outcomes. There is a range of evidence that suggests that positive peer relationships can support children's resilience and well-being through these challenging periods.

A Danish study found that the transition from nursery school to primary school was mediated by the presence of friends (Broström, 2003). The researchers reported that children were more likely to have a positive disposition towards their new school setting if they were transitioning with friends, with higher levels of well-being and confidence reported for these children than their friendless peers. Similar findings have also been reported for later school transitions (Hartup, 1983).

Importantly, children do not seem to need large numbers of friends to smooth the transition. Margetts (2002) found that even having a single familiar friend within the class resulted in higher levels of social skill and confidence, which supported the child to go on to build wider friendship links. In line with this, other studies have posited that the nature of the friendship rather than the number of friends is the important factor in relation to successful school transition. Hartup (1983) suggested that children who had a single supportive, close friendship were better able to adapt to their new school settings than children with large numbers of friends. Ladd, Kochenderfer and Coleman (1996) hypothesized that the ability to share feelings and have these validated by a close peer might be the reason for this positive effect of stable friendship on transition.

Although having a single friend may smooth transition at the time, researchers have found that the characteristics of the chosen friend are also important in relation to later school life. Berndt, Hawkins and Jiao (1999) reported that friendships with peers who had behavioural issues were predictive of later poor behaviour for the child, and children who were friends with sensitive peers were also likely to become more sensitive in their behaviours over time.

Emotional resilience

Perhaps unsurprisingly, children who have friends have been found to be more socially competent than children with limited friends but this social competence brings with it a range of related skills which may also serve to bolster individual resilience. Specifically, popular children have been shown to be more cooperative, more altruistic, more self-confident, and have higher levels of self-esteem (Newcomb and Bagwell, 1996).

Having friends has been linked to increased self-esteem in a number of studies. Vandell and Hembree (1994) found that acceptance by peers was the strongest predictor of positive self-esteem in secondary school age children. Berndt and Keefe (1995) reported that self-esteem was stable for the majority of children across the school year but that friendship quality was a predictor of some changes in self-esteem in relation to academic competence. Children who had difficulties in their friendships reported feeling that they had also become more disruptive and less stable in class; that they were achieving less well.

In relation to well-being, several studies have shown that children list their friends as being an important factor in what makes them *happy*. Westman (1990) asked young adults to think about what made them happy during their childhood. Sixty percent of responses related to friends in some way. In line with this Bagwell and Schmidt (2011) found that children named friends almost as often as they named parents when asked to list people who were important to them.

Finally, friends have been shown to have a key role in emotional support for children. Especially in the case of adolescents, peer relationships have been seen as a safe space in which children can explore who they are and how they express their emotions (Parker and Asher, 1987). This emotional support role is particularly important for vulnerable or at-risk children.

Studies have recorded effects both for children at the time they are experiencing difficulties and for adult outcomes of children who have lived through traumatic events. Positive, stable friendships have been related to reduced stress for children whose parents are divorcing (Wasserstein and La Greca, 1996), whose mothers are ill (Conrad and Hammen, 1993) and who are living in adverse conditions (Criss et al., 2002). A recent Headstart evaluation reported that children with limited or no family support went to friends and to Headstart for emotional support (Williams-Brown and Daly, 2019). Powers, Ressler and Bradley (2009) found that women who had been victims of child abuse were less likely to be depressed if they had had positive friendships at the time of the abuse. The following section looks at other studies which have investigated the longer-term impact of peer relationships and friendlessness.

Emotional adjustment in adult life

Just as we have to be cautious about causality in relation to peer relationships and resilience, so must we be when assessing any link between friendships and later outcomes. Although a number of studies have shown that preadolescent friendship status, and specifically peer rejection, may be predictive of patterns of adjustment in adulthood, it remains unclear whether the friendship experiences are symptoms or causes. Kupersmidt and Coie (1990) suggest that peer relationships may act as a mitigating factor for children with the pre-existing potential to have these negative outcomes, but evidence is lacking to support this claim. What is clear is that children who are isolated or rejected by their peer group are more likely to experience a range of negative outcomes, and these are detailed here.

Parker and Asher's (1987) review reported clear links between rejection by peers in childhood and later criminality, mental health problems and school dropout. More recent research has confirmed that these patterns continue to be recorded (Vargo, 1995). A number of studies have suggested a specific link between childhood aggression, peer rejection and negative consequences in later life. In relation to this, the outcomes recorded include substance abuse, lower academic achievement, delinquency and criminality (Kupersmidt and Coie, 1990).

A further outcome relates to intimate relationships in later life. Researchers have suggested that childhood friendships serve as building blocks for the development of social relationships in adulthood (Bagwell and Schmidt, 2011). Children develop empathy, learn to resolve conflicts and develop trust in these earliest relationships. Rejected or neglected children may not have the chance to learn these skills which may explain the issues observed in later relationships. Given that social isolation in adulthood has been linked to mental health concerns and medical issues, it is possible that this later inability to form social networks is at least in part, responsible for the other negative outcomes recorded.

Individual/group task

Given the benefits outlined in relation to peer friendships, how do you think school staff can support pupils to make and maintain strong and stable friendships?

What works? How can practitioners support pupil-peer interaction?

A range of strategies have been employed by researchers to support children to make and maintain successful friendships. Historically, a focus on social skills training through either active intervention or modelling good behaviour has been suggested. More recently, however, there has been a move away from these adult-led approaches towards strategies that focus on children's own experiences and understandings of their peer relationships. Two examples of this type of study are outlined in this section.

Carter and Nutbrown (2016) conducted a small-scale study that aimed to capture children's views of their friendships and, through understanding their perspectives, develop a *pedagogy of friendship* which could guide practitioner support. Based on the children's responses, the authors suggested that three central ideas are the key to support pupil–peer relationships within early childhood education. First, they emphasised that practitioners need to have knowledge of the friendships of the children they work with, and that this information should come from the children themselves. Second, that practitioners should value and appreciate the friendships of children; understanding the challenges involved in making friends and the effort involved in maintaining friendships. Finally, they suggest that practitioners need to recognise that children have agency in their friendships and so should be given the time, space and opportunity to build bonds independently where possible. Importantly, the children's own voices should underpin the whole process in order to empower them to build their own social competence for later friendships; to support the development of resilience within their peer relationships.

Another study that focuses on children's understandings and supports their agency is Murphy and Schneider (1994). The researchers worked with a group of 12-year olds who had been identified as rejected children. The children were asked to choose a classmate who they would like to be friends with and the child was then guided through the process of engaging with that classmate. Counsellors were available to the child in case of challenges experienced throughout the process. The final results of the study showed that both the previously rejected children and the targeted classmates rated each other more highly as friends following intervention. The process of teaching the children about how to initiate social interactions could also add to their resilience for future peer relationships.

Conclusions

Well-being, resilience and children's friendships are inextricably linked in ways that can affect individuals across their life course. Children start making connections within their first year, and it is clear from the literature that difficulties securing and maintaining these bonds at an early age can be related to problems in later childhood and even into adulthood. Children's friendships have been linked to a number of positive effects including better educational outcomes, less stress during periods of transition and emotional support. Children who do not have stable or positive peer relationships have been found to be more likely to experience a range of negative outcomes in later life.

Although causality remains unclear, the links between negative peer relationships and later negative outcomes, and vice versa, suggests that children who are rejected by their peers or who struggle to maintain friendships should be supported to resolve this. Focusing on children's own understandings of their friends, their individual relationships and what they want to achieve is a strong foundation for successful intervention which can build social competence, individual confidence and equip children with the tools to succeed in future relationships.

Summary points

- Childhood friendships develop at first based upon proximity and availability. As children age, behaviour and characteristics become more important. Aggressive and immature children can struggle to make friends.
- Determining causality is challenging and many researchers are unclear as to whether resilience is built by positive friendships or whether friendships occur more easily for resilient children.
- Childhood friendships have been linked to numerous positive outcomes including a more positive school experience and higher levels of achievement, smoother transition periods, and greater emotional resilience.
- A lack of childhood peer relationships has been found to be predictive of a number of negative outcomes in later life.
- Practitioners can support children to make and maintain successful friendships by listening to the children about their peer relationships and supporting them to have the opportunity and independence to develop these friendships, with guidance and support where required.

Recommended reading

Bukowski, W.M., Newcomb, A.F., and Hartup, W.W. (1996) *The Company They Keep: Friendship in Childhood and Adolescence*. Cambridge: Cambridge University Press.

Meadows, S (2009) *The Child as Social Person*. Hove: Routledge.

Parker, J.G. and Asher, S.R. (1987) Peer Relations and Later Personal Adjustment: Are Low-accepted Children at Risk? *Psychological Bulletin*, **102**(3), 357–389.

Schneider, B.H. (2016) *Childhood Friendships and Peer Relations: Friends and Enemies*, 2nd edition. Abingdon: Routledge.

References

Alvord, M.K. and Grados, J.J. (2005) Enhancing Resilience in Children: A Proactive Approach. *Professional Psychology: Research and Practice*, **36**(3), 238–245.

Azmitia, M. and Montgomery, R. (1993) Friendship, Transactive Dialogues, and the Development of Scientific Reasoning. *Social Development*, **2**(3), 202–221.

Bagwell, C.L. and Schmidt, M.E. (2011) *Friendships in Childhood and Adolescence*. New York: Guilford.

Berndt, T.J., Hawkins, J.A., and Jiao, Z. (1999) Influences of Friends and Friendships on Adjustment to Junior High School. *Merrill-Palmer Quarterly*, **45**(1), 13–4.

Berndt, T.J. and Keefe, K. (1995) Friend's Influence on Adolescents' Adjustment to School. *Child Development*, **66**, 1312–1329.

Brendgen, M. (2012) Genetics and Peer Relations: A Review. *Journal of Research on Adolescence*, **22**, 419–437.

Broström, S. (2003) Problems and Barriers in Children's Learning When they Transit from Kindergarten to Kindergarten Class in School. *European Early Childhood Research Journal*, Research Monograph Series 1, **11**, 51–66.

Cantor, N. and Harlow, R.E. (1994) Social Intelligence and Personality: Flexible Life Task Pursuit. In Sternberg, R.J. and Ruzgis, P. (Eds.), *Personality and Intelligence*, 137–168. New York: Cambridge University Press.

Carter, C. and Nutbrown, C. (2016) A Pedagogy of Friendship: Young Children's Friendships and How Schools Can Support Them. *International Journal of Early Years Education*, **24**(4), 1–19.

Conrad, M. and Hammen, C. (1993) Protective and Resource Factors in High-risk and Low-risk Children: A Comparison of Children with Unipolar, Bipolar Medically Ill, and Normal Mothers. *Development and Psychopathology*, **5**, 593–607.

Criss, M.M., Pettit, G.S., Bates, J.E., Dodge, K.A., and Lapp, A.L., (2002) Family Adversity, Positive Peer Relationships, and Children's Externalizing Behavior: A Longitudinal Perspective on Risk and Resilience. *Child Development*, **73**(4), 1220–1237.

Erwin, P (1998) *Friendship in Childhood and Adolescence*. London: Routledge.

Hartup, W.W. (1983) Peer Relations. In Mussen, P.H (Ed.) *Handbook of Child Psychology*, 4th edition, 103–196. New York: Wiley.

Hill, M., Stafford, A., Seaman, P., Ross, N., and Daniel, B (2007) *Parenting and Resilience*. York: Joseph Rowntree Foundation.

Kupersmidt, J.B. and Coie, J.D. (1990) Preadolescent Peer Status, Aggression and School Adjustment a Predictor of Externalizing Problems in Adolescence. *Child Development*, **61**, 1350–1362.

Ladd, G.W., Kochenderfer, B.J., and Coleman, C.C (1996) Friendship Quality as a Predictor of Young Children's Early School Adjustment. *Child Development*, **67**, 1103–1118.

Li, Y., Lynch, A.D., Kalvin, C., Liu, J., and Lerner, R.M. (2011) Peer relationships as a Context for the Development of School Enagagement During Early Adolescence. *International Journal of Behavioural Development*, **35**, 329–342.

Margetts, K (2002) Transition to School: Complexity and Diversity, *European Early Childhood Education Research Journal*, **10**(2), 103–114.

Meadows, S. (2009) *The Child as Social Person*, Hove: Routledge.

Murphy, K. and Schneider, B.H. (1994) Coaching Socially Rejected Early Adolescents Regarding Behaviours Used by Peers to Infer Liking: A Dyad-specific Intervention. *Journal of Early Adolescence*, **14**, 83–95.

Newcomb, A.F. and Bagwell, C.L. (1996) The Developmental Significance of Children's Friendship Relations. In Bukowski, W.M., Newcomb, A.F., and Hartup, W.W. (Eds.) *The Company They Keep: Friendship in Childhood and Adolescence*, 289–321. New York: Cambridge University Press.

Parker, J. G., & Asher, S. R. (1987) Peer Relations and Later Personal Adjustment: Are Low-accepted Children at Risk? *Psychological Bulletin*, **102**(3), 357–389.

Powers, A., Ressler, K.J., and Bradley, R.G. (2009) The Protective Role of Friendship on the Effects of Childhood Abuse and Depression. *Depression and Anxiety*, **26**, 46–53.

Rees, G., Pople, L., and Goswami, H. (2011) *Understanding Children's Wellbeing*. London: The Children's Society.

Rubin, K., Bukowski, W. and Parker, J. (2006) Peer Interactions, Relationships and Groups. In Damon, W., Lerner, R., and Eisenberg, N. (Eds.) *Handbook of Child Psychology*, 6th edition, 571–645. New York: Wiley.

Snyder, J. and Patterson, G. (1995) Individual Differences in Social Aggression, *Behavior Therapy*, **26**, 371–391.

Vandell, D.L. and Hembree, S.E. (1994) Peer Social Status and Friendship: Independent Contributors to Children's Social and Academic Adjustment. *Merrill-Palmer Quarterly*, **40**, 461–477.

Vargo, B. (1995) Are Withdrawn Children at Risk? *Canadian Journal of School Psychology*, **11**(2), 166–177.

Wasserstein, S.B. and La Greca, A. (1996) Can Peer Support Buffer Against Behavioural Consequences of Parental Discord? *Journal of Clinical Child Psychology*, **25**, 177–182.

Westman, A.S. (1990) Do People's Presence More than Their Parents make Children Happy? *Perceptual and Motor Skills*, **7**, 674.

Williams-Brown, Z. and Daly, J. (2019) The 'resilient' Child: Defining and Supporting Children's Resilience in Educational Practice. In Ward, S. and Simon, C. (Eds.) *A Student's Guide to Education Studies*, 214–223. London: Routledge.

7 Mental health in digital lives

Gavin Rhoades, John Owen and Bill Myers

Introduction

This chapter considers issues around online social media usage and young people's mental health. Many people today experience 'digital' lives that run alongside and intertwined with our 'real' lives. Young people are particularly influenced by their digital lives and for many of them the line between the two is growing increasingly blurred. They have an online world of information at their fingertips, or more likely, their thumbs, that was unimaginable just a few decades ago. The internet provides a wide range of communication channels linking them with people and organisations all over the globe, without needing to know these people before they communicate with them. For the most part, these information sources and communication channels are entirely unmoderated, meaning people can say whatever they like. Today's youth are exposed from a young age to ideas, images, beliefs and ideologies that earlier generations would probably not have encountered until adulthood, if at all. Given this is a recent development, the effects this may have on young people's mental health in the future are unknown. This chapter explores how these digital lives may impact their well-being in their real lives. Issues considered will include our perceptions of reality, social comparisons, peer pressure, radicalisation, self-harming and cyberbullying.

Social media began with the first multi-user online chat system, Talkomatic, created at the University of Illinois in 1973. Since then, the number of social media applications has exploded and user numbers have expanded exponentially. Today 3.2 billion people around the world use social networking sites (SNS) on a daily basis. That equates to 42% of the global population. 90.4% of Millennials are active social media users, compared to 77.5% of Generation X and 48.2% of the Baby Boomer generation (Mohsin, 2019). About 95% of 15-year olds in the UK use SNS every day. Thirty-seven percent of 15-year olds in the UK can be classed as 'extreme internet users' as they are online for over 6 hours per day (Frith, 2017).

Social media permeates most aspects of our online lives, whether it is the news, shopping, religion, entertainment or in the workplace; it is seemingly inescapable. With this growth in reach has come a growth in influence on people and their behaviour. It is this influence that our digital lives exert on our real lives that will be explored in this chapter.

Individual/group task

Think about your own online activities and SNS use. How often do you use social media? How long for each time? Add it all up. Are you above or below the 2 hours 22 minutes average daily use? (Mohsin, 2019).

Benefits of social media and digital technologies

The chapter explores a range of potential negative impacts on young people of SNS and digital technologies. It would be disingenuous however, not to highlight at least some of the areas where social media undoubtedly offers benefits in relation to young people's mental health, especially as young people themselves see social media as a positive influence in their lives.

Benefits include improving social skills online, reducing isolation, developing character and resilience, and learning to collaborate. Young people can have fun, make and maintain friendships and stay connected to family members. They can become part of global communities based on their interests and emerging identities, and find a sense of connection and belonging that can bolster their mental health. Social media can encourage collaborative learning opportunities and foster creativity. Children with disabilities or medical conditions can share experiences with similar peers and find support groups online (raisingchildren.net.au, 2019). Young people with mental health problems can find information and help online; for example, 78% of the young people contacting Childline in the UK now do so online, and the Crisis Text line service in the USA allows young people in any kind of crisis to anonymously talk to trained counsellors via text messages (Frith, 2017).

The digital perceived as reality

A significant school of thought within the social sciences argues that reality is socially constructed. This viewpoint defines reality as "phenomena that we recognize as having a being independent of our own volition (we cannot 'wish them away')" (Berger and Luckmann, 1991, p. 13). Children, like most people living their daily lives, will not routinely stop and ask themselves questions like 'What is reality?' or 'How can I tell what is real?', they just accept everything around them as real. Academics, and philosophers in particular, do tend to ask these questions, and it is important that they do because of the concept of social relativity. What is real to one person, for example a European billionaire businessman, may not be real to an impoverished, orphaned refugee child. This means that these different realities are grounded in different social contexts, or are in other words socially constructed.

Online SNS offer carefully curated windows into peoples' lives which can change users' social contexts and become part of users' realities. This is most easily seen with the followers of celebrity influencers who genuinely feel they have a relationship with the celebrity. Young people especially can be quite naive in their online behaviour, and in their trusting innocence, they tend to find credible things that a more mature, cynical audience would doubt. Young people with developmental delay or additional learning needs may also tend to trust when others would be doubtful. Given that young people's behaviours are often shaped or influenced by their social context, of which social media now forms such a significant part, it is very much the case that for many young people, the boundary between the virtual and the real is no longer distinct. Given that they cannot 'wish away' unpleasant digital experiences it is easy to see the impact this may have on their mental well-being.

Addiction and risk taking in the digital world

One of the most significant dangers facing young people is addiction to technology and the digital world. They may begin to withdraw from everyday life and change their perceptions and values both in the real and online worlds (Vanderhoven, 2014). This can lead to risky behaviours such as publishing inappropriate images, posting harmful comments and shunning friends and family. About 30% of 11- to 16-year olds report one or more experiences linked to excessive internet use such as neglecting friends, schoolwork or sleep (Livingstone and Haddon, 2009).

In terms of other possible effects, particularly on extreme internet users, Shaw and Gant (2004) found a link between internet use and depression, loneliness and stress. A number of studies also suggest that SNS use tends to increase loneliness but can have a positive effect upon social support. Over-use has the potential for social isolation. Valkenburg, Peter and Schouten (2006) identified increased use of SNS as having an indirect effect upon self-respect and psychological mood. This was linked to the number of friends the young people had on the SNS and how the feedback received about one's profile affected their self-esteem.

In addition to potential psychological effects, there is growing concern about the physical impact of excessive 'screen-time', particularly in very young children. One in five children in England are now classed as overweight or obese (Local Government Association, 2018), and it is thought that excessive use of screens may be contributing to rising obesity in children, and when used in the evenings, problems with sleeping. The World Health Organisation recently recommended that children below the age of five should be limited to an hour a day of screen-time and infants should not be exposed to it at all. They also recommend a break from screens every 2 hours for all children and the removal of mobile phones from children during meal times and overnight (WHO, 2019).

Social comparison, envy and depression

The feelings of envy and despair that many people experience when they see the 'perfect lives' of so many other people on SNS are key issues for mental health in digital lives. This is especially true for young people whose perceptions of themselves are often strongly influenced by the opinions of their peers. Many research studies investigating the negative emotional impacts of SNS on the individual are based on social comparison theory, which has three hypotheses (Festinger, 1954). The first hypothesis acknowledges that humans are motivated to evaluate our abilities, characteristics and possessions for our own protection because mis-estimating these can threaten our physical or emotional well-being. Second, we support our assessment by comparing ourselves to others. Third, we prefer to compare ourselves to people we consider to be similar to us. This process has become so embedded that it is often described as a fundamental psychological process related to self-esteem.

Applied to the use of SNS by individuals, social comparison theory explains how other elements can contribute negatively when making personal comparisons. Haferkamp and Krämer (2011) found that, when presented with virtual online profiles of people described as beautiful, participants had a more negative body image afterwards than those who were presented with less attractive profile pictures. Additionally, users often present skewed profiles, editing uploaded information and images to show themselves in a positive light, for example healthy, wealthy, well-informed, popular and beautiful. These comparative opportunities are empirical and can become competitive, for example, number of likes; quantity and quality of comments. The chances of a negative comparison between this legion of positive online profiles and the reality of one's own personal circumstances is likely to be high, and with that negative self-assessment, envy increases, self-esteem lowers and the likelihood of depression increases. Opportunities to raise self-esteem away from the digital world help develop greater resilience to negative comparisons when online.

Individual/group task

Do you know any young people whose online profiles don't match with what you know to be the reality of their lives? Have you ever talked to them about it? What might they say if challenged about the differences? What might their reactions to such questions reveal about the link between their online profiles and their mental images of themselves?

Body image in the digital world

Concerns about the impact of 'air-brushed' models in magazines on impressionable young girls in particular have existed as long as the magazines themselves. With the explosion of the World Wide Web and other media in recent decades, however, the prevalence of such images has grown massively. Marketing campaigns co-ordinate across different media platforms so whether it is billboards in the street, websites on the smartphone or adverts in magazines targeted at young people, these images of unattainable perfection are everywhere.

The increased popularity of smartphones with cameras and apps that can apply filters and manipulate images has led to this issue impacting directly on young people and their peers in the form of altered 'selfies' and the quest to capture the 'perfect' selfies to share on profiles. There is evidence these behaviours have led girls in particular to focus on the 'thin ideal' leading to issues with body esteem (Frith, 2017). Young people do not always understand that these images of perfection are manufactured, and even when they do, they may be more prone to suffer anxiety and depression when they try to match up to them. The Advertising Association conducted research into body confidence with over 1,000 girls aged 10–21 in August 2011. They found that 58% of pre-teen girls understood what air-brushing was, rising to 97% for 16- to 21-year olds. Despite this level of understanding many still aspired to match these published re-touched images, with over a third (37%) of the young women saying they wanted to look like the girls in the images. Fifty-two per cent agreed with the statement "seeing adverts using thin models makes me want to diet/lose weight/feel more conscious of the way I look". Forty per cent of the young women in this study also admitted to air-brushing their own photographs for uploading to social media (Advertising Association, 2011).

Peer pressure and the 'Fear of Missing Out'

Whether it is Game of Thrones, the latest computer game or pop group, if young people are talking about it and one of them knows nothing about it the chances are that the individual will experience characteristics associated with the 'Fear of Missing Out' (FOMO). FOMO has been defined as the psychological state of anxiety caused by thoughts that one's peers within one's social spheres are leading more socially desirable and interesting lives; it has clear parallels with social comparison theory (Przybylski et al., 2013).

Intentionally or not, SNS have created features to entice new users which then induce FOMO. One such feature, 'tagging', which allows users to name fellow users in photographs they upload, may induce non-users who appear in the image to engage so they can be tagged also. When this happens, subconscious peer pressure has procured the SNS another user. Normative social influence, or the desire to fit-in and be like others, has motivated a behavioural, emotional and possibly cognitive change in new user. Engagement with the SNS can then be further induced and maintained by online availability indicators.

To add to the obsessive nature of FOMO, it appears that normative social influence is hard-wired into the brain. Strong correlations have been shown between experiences of FOMO and the frontal-limbic circuits which are the areas of the brain associated with social exclusion (Lai et al., 2016). Normative social influence is particularly strong in young people as they become more influenced by their peers than by their families. As the psychosocial founder Erikson points out, "The growing and developing youths, faced with…[puberty]…are now primarily concerned with what they appear to be in the eyes of others as compared with what they feel they are…" (Erikson, 1963, p. 255). Erikson goes on to explain that through interactions with their peers, through forming groups and adhering to the group norms and styles, often deliberately deviating from the wider societal norms that young people start to find who they are. It is how the young person feels they are being perceived by their peers, that is most important to their sense of self rather than through their familial relationships.

Buglass et al. (2017) found a positive correlation between SNS use and FOMO, lowering self-esteem and increasing online vulnerability. Online vulnerability is the capacity to experience detrimental to one's psychological, reputational or physical well-being as a result of online activities. Their findings further support the FOMO theory of Przybylski et al. (2013) which posits that SNS users can find themselves in a downward cycle of experiencing FOMO where lower self-esteem and peer pressure make young people engage more often in SNS to try and boost their sense of well-being.

Individual/group task

What kind of practical steps do you think could be taken to help a young person who is unhappy through their FOMO?

A reliable source of information about how to overcome FOMO can be found via Psychology Today: https://www.psychologytoday.com/gb/blog/stronger-the-broken-places/201501/10-ways-overcome-fear-missing-out

---

Online relationships with strangers

The most frequent risky online behaviour reported by children in Europe is communicating with people they do not know in the real world (Livingstone and Haddon, 2009). The EU Kids Online study identified that 30% of European children aged 9–16 who use the internet had communicated with someone they had not met face-to-face. Many young people are developing online relationships with people they do not know in the real world through their interactions on SNS, an online gaming site.

In these media, young people meet others whom they do not know and engage in an activity with a common interest. The interactions quickly allow a relationship to develop, for example in a game they may be in the same 'guild', discussing tactics and skills to begin with and then moving on to chatting outside the main game. These relationships provide welcome interactions with like-minded people and can be beneficial, particularly for shy children who struggle to make friends. Children with Special

Educational Needs or Disability may, depending on their needs, be prone to being very trusting and sharing, or may find the social aspect of the games to be challenging. Mazurek and Wenstrup (2013, p. 1259) found that children with Autistic Spectrum Disorder "spent approximately 62% more time watching television and playing video games than in all non-screen activities combined", but spent little time using social media or multi-player games that required them to interact with others.

However, the other person can never genuinely be known or accurately identified because of the ease of anonymity and deception when online. This increases risks for young people who are sharing personal information, intimate thoughts and dreams with others who are effectively strangers. Research in Latvia identified that more than one-half of young people look for new online friends several times each year and more than one-third of them add someone they do not know in the real world to their friends list (Brikse, Inta and Spurava, 2014).

A Japanese study acknowledged that although there were positive opportunities created by accessing SNS, they also offered the danger of establishing undesirable relationships (Ando, Takahira and Sakamoto, 2005). Research in Russia found that making new friends online has an inherent element of risk, but this is not necessarily a negative activity and appears to support the building of resilience as young people explore the boundaries of their social world and learn by both adhering to social norms and taking risks (Soldatova et al., 2014). It can be seen that this is a problem that is not isolated to one country, or region, but is found across the globe.

Grooming and radicalisation

Grooming is the building of a relationship with a child in order to later abuse them. This is generally seen as being for sexual exploitation, but the same process is also used by those who wish to radicalise young people to believe particular doctrines. The grooming process is designed to change the values and perceptions of the 'victim' so that they can be coerced into actions which they would previously have considered to be inappropriate. In order to achieve this, the groomer develops the contact through the chosen media, incrementally drawing their target into an increasingly trusting and dependent relationship. Empathy can be shown about the things in a young person's life that make them unhappy and 'better' alternatives can be suggested.

SNS are designed to encourage the sharing of personal information. This provides a way for online 'groomers' to target young people who make themselves more vulnerable, for example by leaving privacy settings open on their profile. Many gaming sites also include options which allow 'in-game chat' to take place where gamers are encouraged to share personal information. Apparently, innocuous comments about where they and their friends like to hang out in a particular local town or sharing a photograph of themselves in their school uniform where the school name is visible are simple ways in which personal information can be gathered. Over time, a large amount of information can be collated and used to identify where a young person lives, the probable route they walk to school, their favourite activities, who their friends are and what time they are likely to be walking home.

Warning signs of grooming include, amongst others, the following:

- Inappropriate content saved to phones or other devices. Groomers may send pornographic images in order to 'normalise' their requests for pictures;
- Receiving or making calls to numbers that they keep secret;

- Spending an increasing or excessive amount of time online;
- Unexplained gifts. Mobile phones or extra credit vouchers are common;
- The young person becomes withdrawn and shows a distinct change in behaviour.

Victoria State Government (2013)

The National Society for the Prevention of Cruelty to Children (NSPCC) provide statistics from police forces in England and Wales showing over 5,000 crimes of sexual communication with a child being recorded in an 18-month period. They report an almost 50% increase in offences recorded in the 6 months to September 2018, compared to the same period in 2017. There was a 200% rise in recorded instances of Instagram used to target and abuse children over the same time period (NSPCC, 2019). The work of the NSPCC only looks at grooming offences related to sexual exploitation, but it suggests that grooming is on the increase as a way of coercing and changing the values and perceptions of young people and clearly has the potential to damage both their physical and mental health and well-being.

Self-harm and suicide

Self-harm is defined here as intentional, direct damage to one's body tissue without suicidal intent, for example cutting or burning oneself. The stories about the incidence of self-harm and suicide among young people that are regularly presented to the public via established mainstream media outlets such as the BBC are alarming.

Between 2000 and 2014, the proportion of people presenting to hospital departments in the UK after self-harming almost tripled. The most notable increase was in the group of women and girls aged 16–24 years where the figure went from 6.4% in 2000 to 19.7% in 2014 (McManus et al., 2019). However, it is unknown whether this rise reflects an actual rise in self-harming in the community because most people who self-harm do not present to hospitals or tell others about what they are doing. Some of this rise may therefore be due to an increased rate of disclosure.

In 2018, there were 6,507 suicides in the UK, which is equivalent to 11.2 deaths per 100,000 population, significantly higher than in 2017, although the reason for this increase is unknown. Although actual numbers are low, rates among the under 25s, particularly the 10- to 24-year-old female group, saw a significant increase to its highest level since 2012 at 3.3 deaths per 100,000 females in 2018 (ONS, 2019).

The key issues around online activity and self-harm include:

- Ideation, that is putting the thought of self-harm or suicide into the mind of an individual;
- Encouragement or temptation to continue self-harming or suicide via chat rooms or posting on blogs;
- Cessation via online therapeutic opportunities.

In the USA, as early as 2006, it was estimated that there were over 400 self-harming message boards and most of these were frequented by females between the age of 12 and 20 years. Although they may provide some support for already socially isolated individuals they may also have encouraged or at least normalised self-harming behaviour, or added alternative harming methods to the behavioural repertoire (Whitlock, Powers and Eckenrode, 2006). Daine et al. (2013) added further concerns over online activity regarding the discouragement of disclosure or seeking professional help and the potential for cyberbullying. The latter has been found to be highly correlated with increased risk of self-harm, suicide ideation and depression. A short but uncomfortable internet search uncovers many easily accessible forums discussing the efficacy of numerous methods of committing suicide. Finding information from groups that seek to intervene in a more positive manner, such as the Samaritans, can be harder to locate. Unfortunately, it seems to take a tragic death to motivate SNS policy changes, such as the suicide of 14-year-old Molly Russell in 2017. The subsequent discovery by her parents of her Instagram accounts containing numerous graphic images of self-harm and references to depression and suicide, led Instagram to ban all images of self-harm.

As both self-harm and suicidal thoughts are intensely private matters for the individual, providing emotional and psychological support to vulnerable young people can be extremely challenging. In the case of self-harm, behavioural patterns may be well established and therefore more difficult to eliminate, however, monitoring online activity may allow earlier intervention. Schools can track pupils' use of their systems and parents have tools available to track their children's online activity, if they are aware of them. Such monitoring might flag up concerns earlier allowing more timely interventions.

Individual/group task

Consider the scenario... as a professional, a disclosure is made that a young person you work with is self-harming. We know that self-harm is frequently a pre-cursor to suicide. What actions would you take?

Review the Samaritans website – www.samaritans.org.uk – to learn more about crisis support.

Cyberbullying

One definition of cyberbullying is "violence committed by perpetrators and bystanders using information and communication technology and various functionalities of the Internet" (Barlińska et al., 2013). Traditional school-yard bullying can be very harmful both physically and emotionally, but the victim usually escapes at the end of the school day. Unfortunately, "…cyberbullying has the potential of following the victim everywhere there is internet or a mobile phone signal. Likewise, with time: places of refuge and safety exist no more" (Duncan and Myers, 2016, p. 136). It is this relentless nature of cyberbullying that can make it so insidious, along with the cloak of anonymity it allows the perpetrators to hide behind.

A recent report highlighted that English schools had more cyberbullying and misuse of SNS than any other developed country (OECD, 2019). About 14% of headteachers sampled in England reported regular incidents of cyberbullying in their schools compared to 11% in Australia, 10% in the USA and 9% Belgium. In Vietnam, Chinese Taipei, Slovak Republic, Russia, Portugal, Lithuania, Kora, Kazakhstan, Finland and Chile, there were no incidents reported. While the UK has the highest level of reported online bullying in this study, it is clearly not unique and may be representative of other bullying, behaviours and pressures exhibited within these societies. The challenge confronting the education system is that while cyberbullying undoubtedly impacts on the school environment, it seldom happens on the premises and all the limitations that schools can place on access to mobile technology whilst onsite have little effect on cyberbullying outside the school gates.

Cyberbullying can occur via various media, including mobile phone calls, instant texts or messaging, emails, online fora and blogs, but a significant proportion comes through SNS such as Facebook. Titcomb (2018) points out that more than half a million children are using Facebook at least once a month, many of them whilst they are below the SNS minimum age. This leaves a considerable number of children vulnerable to a key source of cyberbullying.

The strongest predictor of perpetrating cyberbullying is having previously been the victim of cyberbullying (Hood and Duffy, 2018). Two potential approaches to addressing the problem were identified. The first was reducing the moral disengagement of the perpetrator, by making them understand that they are morally responsible for their actions and the consequences of their actions. The second was that effective parental monitoring weakened the cyberbully–victim relationship. Together these offered hope that home and school interventions via pastoral support and parental education could be potentially effective approaches to reduce cyberbullying.

Individual/group task

The Young Minds website provides support for people who are experiencing cyberbullying:
   https://youngminds.org.uk/blog/online-pressures-tackling-cyberbullying/
   Young people are advised how to deal with cyberbullying – do the suggestions on this website, in your opinion, provide the level or type of support required?
   Young people are advised not to ignore or retaliate as these can have detrimental and unwanted consequences – what do you think these consequences might be?

Conclusion

There is no doubt that billions of people around the world enjoy using social media. It has reunited long lost family members, facilitated emergency information campaigns and supported freedom of speech in countries with repressive authoritarian regimes. Conversely, it has also been the source of much unnecessary mental anguish for many millions of people. Young people are particularly at risk of developing or exacerbating mental ill-health issues as a consequence of their interactions in the digital world.

The different online behaviours and their associated risks to mental health which have been considered in this chapter are not restricted to any one country or region. They are classless, gender-less and very hard for responsible adults to identify, due to their discreet nature. They have been identified in studies carried out across the developed world. Most law enforcement, legislation and support are provided at a national level, while those who are creating the risks for the young people are frequently operating across national boundaries. This presents significant challenges in supporting young people to be safe online.

Young people must be given appropriate guidance to enable them to identify and reduce the risks they face, while still being able to get the most from the technologies available to them. Some clear guidance regarding what to look for, what to avoid, how to behave and what to do if something does not seem appropriate would help young people to develop their own capabilities with reduced risks.

Summary points

- Social media usage is incredibly widespread and popular, and although the exact SNS might change over time, it seems unlikely that social media itself will ever fall out of popular usage.
- Many young people all around the world are using social media every day, some starting at very young ages, and they see it as a positive part of their lives.
- Many young people are susceptible to risks to their mental health from activities in the digital world, due to both innocence and bad actors (such as groomers or criminals).
- Problems considered in this chapter include depression, envy, despair, anxiety, stress, body-image issues, isolation and fundamental changes to personalities through the hijacking of personal values.
- There are growing concerns over excessive screen time potentially leading to obesity, disruption to sleep and other social and emotional problems, but further research is needed in this area.
- The use of these technologies must be mediated and young people need support to develop sufficient digital skills so they can use them safely.

If you or anyone you know are being affected by the issues discussed in this chapter please refer to one of the organisations that offer help and support at the end of this book.

Recommended reading

Frith, E. (2017) *Social media and children's mental health: A review of the evidence.* [online] London: Education Policy Institute.

Livingstone, S. (2019) *Global kids online research project.* [online] Available at: http://globalkidsonline.net/.

OECD (2019) *Children & young people's mental health in the digital age: Shaping the future.* [online] Paris: OECD.

References

Advertising Association (2011) Pretty as a picture. [online] Available at: https://www.adassoc.org.uk/wp-content/uploads/2017/10/Pretty-as-a-picture.pdf.

Ando, R., Takahira, M., and Sakamoto, A. (2005) Effects of Internet use on junior high school students' loneliness and social support. *The Japanese Journal of Personality*, **14**(1), pp. 69–79.

Barlińska, J., Szuster, A., and Winiewski, M. (2013) Cyberbullying among adolescent bystanders: Role of the communication medium, form of violence, and empathy. *Journal of Community & Applied Social Psychology*, **23**, pp. 37–51.

Berger, P. L., and Luckmann, T. (1991) *The social construction of reality: A treatise in the sociology of knowledge (No. 10).* London: Penguin.

Brikse, Inta and Spurava, Guna (2014) *Kids online – safety and risks: Full findings from children survey of 9- to 16-year-olds in Latvia.* Faculty of Social Sciences. Riga: University of LatviaRiga. [online].

Buglass, S. L., Binder, J. F., Betts, L. R., and Underwood, J. D. (2017) Motivators of online vulnerability: The impact of social network site use and FOMO. *Computers in Human Behavior*, **66**, pp. 248–255.

Daine, K., Hawton, K., Singaravelu, V., Stewart, A., Simkin, S., and Montgomery, P. (2013) The power of the web: A systematic review of studies of the influence of the internet on self-harm and suicide in young people. *PloS one*, **8**(10), e77555.

Duncan, N., and Myers, B. (2016) Bullying in schools–or bullying schools? In Richards G. (Ed.), *Key issues for teaching assistants* (pp. 134–144). London: Routledge.

Erikson, E. (1963) *Childhood and society.* New York: W.W. Norton.

Festinger, L. (1954) A theory of social comparison processes. *Human Relations*, 7(2), 117–140.

Haferkamp, N., and Krämer, N. C. (2011) Social comparison 2.0: Examining the effects of online profiles on social-networking sites. *Cyberpsychology, Behavior, and Social Networking*, **14**(5), 309–314.

Hood, M., and Duffy, A. L. (2018) Understanding the relationship between cyber-victimisation and cyber-bullying on social network sites: The role of moderating factors. *Personality and Individual Differences*, **133**, 103–108.

Lai, C., Altavilla, D., Ronconi, A., and Aceto, P. (2016) Fear of missing out (FOMO) is associated with activation of the right middle temporal gyrus during inclusion social cue. *Computers in Human Behavior*, **61**, 516–521.

Livingstone, S., and Haddon, L. (2009) EU kids online. *Journal of Psychology*, **217**(4), 236.

Local Government Association (2018) *Healthy weight, healthy futures: Local government action to tackle childhood obesity.* [online] Available at: https://www.local.gov.uk/healthy-weight-healthy-futures-local-government-action-tackle-childhood-obesity-0.

Mazurek, M., and Wenstrup, C. (2013) Television, video game and social media use among children with ASD and typically developing siblings. *Journal of Autism and Developmental Disorders*, **42**, 1258–1271.

McManus, S., Gunnell, D., Cooper, C., Bebbington, P., Howard, L., Brugha, T., Jenkins, R., Hassiotis, A., Weich, S., and Appleby, L. (2019) Prevalence of non-suicidal self-harm and service contact in England, 2000–2014: Repeated cross-sectional surveys of the general population, *The Lancet*, **6**(7), 573–581.

Mohsin, M. (2019) *10 Social media statistics you need to know in 2019.* [online] Available at https://www.oberlo.co.uk/blog/social-media-marketing-statistics [Accessed 21 September 2019].

NSPCC. (2019) News report 1st March 2019. [online] Available at: https://www.nspcc.org.uk/what-we-do/news-opinion/over-5000-grooming-offences-recorded-18-months/ [Accessed 21 September 2019].

Office for National Statistics (ONS) (2019) *Suicides in the UK: 2018 registrations.* London: ONS. [online] Available at: https://www.ons.gov.uk/peoplepopulationandcommunity/birthsdeathsandmarriages/deaths/bulletins/suicidesintheunitedkingdom/2018registrations [Accessed 20 September 2019].

Przybylski, A. K., Murayama, K., DeHaan, C. R., and Gladwell, V. (2013) Motivational, emotional, and behavioral correlates of fear of missing out. *Computers in Human Behavior*, **29**(4), 1841–1848.

Raisingchildren.net.au (2019) Social media benefits and risks: Children and teenagers. [online] Available at: https://raisingchildren.net.au/teens/entertainment-technology/digital-life/social-media#social-media-benefits-for-your-child-nav-title.

Shaw, L. H., and Gant, L. M. (2004) In defense of the internet: The relationship between Internet communication and depression, loneliness, self-esteem, and perceived social support. *Internet Research*, **28**(3), 157–171. doi:10.1089/109493102753770552

Soldatova, G., Rasskazova, E., Zotova, E., Lebesheva, M., Geer, M., and Roggendorf, P. (2014) *Russian kids online: Key findings of the EU kids online II survey in Russia.* Moscow: Foundation for Internet Development.

Titcomb. J. (2018) Half a million British children under 12 use Facebook despite being underage *The Telegraph* [28th August 2018]. [online] Available at: https://www.telegraph.co.uk/technology/2018/08/28/half-million-british-children-12-use-facebook-despite-underage/ [Accessed 15 September 2019].

Valkenburg, P. M., Peter, J., and Schouten, A. P. (2006) Friend networking sites and their relationship to adolescents' well-being and social self-esteem. *Cyber Psychology & Behavior*, **9**(5), 584–590.

Vanderhoven, E. (2014) Educating teens about the risks on social network sites. An intervention study in secondary education. *Comunicar*, **22**(43), 123–132.

Victoria State Government (2013) *Online grooming.* [online] Available at: https://www.education.vic.gov.au/Documents/about/programs/bullystoppers/smgrooming.pdf [Accessed 21 September 2019].

Whitlock, J. L., Powers, J. L., and Eckenrode, J. (2006) The virtual cutting edge: The internet and adolescent self-injury. *Developmental Psychology*, **42**(3), 407–417.

World Health Organization (WHO), (2019) *To grow up healthy, children need to sit less and play more.* [online] Available at: https://www.who.int/news-room/detail/24-04-2019-to-grow-up-healthy-children-need-to-sit-less-and-play-more

Section 3

Examples of practice interventions that support children and young people's well-being and resilience

8 Well-being and outdoor learning

Gary Beauchamp, Susan Davis, Chantelle Haughton, Cheryl Ellis, Dylan Adams, Sian Sarwar, Sandra Dumitrescu and Jacky Tyrie

Any consideration of children being outdoors must take account of nature's ability to invoke "feelings of wonder, wonderment, awe, joy and inner peace" (Schein, 2018, p. 86). In recent years, it has become more apparent that these benefits, as perceived by those involved, can have a positive impact on learning outdoors, such as improving children's cognitive development, health/well-being and resilience (Wilson, 2008; Education Scotland, 2015). It has been proposed that outdoor learning is a cultural construct, which is "thought about and applied in different ways within and between countries" (Higgins and Nicol, 2002, p. 1). But, Prince et al. (2013, p. 186) argue that "young children learning and playing in the outdoors can transcend traditional compartmentalisations". The benefits are being increasingly recognised in education policy within the devolved education systems of the UK (Bratton et al., 2005; DCELLS, 2008; Learning and Teaching Scotland, 2010), as well as their inspectorates (e.g. Estyn, 2011). Such aspirations, and government support, suggest that gradually learning outside of the classroom is becoming a fundamental part of effective early years education and, indeed, across the primary school.

In Wales, there has been a long history of valuing education to the extent that "the appetite and respect for education is second to none" (Jones, 1997, p. 2). Beauchamp and Jephcote (2016, p. 113), however, suggest that this appetite "was for a Welsh education, reflecting both the culture and, as a visible symbol, the Welsh language". Nevertheless, education in Wales was practically indistinguishable from that in England before a narrow public vote for devolution in a second referendum in 1997 (devolution was significantly rejected by the Welsh people in the first referendum in 1979). Even then, it was not until 1999 that limited powers (including education) were devolved to the new Welsh Assembly Government, now called Welsh Government. Since that time, successive governments have made significant changes to education policy, in Welsh and English-medium schools, beginning with the introduction of a Foundation Phase, "a flagship policy of early years education (for 3 to 7-year old children) in Wales" (Maynard et al., 2013, p. ii). At the time of writing, the curriculum for all schools in Wales has been subject to a radical overhaul, with a new curriculum developed by teachers, with Areas of Learning and Experience instead of subjects, is due to be introduced in 2022. Chapter 13 discusses the history of Welsh educational policy in further detail.

Beyond educational settings, organisations such as the Suzuki Foundation (2015) have championed the cognitive and emotional health benefits of spending time outdoors, stating that this increases creativity, curiosity and problem-solving abilities. Internationally, Scandinavian ideas on early education equate time spent outdoors with quality learning, and the well-being aspects of fresh air and space to run around are also well documented (Magnussen, 2011; Bentsen and

Jensen, 2012). Additionally, Adams and Beauchamp (2019) suggest that specific activities, such as music-making outdoors, can lead to 'spiritual moments'. In a study with primary school children making music at a variety of outdoor locations in Wales (including a beach, woodland and a neolithic chamber), they gave many examples "whereby they are able to stand outside of themselves and experience a heightened reality" (Adams and Beauchamp, 2019, p. 271). A typical example from the pupil interviews was:

> I haven't done anything like that before, so it feels like a new person's come out of me and just taken over. It feels like another side of me that I hadn't known. (School 2, pupil 2).
>
> (Adams and Beauchamp, 2019, p. 271)

An added bonus data analysis from this project suggested the activities also perceived by the children and their teachers to improve their well-being.

Individual/group task

Before you read further, consider your own experience of learning and playing outdoors and any impact (positive or negative) on:

1.   you and
2.   your ideas of how children learn.

This chapter explores ideas on the importance of the outdoors in promoting and developing young children's health, well-being, resilience and learning. We will use case studies from Wales, where a new teacher-led curriculum is being developed, to examine key pedagogic theories, including Grit theory, the concept of risk and mindfulness. Examples will be drawn from the work of a team of lecturers who work with a range of alternative approaches in the outdoors. The impact of community engagement in developing a university's Outdoor Learning Centre (OLC) will be examined, which led to a previously unused strip of ancient Welsh woodland on campus being developed to introduce a suite of log circle classrooms and a log cabin largely funded by charitable trusts. The chapter highlights how subsequent projects put health and well-being at their heart for all involved.

The importance of the outdoors in promoting and developing young children's health, well-being, resilience and learning

Although we are beginning to see a greater emphasis on outdoor pedagogy, play and learning in the UK, we still have some way to go to equal the level of priority attached in other countries. For instance, outdoor learning has a long tradition in countries such as Norway (Borge, Nordhagen and Lie, 2003), where it is seen as an integral part of everyday education. The tradition of outdoor play throughout the year is strongly embedded in Norwegian outdoor traditions (Moser and Martinsen, 2010), even with very young children in kindergartens (Kaarby and Tandberg, 2017). This is important because evidence suggests that outdoor play benefits holistic child development and well-being (Norðdahl and Jóhannesson, 2015; Kemble et al., 2016).

Wilson (2008) suggests that young children need to build their own knowledge and develop a sense of 'rightness' when they respond to and embrace the natural world. Early positive experiences with nature foster curiosity and an appreciation of nature. Research continues to show that engagement with the outdoors is beneficial to children in a multitude of ways (McClain and Vandermaas-Peeler, 2015; Bento and Dias, 2017). Moving learning outside is, however, not as simple as it seems. For instance, although Burriss and Burriss (2011, p. 2) contend that "outdoors becomes a natural extension of the indoor classroom", Waite (2011, p. 14) provides the important caveat that "the value of working outside the classroom is in providing pupils with experiences that are different from those inside it. ... We want them to learn to behave in ways that are different to classroom behaviour".

Resilience/grit theory

To benefit from the outdoors, children need to embrace it fully and with confidence. In our projects, many children seemed comfortable in the outdoor space. Some children, however, were initially reluctant to 'explore', especially within the confines of a 'forest' (in reality a small wood on the university campus, but with tall trees). This understandable reluctance in a new environment with large trees towering above and around them, shown in hesitancy and nervousness, can, however, be overcome with persistence. For instance, a child in our forest school showed great distress at the sound of fallen twigs being crunched under foot and was also 'terrified' of insects. The same child, a few weeks later, was climbing trees and whittling wood with enthusiasm. It is therefore very important to allow children time and space, to overcome fears and build their own strategies and points of reference in relation to being outdoors, in effect empowering them to develop 'grit'.

There are varying ideas on the notion of 'grit' and the term 'grit theory' is becoming more apparent in relation to ideas on children's resilience (see more in Chapter 2) and subsequent educational achievement as a result (Duckworth, 2019). Originating from personality theory (Muenks et al., 2017), grit is here defined as "perseverance and passion for long-term goals" (Duckworth et al., 2007, p. 1087), by maintaining effort over long periods "despite failure, adversity and plateaus" (p. 1088). Kirchgasler (2018, p. 694), however, suggests that "grit is more than a psychological quality; it is also a metonym for the autonomous individual". However, we define it, grit theory suggests that challenges and problems are inevitable, but can be overcome with stamina and perseverance, like our children in the woods in the example above. Thus, when a child struggles with a problem, this should be seen as a positive and not a reason to give up – the idea here being that children need to believe that they have the ability to problem solve, even if initially they may find a situation challenging. Therefore, the idea of teaching children that overcoming mistakes is a normal part of everyday learning.

Individual/group tasks

1. Consider how you currently respond to experience of failure in the setting/placement/classroom or other experience. Do you think that 'grit' is a good thing and can it be taught?
2. Duckworth et al. (2007) conclude that:

    as educators and parents, we should encourage children to work not only with intensity but also with stamina. *In particular, we should prepare youth to anticipate failures and misfortunes* and point out that excellence in any discipline requires years and years of time on task. (Our italics)

Discuss:
- Can children be prepared for failure and misfortune?
- How realistic is it for teachers to allow children 'years and years' of failure if needed?
- Should grit theory be incorporated into setting, placement, school or other activity planning?
- If so, how should this be facilitated?

Figure 8.1   Ready for the 'swamp of biting mud'.

In this context, 'grit theory' can be applied to outdoor learning and play. The outdoor setting can not only allow children freedom and space (something which can be limited within an indoor setting), but also present multiple and different challenges to be overcome both individually and collectively. In relation to grit theory, outdoor play can empower children to work outside their comfort zone, especially in relation to developing physical skills such as those needed to climb trees or jump across puddles. In addition, as Barnes and Shirley (2007) suggest, being outdoors can make things 'strangely familiar', where new experiences (in our case outdoors) bring fresh perspectives to familiar aspects of life, requiring a new application of grit. In a recent project in the woodlands, grit was required to overcome the weather, the terrain, the bumpy ground and even the 'swamp of biting mud', which tried to bite off the children's wellies!

But what about risk?

In such activities, however, there will be inevitable concerns amongst teachers in some countries, including the UK, about risk. Although young children are capable of making risk judgements (Little and Wyver, 2010), it is suggested that "risk-averse responses to children's play are increasing in many western countries" (Sandseter, Little and Wyver, 2012, p. 168). Mortlock (1984) looked at the benefits of risk taking in outdoor play and set out ideas on four basic *adventure states*. These progressed in intensity from everyday *play*, where there is easy participation and is very much within a child's skill level. *Adventure play* is seen as the next level whereby the child is using more in-depth skills but maintaining control. *Frontier adventure play* is categorised as 'peak experience' and seen as challenging and adventurous, and the participant is very much close to physical limits – there is a risk here of a child pushing themselves too far, for example falling/failing, which could lead to stage four – *misadventure*, the child being hurt by the adventurous play. Mortlock (1984), however, argues that it is within the *frontier adventure state* that children develop the most. It could be suggested, that they have to display the most grit. Thus, it could be argued that the children who stretch themselves through the most through 'gritty' outdoor play are in effect the most resilient in this context, learn the most about the outdoor setting and indeed themselves/their own abilities.

Case study

In a woodland project with 4- to 6-year olds in the university woodlands (the 'forest'), children were given some time for free play. There were some perceived risks in the required risk assessment (such as slippery slopes and a running stream) but having put in place appropriate adult supervision the children were allowed to play. We offered guidance and rules for the children not to touch anything 'sharp, shiny or strange', but report it to an adult. We explained that in the woods we sometimes find things like broken glass, cans and so on. Although we had removed most detritus before sessions, the children sometimes found things in the undergrowth. When it is obviously litter the children simply report it, but recently the children were digging up some mud and found 'treasure'. Looking from a distance, we could see there were conflicting ideas about what to do and eventually despite them realising it was not a broken bottle (so not sharp it was shiny and glass), they reported it. But this seemed to cause some disappointment to those in the group defining it as treasure!

As the play was often out of direct adult sight, what became apparent was the emergence of peer support. Field notes and recordings showed the children offering reassurance to each other about the environment, helping each other overcome feelings of uncertainty and sharing ideas for play. It was interesting to note how children showed different competencies and confidence from the classroom: those confident in the classroom were sometimes timid in the woods and vice versa. Indeed, the teachers were surprised by the different competencies and confidence they saw in the forest. For example, one 6-year-old boy who in the classroom could clearly define 'predator' as if he was reading from a dictionary was scared and timid in the woods. Another boy, who was described to us by the teacher as having limited language and some behaviour challenges, was immediately confident and capable at exploring in the woods and using tools was able to help the first child. They had never before forged a friendship before, yet in the woods they often spent time together.

We could therefore conjecture that risk in the forest may provide opportunity to nurture a community of care: the children were often helping each other; pointing out the brambles at their eye level, the tree roots obstacles in the pathways, the slippiness of the slope. This risk also provided opportunities for children to develop grit and new friendships to help overcome challenges they may not have done on their own. Outdoor play here also accords with Noddings' (2002, p. 283) conception of education as "a constellation of encounters, both planned and unplanned, that promote growth through the acquisition of knowledge, skills, understanding and appreciation".

Impact of community engagement in developing a University Outdoor Learning Centre (OLC)

For many years, an ancient woodland was a forgotten part of the university campus. Most staff did not know that it existed and assumed it was just some trees forming a border between the campus and nearby houses – in reality it is about 2 hectares. Some of the lecturers, however, realised its potential. This was noted in a field note from a project, where a lecturer wrote "This natural space provides a magical spot an acorn's throw away from the hustle and bustle of the car park, which almost feels near, yet distant, and peaceful, yet exciting simultaneously". The woodland site, and a new Outdoor Learning Centre (OLC), where the activities described in this chapter took place, could not have been developed by the university alone. In line with the university 'third mission' of embracing and further extending social justice and community engagement, money was raised through internal and external grants, with the aim of providing a centre which would extend our work with schools, other agencies (such as Public Health Wales, National Resources Wales, Outdoor Learning Training Network Wales, Play Wales), children and their families and partners within our local and professional communities. For instance, in the short term, this approach provided local children from a Community First-funded area (at the time a Welsh Government-funded community focussed programme aimed at reducing poverty, closed in 2018) and their teacher with a positive opportunity to experience mindfulness (of which more below) for the first time. In the longer term, it also allowed children from a very early age to experience university, to provide new aspiration for life-long learning and perhaps even want to attend university in the future. This setting also provided our own undergraduate students with opportunities to work with children, as well as to gain additional qualifications such as Forest School and First Aid. It also allowed opportunities to run Continuing Professional Development (CPD) course for staff in local schools and early years' settings. One example of this was the development of the concept of mindfulness in nature. Below is a picture of the OLC in the woodland setting.

Figure 8.2   The Outdoor Learning Centre (OLC) with woods in the background.

Mindfulness in nature

Although Uusberg et al. (2016) remind us that a precise definition of mindfulness remains contested, they argue that it is "a holistic state of awareness, facilitated by the interplay of such components as attention, attitude, and intention" (p. 94). More simply, Thompson (2017) considers mindfulness as something that we need to 'simply do'. In essence, it can be as simple as taking the time to reflect and essentially notice what is going on around us. In relation to nature and the outdoors, it would be simply enjoying and taking time to 'be' in natural surroundings. Whatever the definition, Willert, Wieclaw and Thulstrup (2014, p. 720) argue that "the combination of nature and mindfulness seemed obvious".

Individual/group task

On your own, or with others, consider your own definition of mindfulness and how important being in natural settings is to your understanding of its effectiveness with a chosen age group.

Giving children time to reflect within the busy school day is often seen as a luxury, but the importance of thinking time and space should not be underestimated. The use of mindfulness within the school day is beginning to become more apparent and the benefits of this are being documented. Bostic et al. (2015) noted that practising mindfulness frequently, even for short periods results in health benefits and changes in their body's reactivity to stress. Huppert and Johnson (2010) found that when practising mindfulness with adolescent boys within a school mindfulness group, there was a significant improvement in their psychological well-being, especially in relation to their emotional stability. In a very small-scale study (11 children in one school in England) McCree, Cutting and Sherwin (2018) suggested that self-regulation and resilience were developed in children aged 5–7 years through weekly Forest school learning sessions. We should, however, note that these qualitative studies only attempt to measure perceptions, so we should remember this and consider how far it may apply outside the sample groups.

Being outdoors in nature can help children to consciously or unconsciously become aware of their surroundings, enabling them to experience calm, rest and contemplation. Van Gordon, Shonin and Richardson (2018) propose that as well as being calming, spending time in nature can, paradoxically, also be energising. Quietly appreciating the natural world can be seen as mindful awareness. Within the school day, children are rarely given opportunities to just sit, do nothing and appreciate their surroundings. Such an approach could be useful as Van Gordon, Shonin and Richardson (2018) highlight the importance of embracing and relaxing into a natural environment, which can enhance meditative awareness simply by the act of sitting under a tree and contemplating upon its beauty and properties. The idea of allowing time for mindful musing can help children to become connected to a natural environment and give them the opportunity and time to appreciate the beauty or quiet within the school grounds, park or forest.

The idea of nature connectedness is also apparent when children have contact with nature through their senses and emotions. Van Gordon, Shonin and Richardson (2018) call this "mindfulness-enhanced nature connectedness", a process of allowing the outdoor space to *wash over us* by engaging our senses in, listening to the sounds of bird song or feeling the wind gently whistling past us, through the trees. This is aligned to the term 'forest bathing' which is based on the Japanese practice of Shinrin-Yoku the translation is taking in the Forest atmosphere or Forest bathing, and simply demonstrates how being in a forest or green space, can be an immersive experience for the senses, and which has been shown to foster calm and help rebalance emotions (Park et al., 2010; Tsunetsugu et al., 2010). This could be labelled as yet another new alternative therapy, though it can be classified simply as a return to a more holistic and natural state of being and one which can be afforded to children, just by allowing them to spend more quality time in nature.

Case study: mindfulness

The Youth Mindfulness programme is a series of 16 designed lessons with local children guided by our lecture team, supported by our undergraduate students. One project with a class of 6- or 7-year-old children serves to explain the process and impact of this programme.

From the outset, the class teacher was open to wanting to work with us for support and to learn more about alternative approaches to working within her class and teaching. She approached us initially with a cry for help for ideas and asked about the possibilities of working with us to support her CPD. She shared that she was feeling pressured by workload and that many of the children in her class had a range of needs, pressures and difficult circumstances in their lives. She said that she wanted to explore new ways of tackling management strategies for her and the children and how she could support the children and herself through self-regulating approaches.

An extract from a lecturer's field note explains that

> Children were excited to be on a trip away from school into somewhere different, the children ooze out of the minibus and surge onto the balcony of our Outdoor Learning Centre (OLC) sheltered by the old oak tree, surrounded by the birdsong with the view of the old woods and the breeze combined, quickly switch the vibe into a natural sense of awe and calmer excitement in noticing and inhaling the environment.

As the weeks progressed, it felt important to dwell on what was happening during the process of it all, rather than what everyone was going to get out of it at the end. It felt clear that the mindfulness approach in this context positively outweighs the emphasis elsewhere on learning outcomes and, crucially, positively impacts holistic development. The lecturers noted:

- The sense of joy, excitement, thought and surprise on the children's faces.
- The incredible sense of calm amongst us all as a community in practice.
- The philosophical, sincere and creative responses from the children in the discussions that gripped us all about what they thought of their minds, their thoughts and the environment around us also I felt surprised by how the teacher seemed surprised by this.
- The children's positive perceptions about visiting Forest University.
- The strong sense of authentic learning for all of us involved.

At the end of the project, the teacher and the children reported a range of positive emotional and cognitive outcomes from taking part in the series of lessons in the outdoors. The children and the teacher talked about positive impact on their emotional well-being, self-regulation, self-awareness and knowledge and about training their minds.

Critical note: It should be remembered that these responses came at the end of the project after an extended period of visits. Even then, we cannot guarantee that all children experienced the benefits from the start, or even at the end. In all research, we need to be careful to consider all perspectives, even if they do not accord with our own beliefs, the overall findings or existing literature.

Conclusion

In this chapter, we have examined some of the benefits of learning and playing outdoors. We have seen that it can help to develop perseverance, or grit, which may be beneficial in other facts of children's life and learning. Other benefits include developing mindfulness and the potential benefits of children taking risks in outdoor settings. In many school settings in the UK, despite evidence from other countries, finding time for such activities can be challenging (particularly when not embedded in curriculum), but *you* can play your part in meeting this challenge for the benefit of the children in your care.

Summary points

- Outdoor learning is recognised as being important to children's development and is a statutory requirement of curricula throughout the UK.
- Despite an increased attention on outdoor learning in the UK over the past ten years, the UK still lacks behind countries such as Norway in prioritising outdoor nature activities.
- Outdoor learning in nature spaces can have a positive effect on children's health and well-being.
- Outdoor learning allows for pedagogical approaches that differ from traditional classroom pedagogy.
- Playing outdoors can provide a healthy element of risk for children and allow them to develop qualities such as resilience and perseverance.
- Mindfulness in nature can improve children's well-being and increase their sense of 'ature-connectedness'.
- Although there are many perceived benefits from outdoor activities, not all children will feel the same and we should be careful to remember this – for example, it is just as easy for a child to be excluded from activities (such as play) in the woods (or other outdoor setting) as well as the playground or the classroom.

Recommended reading

Hayhow, D. B., Eaton, M. A., Stanbury, A. J., Burns, F., Kirby, W. B., Bailey, N., and Dennis, E. B. (2019). State of nature 2019. Available online at: https://nbn.org.uk/wp-content/uploads/2019/09/State-of-Nature-2019-UK-full-report.pdf Accessed 11 December 2019.
Huppertz, M., and Schatanek, V. (2018) *Mindfulness in nature* (English edition). Paderborn: Junfermann.

Richardson, M., Sheffield, D., Harvey, C., and Petronzi, D. (2016). The impact of children's connection to nature: A report for the royal society for the protection of birds (RSPB). Available online at: https://www.rspb.org.uk/globalassets/downloads/documents/positions/education/the-impact-of-childrens-connection-to-nature.pdf Accessed 11 December 2019.
Sobel, D. (2008). *Childhood and nature: Design principles for educators.* New York: Stenhouse Publishers.
Waite, S. (Ed.). (2017). *Children learning outside the classroom: From birth to eleven.* London: Sage.
Wilson, R. (2018). *Nature and young children: Encouraging creative play and learning in natural environments.* London: Routledge.

References

Adams, D., and Beauchamp, G. (2019) Spiritual moments making music in nature. A study exploring the experiences of children making music outdoors, surrounded by nature. *International Journal of Children's Spirituality*, **24**(3), 260–275.
Barnes, J., and Shirley, I. (2007) Strangely familiar: Cross-curricular and creative thinking in teacher education. *Improving Schools*, **10**(2), 162–179.
Beauchamp, G., and Jephcote, M. (2016) Teacher education in Wales: Towards an enduring legacy, in Beauchamp et al. (Eds.) *Teacher education in times of change.* Bristol: Policy Press. pp. 109–124.
Bento, G., and Dias, G. (2017) The importance of outdoor play for young children's healthy development. *Porto Biomedical Journal*, **1**(2), 157–160.
Bentsen, P., and Jensen, F.S. (2012) The Nature of Udeskole: theory and practice in Danish schools. In *Journal of Adventure Education and Outdoor Learning*, **12**(3), 199–219.
Borge, A., Nordhagen, R., and Lie, K. K. (2003) Children in the environment: Forest day-care centers: Modern day care with historical antecedents. *History of the Family*, **8**, 605–618.
Bostic, J.Q., Nevarez, M.D., Potter, M.P., Prince, J.B., Benningfield, M.M., and Aguirre, B.A. (2015) Being present at school. Implementing mindfulness in schools. *Child & Adolescents Psychiatric Clinics*, **2**(2), 245–259.
Bratton, C., Crossey, U., Crosby, D., and McKeown, W. (2005) *Learning outdoors in the early years.* Available online at: http://ccea.org.uk/sites/default/files/docs/curriculum/area_of_learning/fs_learning_outdoors_resource_book.pdf Accessed 29 September 2018.
Burriss, K., and Burriss, L. (2011) Outdoor play and learning: Policy and practice, *International Journal of Education Policy and Leadership*, **4**, 6(8).
DCELLS (2008) *Foundation phase: Framework for children's learning for 3- to 7-year-olds in Wales.* Cardiff: WAG.
Duckworth, A.L. (2019) *Grit. Why passion and persistence are the secrets to success.* New York: Vermillio.
Duckworth, A.L., Peterson, C., Matthews, M.D., and Kelly, D.R. (2007) Grit: Perseverance and passion for long-term goals. *Personal Social Psychology*, **92**(6), 1087–1101.
Education Scotland (2015) Education matters, taking learning outside. Available online at: www.educationscotland.gov.uk/earlyyearsmatters/t/takelearningoutside.asp.
Education Scotland (2015) Outdoor learning, practical guidance, ideas and support for teachers in Scotland. Available online at: https://education.gov.scot/improvement/documents/hwb24-ol-support.pdf.
Estyn (2011) *Outdoor learning: An evaluation of learning in the outdoors for children under five in the foundation phase.* Cardiff: Estyn.
Higgins, P., and Nicol, R. (2002) *Outdoor education: Authentic learning in the context of Landscapes* (Volume 2). Sweden: Kisa.
Huppert, F.A., and Johnson, D.M. (2010) A controlled trial of mindfulness training in schools: The importance of practice for an impact on well-being. *The Journal of Positive Psychology*, **5**(4), 264–274.
Jones, G. E. (1997) *The education of a nation.* Cardiff: University of Wales Press.
Kaarby, K., and Tandberg, C. (2017) The belief in outdoor play and learning. *Journal of the European Teacher Education Network*, **12**, 25–36.
Kemble, M. K., Oh, J., Kennedy, E., and Smith-Bonahue, T. (2016) The power of outdoor play and play in natural environments. *Childhood Education*, **92**(6), 446–454.
Kirchgasler, C. (2018) True grit? Making a scientific object and pedagogical tool. *American Educational Research Journal*, **55**(4), 693–720.
Learning and Teaching Scotland (2010) *Curriculum for excellence through outdoor learning.* Available online at: https://www.educationscotland.gov.uk/Images/cfeoutdoorlearningfinal_tcm4-596061.pdf Accessed 29 September 2018.

Little, H., and Wyver, S. (2010) Individual differences in children's risk perception and appraisals in outdoor play environments. *International Journal of Early Years Education*, **18**(4), 297–313.

Magnussen, L. (2011) Play – The making of deep outdoor experiences. *Journal of Adventure Education and Outdoor Learning*, **12**(1), 25–39.

Maynard, T., Taylor, C., Waldron, S. Rhys, M., Smith, R., Power, S., and Clement, J. (2013) *Evaluating the foundation phase: Policy logic model and programme theory*. Cardiff: Welsh Government.

McClain, C., Vandermaas-Peeler, M. (2015) Social contexts of development in natural outdoor environments: Children's motor activities, personal challenges and peer interactions at the river and the creek. *Adventure Education and Outdoor Learning*, **16**, 31–48.

McCree, M., Cutting, R., and Sherwin, D. (2018) The hare and the tortoise go to forest school: Taking the scenic route to academic attainment via emotional wellbeing outdoors. *Early Child Development and Care*, **188**(7), 980–996.

Mortlock, C. (1984) *The adventure alternative*. Cumbria: Cicerone Press.

Moser, T., and Martinsen, M. (2010) The outdoor environment in Norwegian kindergartens as a pedagogical space for toddlers' play, learning and development. *European Early Childhood Education Research Journal*, **18**(4), 457–471.

Muenks, K., Wigfield, A., Yang, J., and O'Neal, C. (2017) How true is grit? Assessing its relations to high school and college students' personality characteristics, self-regulation, engagement, and achievement. *Journal of Educational Psychology*, **109**(5), 599–620.

Noddings, N. (2002) *Starting at home. Caring and social policy*. Berkley and Los Angeles: University of California Press.

Norðdahl, K., and Jóhannesson, I. Á. (2015) Children's outdoor environment in Icelandic educational policy. *Scandinavian Journal of Educational Research*, **59**(1), 1–23.

Park, B.J., Tsunetsugu, Y.A., Kasetani, T.A., Kagawa, T.A., and Miyazaki, Y.A. (2010) The physiological effects of Shinrin-yoku (taking in the forest atmosphere or forest bathing): Evidence from field experiments in 24 forests across Japan. *Environmental Health* Preventative Medicine, 15, 18–26.

Prince, H., Allin, L. and Hansen Sandseter, E.B. (2013) Editorial: Outdoor play and learning in early childhood from different cultural perspectives. *Journal of Adventure Education and Outdoor Leaning*, **13**(3), 183–188.

Sandseter, E., Little, H., and Wyver, S. (2012) Do theory and pedagogy have an impact on provisions for outdoor learning? A comparison of approaches in Australia and Norway. *Journal of Adventure Education and Outdoor Learning*, **12**(3), 167–182.

Schein, D. L. (2018) *Inspiring wonder, awe, and empathy: Spiritual development in young children*. St. Paul, MN: Redleaf Press.

Suzuki Foundation. (2015) Available online at: http://wwwdavidsuzuki.org/ Accessed 11 October 2019.

Thompson, C. (2017) *Mindfulness and the natural world*. London: Quarto Nows.

Tsunetsugu, Y., Park, B.J., and Miyazaki, Y. (2010) Trends in research related to 'Shinrin-yoku' (taking in the Forest atmosphere or Forest bathing) in Japan. *Environmental Health Preventative Medicine*, **15**, 27–37.

Uusberg, H., Uusberg, A., Talpsep, T., and Paaver, M. (2016) Mechanisms of mindfulness: The dynamics of affective adaptation during open monitoring. *Biological Psychology*, **118**, 94–106.

Van Gordon, W., Shonin, E., and Richardson, M. (2018) Mindfulness and nature. *Mindfulness in Practice*, **9**(5), 1655–1658.

Waite, S. (2011) *Children learning outside the classroom*. London: Sage.

Willert, M., Wieclaw, J., and Thulstrup, A. (2014) Rehabilitation of individuals on long-term sick leave due to sustained stress-related symptoms: A comparative follow-up study. *Scandinavian Journal of Public Health*, **42**(8), 719–727.

Wilson, R. (2008) *Nature and young children, encouraging creative play and learning in natural environments*. London: David Fulton Publishers.

9 The role of mindfulness in supporting well-being in young children

Chris Ludlow

Introduction

In this chapter, I initially provide a brief overview of the history of mindfulness and the potential benefits identified by research with adults, and identify a definition of mindfulness and why it has been considered as a strategy that might be used to promote positive mental health in children. I will then review results from mindfulness training (including my own) with children that has taken place with different groups of children from a diverse range of cultural and socio-economic circumstances. Within the literature, I will consider specific issues that mindfulness training in children successfully addresses and where there is a need for greater research. I discuss the potential limitations of the research and where there is limited evidence for benefits of mindfulness for children. Within the chapter, I will also outline the basic components of a mindfulness programme that can be used by parents or teachers alike.

The use of mindfulness to promote well-being

The use of mindfulness-based programmes to promote well-being among adults has rapidly increased in recent years. Digital applications such as Headspace, Calm and Buddhify have become more widely used and have brought mindfulness meditation into mainstream use, making it part of a wider conversation about mental health and well-being. Among adults, there is a growing body of evidence from research (Kabat-Zinn, 1996; Gazella, 2005; Lampe and Engleman-Lampe, 2012) that attests to the positive impact mindfulness can have on adult mental health. As well as the more recently available digital programmes, over the past quarter of a century, mindfulness techniques have been increasingly taught to adults in a wide variety of settings, largely in the USA.

Mindfulness-based programmes such as the Mindfulness-Based Stress Reduction (MBSR) Programme, also known as the Stress Reduction and Relaxation Programme, designed by American scientist and a man who previously identified himself as Buddhist, Jon Kabat-Zinn was one of the first programmes to use mindfulness to promote well-being. The strategies it uses have been taken out of its original context by other professionals and used in other settings including prisons and schools. Jon Kabat-Zinn founded the Centrer for Mindfulness in Medicine, Health Care and Society and was the Director of the Center's MBSR programme which began delivery in 1979 (Proulx, 2003). The Center delivered MBSR courses in inner city locations and within the prison system. Its use spread and hundreds of clinics use the MBSR model along with prisons across

America (Gazella, 2005). It is a programme that is often adapted for use in a range of settings involving different social groups alongside institutions like sports teams (Kabat-Zinn, 1996). This is a trend that has been continued by organisations like Headspace who have collaborated with companies like Nike and Virgin as well as the Los Angeles Lakers Basketball team to promote the use of mindfulness techniques.

A study of the benefits of mindfulness to sporting performance (Ajilchi et al., 2019) found that as Basketball players became more mindful, there was an improvement in their ability to concentrate and not allow other emotions to disrupt their focus. This led to an increase in scores measuring mental toughness. While the same limitations are evident in this study as elsewhere (small sample size and a lack of follow-up data), it is interesting to note that the improvements noted are consistent with other studies. In a study of female high school athletes, the athletes reported that there had been an improvement in emotional awareness, staying focused and team bonding (Worthern and Luiselli, 2016). The Chicago Bulls and subsequently the Los Angeles Lakers began using mindfulness techniques in the late 1980s and during the 1990s, reporting tangible benefits for emotional regulation and team bonding (Lingtao and Zellmer-Bruhn, 2019). It should be noted that both teams enjoyed extraordinary success over that period, winning 11 titles between them (Lingtao and Zellmer-Bruhn, 2019).

As I have previously alluded to, with potential benefits to team bonding and the ability of an individual to focus, the use of mindfulness has been adopted by some quarters of the corporate world. In an article written for the Harvard Business School, Yu Lingtao and Mary Zellmer-Bruhn make explicit their belief that a team in any organisation trained in mindfulness is likely to perform better than a team who haven't (Lingtao and Zellmer-Bruhn, 2019).

The popularity of Mindfulness Meditation as an effective tool to promote well-being may in part be as a result of its techniques being packaged into manageable chunks of time for 'time poor' societies. Mindfulness-based programmes such as Jon Kabat-Zinn's MBSR Programme and Headspace's 'Take Ten' programme are designed for implementation as a manageable part of a daily routine Furthermore, the popular appeal of mindfulness reflects two interrelated trends: the steady increase in consumer demand for alternative ways of promoting positive health (Eisenberg et al., 1998 cited in Barker, 2014), and the increase of information in both the print and digital media, including a range of social media platforms (Seale, 2003 cited in Barker, 2014).

The use of mindfulness with children

As a result of the perceived benefits for adults and in response to widespread concerns about mental health in children and young people, there has been a growth in the number of programmes incorporating mindfulness-based techniques that are designed specifically for children. In a Yougov Poll conducted in 2013, many children reported that they felt worried or sad at least once a week with a number of children reporting that they felt sad once every two to three days (Yougov, 2013). The number rose to nearly a quarter by the time children were 11. More recent statistics released by the NHS in 2018 show a rise in children suffering from mental health disorders since 2004 (Mental Health Foundation, 2018) with 1 in 8 children between the ages of 5 and 19 being diagnosed with a specific mental health disorder (Mental Health Foundation, 2018). This, of course, does not account for children who suffer from their mental health in more general terms without a diagnosis. The school setting has been identified as a good place to deliver mindfulness training to children due to the fact that children from the age of 5 spend between 5 and 7 hours in school (Sheinman et al., 2018) with additional time in wrap around care for some. Organisations like the Mindfulness in Schools Project, Relax Kids and Thought Bubbles Education have produced programmes designed to be delivered to school age children. In fact, this type of learning may be valuable as childhood is a time of significant vulnerability to life's events (Sacks et al., 2014, cited in Sheinman et al., 2018). A recent report published by True Activist (2019) suggests that in the UK, 370 primary schools are incorporating Mindfulness Meditation into their curriculum. You would have read in Chapter 8 about mindfulness in nature and how outdoor learning lends itself to mindfulness practice. Studies on the effects of mindfulness on children are not as extensive as work with adults but the number of programmes aimed at children and the number of studies is growing (Sheinman et al., 2018). This is particularly the case in developed countries including the UK and the initial results are promising (Weare, 2013). In the growing evidence from research on the topic, mindfulness programmes are popular with staff and children with some tangible benefits that might lead to improved well-being. The evidence suggests that some interventions for children and young people can have at least a modest impact on improved mental health and well-being, reduce stress, anxiety and depression, and enhance academic, cognitive, social and emotional skills (Weare, 2013). This view is supported by Broderick and Metz (2009) who reviewed the Learning to BREATHE programme. The mindfulness-based programme was implemented with just over a hundred students who were approximately 17 years of age in America. When compared to a control group, students who had undertaken the programme reported an increase in feelings of calmness, relaxation and self-acceptance. In addition to this, there was also an increase in emotion regulation after the programme had been completed. Children completing the programme felt that they were more aware of their feelings and more able to let go of thoughts or feelings that caused them unhappiness (Broderick and Metz, 2009). Some students also reported some physical benefits including feeling more awake and fewer minor aches or pains (Broderick and Metz, 2009). The study was limited in similar ways to other studies about mindfulness interventions; the group tested was a fairly homogenous one and limited in size. Further research could focus on the impact of these interventions upon a more diverse ethnic and social group.

Similar programmes could also be trialled with much younger students. However, the authors of the study suggest that the benefits that mindfulness-based programmes have brought to adults like improved attention, concentration and creativity are central to the 'goals of education' (Broderick and Metz, 2009). Given what we know about the benefits of early intervention in other areas of learning like speech therapy, it would seem to make sense to begin to think about giving children some basic contemplative skills that they can then build upon at an early stage in their education. Getting children into the habit of thinking about their mental well-being as well as their physical well-being at an early age may help improve their chances of better mental health in the future.

An adapted version of the MBSR Programme was used in a larger-scale research project involving more than 300 pupils, largely from minority ethnic backgrounds in Baltimore involving a randomized control group (Sibinga et al., 2013). While the authors acknowledge the limitations of this study, including missing data due to pupil absences, the findings were both positive and highlighted the potential effect that mindfulness can have in supporting different areas of a student's well-being. The majority of students came from poor socio-economic backgrounds with high levels of childhood trauma (Sibinga et al., 2013). The students (mean age – 12 years) were measured both at the beginning and end of the programme against a variety of scales including the ten-item Children's

Acceptance and Mindfulness Scale, Multidimensional Anxiety Scale for Children and the Positive and Negative Affect Schedule among others (Sibinga et al., 2013) in order to assess the effect of the intervention across a range of areas of well-being. Post-programme results suggest that the students who undertook the mindfulness programme experienced significantly lower levels of somatization, depression, negative affect, negative coping, rumination, self-hostility and post-traumatic symptom severity (Sibinga et al., 2013). These results appear to support the need for more research into the potential for mindfulness as a tool to support well-being in children including the need for longitudinal research on the longer-term benefits of mindfulness programmes for children on their well-being in adulthood.

For this exercise, find yourself a place where you are unlikely to be disturbed wherever you are. If you are in the house, this might be the bedroom but if you are outside, this could be a park bench or another suitable space. Take a moment to pause, put down your phone, laptop or anything else that might disturb you and with your eyes open, gently focus your attention on your breathing. Just spend a moment being aware of each in-breath and each out-breath and, after a few moments, gently close your eyes. Bring your attention to the environment around you. Think about the different noises you can hear and spend a few moments resting in your sense of hearing before slowly and gently returning your attention to the in-breath and out-breath, counting each one up to a count of six if you find this helpful. After a few moments, gently open your eyes and pause before gradually rising and continuing your day.

Evidence from my own research, based on information provided by practitioners delivering the programme, suggests that the introduction of simple mindfulness skills enabled children to focus and settle into their learning effectively (Ludlow, 2016). Practitioners in the year one class felt that the programme provided a nice bridge between lunchtime and the afternoon activities. This is a potentially important benefit for children as, for a child, an inability to focus may result in underperformance at a certain task. In addition, an inability to become immersed in a subject can result in a child not being in the best position to fully understand or enjoy it. It may also result in an inability to 'switch off' which may affect sleeping patterns with a subsequent emotional and physical impact. It can be hard to switch off when you're permanently plugged in (Puddicombe, 2012).

Mindfulness interventions would appear to be starting to find ways to help students learn to pay mindful attention and there is now evidence of the impact of mindfulness training on awareness and clarity (Weare, 2013). Within my own research, the practitioners who delivered the programme felt that the skills children developed gave them strategies that they could use independently of the school-based sessions (Ludlow, 2016). Furthermore, the practitioners reported that some children actively welcomed the opportunity to spend time quietly, focusing on the breath (Ludlow, 2016).

As with many studies on the benefits of mindfulness, this study explored the benefits of using mindfulness as a treatment for problems that children had and were experiencing. However, the potential academic benefits that may result from mindfulness practice cannot be ignored and it must be said that due to the pressure on all schools to improve their pupil's academic performance, mindfulness programmes will be more attractive to schools if these benefits can be demonstrated. In drawing together various strands of research, it would appear that results from research evidence an improvement in executive functioning similar to that experienced by adults who have been exposed to mindfulness training. Of all the potential benefits of mindfulness I have discussed, the ability to improve children's ability to sustain their attention appears particularly prescient to our society. The distractions for everyone, including children, are multiple. Mobile phones and games consoles are ubiquitous and their primary function, they also enable access to the internet and an enormous array of other applications. Many of these operations require only fleeting attention and our minds can become used to an almost permanent level of distraction. There are inevitably some consequences that are problematic for our mental health and at times our academic performance; the mind may struggle to maintain focus on a specific activity.

As a result of this potential benefit, at least one study has sought to measure the benefits of mindfulness practices upon children who suffer from Attention Deficit Hyperactivity Disorder (ADHD). Treatment for ADHD has previously focused on the use of medication and behavioural parent training (Oord et al., 2012). Mindfulness training presents a third option to be explored. Results from the study based on an 8-week course for both children and their parents suggest that, from a parental perspective, children's ADHD symptoms significantly reduce as a result of mindfulness training (Oord et al., 2012). Furthermore, parents who also suffered elements of ADHD reported that their own symptoms were reduced (Oord et al., 2012). The study demonstrated some limitations; teachers did not report any difference in the behaviours of the children with ADHD in a school setting (Oord et al., 2012).

Mindfulness and the curriculum

The challenge for the researcher when discussing the benefits of mindfulness for children, is the variation both in content and in the method of delivery. It is evident in the literature that mindfulness in education can take many forms, and programmes apply a variety of styles and components to cultivate it (Sheinman et al., 2018). These range from whole school programmes to work with classes, groups of children or, in the case of some digital programmes, individual children. Evidence from my own research suggests that a simple 'build-up' of basic mindfulness skills with a focus on the breath, is effective and easy to deliver within the curriculum (Ludlow, 2016). Furthermore, practitioners liked the links with other areas of the curriculum, like Physical Education and aspects of the science curriculum (Ludlow, 2016). In addition, the timings of the sessions, between 3 and 5 minutes were easy to implement within a hectic curriculum schedule (Ludlow, 2016).

It might be said that the feasibility of introducing mindfulness-based approaches in schools deserves extra scrutiny following the UK government's own targets for supporting positive mental well-being for young people (DoHSC and DfE, 2018). In response to a consultation about the proposals in their 2017 Green Paper, the government re-iterated their aim to introduce a senior leader for children's mental health in every school (DoHSC and DfE, 2018). They proposed that from 2019, one-fifth of schools would have access to training for this provision with other schools having access to training at a later date (DoHSC and DfE, 2018). These proposals, while constituting a promising start, should be seen within the context of budgetary constraints and pressure for improved outcomes from statutory assessments. These facets of school life compete for a finite amount of time so strategies to support mental well-being that are put in place must be effective, relatively inexpensive and possible to fit into a hectic curriculum. In the main, mindfulness-based programmes have the potential to fulfil at least the last two of those criteria, while their effectiveness remains an area for ongoing research. One specific area of research, moving forward, might be an exploration of *how long* it is necessary for children to participate in a mindfulness programme for it to be an effective strategy to promote positive well-being.

While there are obvious training implications for teachers and other practitioners, the basic tenets of mindfulness are not overly complicated to deliver and do not necessarily rely on expensive resources or time-consuming bureaucracy. For schools, at a time when budgets are stretched, this makes both educational and fiscal sense. Across the majority of programmes in the literature, mindfulness training for children included similar components based on Kabat-Zinn's definition of mindfulness as, paying attention to the present moment without judgement (Kabat-Zinn, 1996). Indeed, the principles and approaches common to programmes either designed or inspired by Kabat-Zinn were brought together in a programme delivered to children in a number of elementary schools in America in the mid-90s. The results of this research were retrospectively analysed in 2017 (Cheek et al., 2017). While the programme included some physical, yoga-inspired activities, it included a core set of skills that are taught in programmes currently delivered. A typical session for children might include:

- Gentle stretching to help children to settle before sitting in a comfortable position.
- Slowly breathing in for a count of five or more before gently exhaling, counting out as they breathe.
- Gently closing the eyes and bringing their attention to the breath (breathing as normal), counting both the in-breath and the out-breath.
- Slowly returning their attention to the world around them to focus on their primary senses.
- Gently opening their eyes.

Many mindfulness programmes also encourage children to apply these skills to walking and eating meditations. This has the potential to fulfil a broader range of well-being outcomes for children. Eating at a slower rate and gaining a greater understanding of where food comes from, might point to mindfulness-based interventions being used to promote healthier eating and as a potential intervention for children with eating disorders alongside other more conventional therapeutic approaches. Perhaps, a point worth mentioning is that mindfulness-based approaches to children's well-being need not be either a sole approach that is adopted or a replacement for other approaches. Research about mindfulness tends to naturally focus on the outcomes of mindfulness in isolation whereas future research might consider it as a basis for part of a range of strategies to promote positive well-being in children.

This exercise can be done when walking. This might be a time when you are walking to or from work or it might be integrated into your break or lunchtime. It can also be conducted outside of work but is easier to practice if you are alone. Please ensure you are in a relatively safe space, like a park or a garden as opposed to a busy road.

As you are walking, turn your attention to your breathing and take some deep breaths, slowly breathing in through your nose and out through your mouth. The emphasis is on breathing *slowly* as opposed to panic breaths. After repeating three or four times, gradually slow your walking pace and while continuing to look straight ahead, inwardly turn your attention to your feet. Focus your attention on each step, thinking about which part of each foot is striking the ground, how your footwear feels and what the ground feels like under your feet.

  After a few moments of focussing on each step, slowly bring your attention to your other senses, pausing for a few moments on each sense. Slowly think about what you can hear, see and smell in the environment around you. After pausing to focus on each sense, return your attention to your breathing, pausing to focus on each in-breath and out-breath up to six or ten or until you are ready to continue with your day.

Outcomes from research

The literature about mindfulness training for children suggests that it may be beneficial in the short term, as an immediate treatment for stressors and in the longer term as a strategy for developing and maintaining good mental health. Indeed, a recent study of mindfulness training in Israeli schools suggests that some groups of children were able to use mindfulness techniques and strategies in their daily lives away from the classroom (Sheinman et al., 2018). The benefits might also be multi-faceted as a positive impact on children's mental health and well-being might also affect other areas of their life, including the academic. Indeed, mindfulness supports a holistic view of education as impacting on the whole child and not just restricted to promoting achievement in specific academic areas. Much of the discussion regarding mindfulness and its impact on children has focused on its use as a tool to prevent and treat mental health issues however it might also be something that assists children in flourishing by creating an optimum mental state (Weare, 2013). Mindfulness has been linked to improving pupil's ability to avoid impulsive behaviour, improve the choices they make and improve their goal setting and resilience (Weare, 2013). The potential benefits of mindfulness as a tool to improve behaviour through better emotional regulation and an increased sense of empathy has influenced specific elements of educational programmes unrelated to well-being. Lampe and Engleman-Lampe (2012) hypothesize that mindfulness leads people to act from compassion and the insight it brings can lead to ethical intention and ethical action. It is important that the positive impact of mindfulness on children's emotional and social well-being is not viewed in complete isolation from wider outcomes like the academic. A holistic view of the child implies direct connectivity between all aspects of their personality and their ability to function across different areas of their lives. In a study that examined the effects of a mindfulness-based programme (CalmSpace) on young children, Janz et al. (2019) noted that up to this point there has been little research on the effects of mindfulness on children in the early years. This is despite the fact, that early childhood is characterised by the development of self-regulation and executive functioning (Janz et al., 2019), reinforcing the point made earlier in this chapter, suggesting mindfulness might be a worthwhile activity from a young age. The study examined the effects of a mindfulness-based programme that was embedded in the school curriculum as a regular lesson or intervention. When compared to a control group, results from the study suggest that a mindfulness-based intervention delivered by teachers can improve children's executive functioning and ability to maintain attention, at least in the short term. Using the Strengths and Difficulties Questionnaire – teacher form (SDQ) (Janz et al., 2019), children's behaviours were measured from the teacher's perspective. The teacher's perspective of the pupil's behaviour after participating in the programme mirrored the positive impact the programme had on children's executive functioning.

This suggests that a mindfulness-based programme can improve children's emotional self-regulation; children who were considered impulsive showed considerable improvements in managing their feelings (Janz et al., 2019). The findings of this study echo the potential benefits of mindfulness in schools found in other studies of the topic, however, it is still limited by sample size and while there are general improvements in aspect of executive functioning that *might* improve academic performance, there is little evidence to show a direct impact (Maynard et al., 2017). In the literature regarding the impact of mindfulness upon children and adults, the impact on performance tends to be isolated to specific tasks rather than a more general increase in grades. This does not necessarily mean that mindfulness doesn't impact on academic performance but rather that few studies have used it as a primary measure and it may be the case that more research of the impact of mindfulness needs to take place where the programmes have been implemented for a longer period of time (Janz et al., 2019).

As well as being aware of the potential limitations of mindfulness, practitioners might also consider when mindfulness could cause distress and have a negative impact. A study examining the benefits of the daily use of the Calm mindfulness app found that for some adults who were feeling particularly low and experiencing poor mental health, daily meditation didn't work as they became more aware of difficult thoughts and the subsequent distress was too severe to manage. This appeared to amplify their negative thoughts and feelings (Clarke and Draper, 2020). Practitioners may need to consider if mindfulness will support the well-being of all pupils and whether or not daily use is the most beneficial course of action.

Conclusion and further discussion

In conclusion, the evidence base for the use of mindfulness as a tool to promote children's well-being indicates that mindfulness can have a positive effect on children's ability to emotionally self-regulate and improve their ability to focus more effectively. Mindfulness in schools remains a relatively recent phenomenon and its use in early years' settings and with younger children in general remains limited. In short, further evidence is needed from independent evaluators to effectively evaluate the impact of mindfulness upon social and emotional outcomes for children's well-being (Maynard et al. 2017).

What is evident from the literature is that delivering mindfulness training in schools is, at least a viable option even within a pressurised curriculum that includes high stakes testing (Cheek et al., 2017). Mindfulness skills are not overly complicated, they don't require children to complete assessments and they are not a burden on resources or time. Approaching mindfulness for children with cautious optimism may be the best approach as the body of research continues to grow and provide us with more detailed evidence of how and what works when supporting well-being in children. Important questions remain, particularly regarding the impact of introducing mindfulness to children at an earlier age and whether the effects of mindfulness for children continue into adulthood.

The variety in how and when mindfulness training is delivered means measuring its impact can be challenging. However, this variation in delivery and the research information it provides also allows practitioners and academics to analyse and discuss the optimum methods of delivery and the age range for whom it might be most effective. In the future, results of research with a neuroscientific basis might provide a clearer picture of the benefits of mindfulness training for children particularly when synthesised from research based on self-report and observation. Meanwhile, the literature attests to some common benefits across groups of children from different cultures and socio-economic circumstances. This means that mindfulness training should be something that parents, teachers and schools consider as a valid course of action to support children in developing and maintaining positive well-being and good mental health. As posited previously, it might better be regarded as a strategy for promoting well-being that exists alongside other strategies and an effective way to introduce the idea that looking after children's mental health is important. A further, layered approach is another possibility, in which a mindfulness-based programme acts as a foundation for positive well-being from which other approaches, whether dietary or athletic, then emerge.

Summary points

- There are concerns about mental health and well-being for children in the UK. Following its adoption more widely by adults, mindfulness is regarded as a strategy that could also be used to improve children's well-being.
- It is possible for children to learn basic mindfulness skills and there are different programmes for children currently in use in school or early years' settings.
- Mindfulness exercises can be introduced to children in different ways and at different times throughout the curriculum.
- While there are limitations to current research about mindfulness for children, new research is emerging all the time and there is an increasing body of research from neuroscience.
- There are some common themes from research about the potential benefits for children including a positive impact upon the ability of children to regulate their emotions and behaviour.
- In the future, mindfulness-based programmes could be used as part of a multi-layered approach to enhance well-being children. Such programmes could potentially be used to target specific areas of children's well-being for example around issues with eating, sleeping or behavioural disorders.

Recommended reading

Hanh, T.N. (2016) *How to Walk (Mindful Essentials)*. Berkeley, California Parallax Press.
Puddicombe, A. (2011) *The Headspace Guide to Mindfulness & Meditation: 10 Minutes Can Make All the Difference*. London: Hodder and Staughton.
Willard, C. and Saltzman, A. (Eds.) (2015) *Teaching Mindfulness Skills to Kids and Teens*. New York: The Guilford Press.
Williams, M. and Penman, D. (2011) *Mindfulness: A Practical Guide to Finding Peace in a Frantic World*. London: Piaktus.

References

Ajilchi, B. et al. (2019) Applying mindfulness training to enhance the mental toughness and emotional intelligence of amateur basketball players. *Australasian Psychiatry*, **1** (3), p. 291.
Barker, K.K. (2014) Mindfulness meditation: Do-it-yourself medicalization of every moment. *Social Science & Medicine* **106**, pp. 168–176.

Broderick, P. C. and Metz, S. (2009) Learning to BREATHE: A pilot trial of mindfulness curriculum for adolescents. *Advances in School Mental Health Promotion*, **2** (1), pp. 35–46.

Cheek, J. et al. (2017) Creating novel school-based education programs to cultivate mindfulness in youth: What the letters told us. *Journal of Child & Family Studies*, **26**(9), pp. 2564–2578.

Clarke, J. and Draper, S. (2020) Intermittent mindfulness practice can be beneficial, and daily practice can be harmful. An in depth, mixed methods study of the 'Calm' app's (mostly positive) effects. *Internet Interventions*, **19**, p. 10293.

Department of Health and Social Care and Department of Education (DoHSC and DfE) (2018) Government response to the consultation on *Transforming Children and Young People's Mental Health Provision: a Green Paper and Next Steps*. Available at: https://assets.publishing.service.gov.uk/ Accessed 7 January 2020.

Gazella, K. A. (2005) Jon Kabat-Zinn, PHD bringing mindfulness to medicine. *Alternative Therapies in Health and Medicine*, **11** (3), p. 57.

Janz, P., Dawe, S., and Wyllie, M. (2019) Mindfulness-based program embedded within the existing curriculum improves executive functioning and behavior in young children: A waitlist controlled trial. *Frontiers in Psychology*, **10**, p. 2052.

Kabat-Zinn, J. (1996) *Full Catastrophe Living: How to Cope with Stress, Pain and Illness using Mindfulness Meditation*. London: Piatkus.

Lampe, M. and Engleman-Lampe, C. (2012) Mindfulness-based business ethics education. *Academy of Educational Leadership Journal*, **16** (3), pp. 99–111.

Lingtao, Y. and Zellmer-Bruhn, M. (2019) What mindfulness can do for a team. *Harvard Business Review Digital Articles*, pp. 2–5.

Ludlow, C. (2016) A narrative exploring the development of a mindfulness programme for children aged five to seven. Masters in Education, Birmingham City University.

Maynard, B.R., Solis, M., Miller, V., and Brendel, K.E. (2017) Mindfulness-based interventions for improving cognition, academic achievement, behavior and socio-emotional functioning of primary and secondary students. *Campbell Systems Review*, **13**, pp. 1–147.

Mindfulness and meditation will now be part of the curriculum in 370 schools in England. Available at: http://www.trueactivist.com/?s=Mindfulness+for+children Accessed 1 September 2019.

Oord, S., Bögels, S., and Peijnenburg, D. (2012) The effectiveness of mindfulness training for children with ADHD and mindful parenting for their parents. *Journal of Child & Family Studies*, **21** (1), pp. 139–147.

Proulx, K. (2003) Integrating mindfulness-based stress reduction. *Holistic Nursing Practice*, **17** (4), pp. 201–208.

Puddicombe, A. (2012) *Get Some Headspace*. London: Hodder and Stoughton.

Sheinman, N. et al. (2018) 'Preliminary Investigation of Whole-School Mindfulness in Education Programs and Children's Mindfulness-Based Coping Strategies', *Journal of Child & Family Studies*, 27(10), pp. 3316–3328.

Sibinga, E. M. S. et al. (2013) 'School-based mindfulness instruction for urban male youth: A small randomized controlled trial', *Preventive Medicine*, 57(6), pp. 799–801.

The Mental Health Foundation (2018) What new statistics show about children's mental health. Available at: https://www.mentalhealth.org.uk/ Accessed 6 November 2019.

Weare, K. (2013) Developing mindfulness with children and young people: A review of the evidence and policy context. *Journal of Children's Services*, **8** (2), pp. 141–153.

Worthern, D., and Luiselli, J.K. (2016) Attitudes and opinions of female high school athletes about sports-focused mindfulness training and practices. *Journal of Clinical Sport Psychology*, **1** (10), pp. 177–191.

YouGov. (2013) *YouGov-Survey-Big-Lottery-Fund-Children's-Worries-131107*. Available at: https://yougov.co.uk/ Accessed 6 November 2019.

10 Education and social work working collaboratively to support vulnerable families
Benefits and tensions

Michael Jopling and Sharon Vincent

This chapter examines two innovative programmes aimed at improving support and provision for vulnerable families, and promoting their well-being and resilience. It focuses on the benefits, tensions and challenges associated with the inter-agency collaboration which was central to the two programmes and, arguably, all effective support for vulnerable children, young people and families. After a brief discussion of the terms *vulnerable* and *inter-agency collaboration*, we focus on what our research into the programmes told us about how education and social work professionals collaborate both with each other and (less commonly) with the families with whom they work, both of which are relatively unexplored areas.

Vulnerability and interagency collaboration

We have written elsewhere about the ubiquity of the use of the terms *vulnerable* and *vulnerability* to describe disadvantaged individuals, children, young people and families in social and education policy in the UK and Europe, and the need to use the terms more carefully (Jopling and Vincent, 2020). Ecclestone (2016) and Ecclestone and Lewis (2014) have valuably questioned the application of the terms and their use in creating a therapeutic emphasis in social justice (Frawley, 2015) and diverting resources away from those most in need (Brown, Ecclestone and Emmel, 2017). Potter and Brotherton (2013) have similarly asserted that popular discourse has increasingly blurred the extreme positions of blame (associated broadly with neoliberalism, a political philosophy based on applying market economics and competition to all areas of society) and compensation (associated with social democratic approaches) in relation to vulnerable individuals. This has often led to *vulnerability* being emptied of meaning, allowing policy to ignore it. Informed by these arguments, our starting point is the definition of *vulnerability* used in the larger of the two programmes we draw on in this chapter: any families with children from 0 months to 18 years of age who might require some form of multi-agency support. This also helps us to focus on the benefits and challenges involved in such collaboration, focusing on two key agencies: education and social work.

Multi-agency, or inter-agency, collaboration and partnership has been the subject of intense policy interest since the early 2000s, represented most clearly by the key New Labour policy, *Every Child Matters* (DfE, 2004). Powell and Glendinning (2002, p. 3) offered a contemporaneous, minimal definition which suggested that such partnership requires:

> the involvement of at least two agents or agencies with at least some common interests or interdependencies and [...] a relationship between them that involves a degree of trust, equality or reciprocity.

In their slightly later review of the literature relating to inter-agency collaboration, Warmington et al. (2004, p. 7) found it to be idealised and immature, focused on promoting models of good practice and tending "to under-acknowledge interagency working as a site of tensions and contradictions". Taylor and Thoburn (2016, p. 8) suggest that we have not moved much further and that much writing on inter-agency and inter-professional working still "focuses on the role and effectiveness of protocols and procedures, especially with respect to formal child protection services".

While there is an extensive literature exploring school to school collaboration (e.g. Rincon-Gallardo and Fullan, 2016), little research has focused specifically on collaboration between teachers and social workers. However, there has been particular interest in inter-professional collaboration among researchers in Norway in recent years. Focusing on collaboration in health and social welfare, Willumsen et al. (2012) concluded that it remains crucial to improve our knowledge about how best to establish and maintain high-quality services. In their study of a municipal child welfare service, Hesjedal et al. (2015) identified three themes: personal commitment; creating a positive atmosphere; and pulling together towards future goals, which supported successful inter-professional collaboration, but concluded, like Willumsen et al. (2012), that facilitating factors have generally been under-reported in the literature. However, these frameworks seemed inadequate as a theoretical framework for our research because their focus on inter-professional working underplayed the role of service users, in our case the families themselves, in the collaborations, as Willumsen et al. (2012) acknowledged. Ahgren et al.'s (2009) study of collaboration between professional groups represent one of the few exceptions to this. However, their framework, which distinguished between the structure, process and outcome of welfare service integration, was too general for our purposes. Therefore, we decided to draw on Smith's (2013) implicit framework to guide our analysis because it was flexible enough to allow us to assess the extent to which families themselves were able to be involved in effective collaboration. Smith (2013) emphasised four factors:

- establishing a common sense of purpose
- mediation between different interests
- acknowledging conflict and complexity
- developing mutual trust and respect

This enabled us to put the family at the centre of our analysis as partners in, rather than barriers to, collaboration, allowing us to focus on how their well-being and resilience were improved.

Individual/group task

The research cited above only identified some of the factors involved in successful collaboration between professions. What else do you think is important in facilitating collaboration which aims to improve families', children's and/or young people's well-being and resilience?

Underlying research

This chapter is based on the findings from two research projects which assessed the impact of two reform programmes, focused on improving provision and support for vulnerable families, conducted in two areas of high deprivation in North West England between 2014 and 2017.

Both projects used mixed methods which brought together qualitative research which aims to seek the view of and understand the lived experiences of participants, in our case children, young people, families and professionals, with analyses of quantitative outcome data which comprised routine numerical administrative data held by organisations such as schools, social care organisations, health services and the police. Programme A was designed by a single local authority to bring about cultural transformation through the development of an integrated, early intervention and prevention framework to promote the well-being and resilience of all vulnerable families with children from 0 months to 18 years of age. The programme combined new and existing initiatives, including the national troubled families programme which aimed controversially to *turn around* 120,000 families regarded as both experiencing and causing serious social problems, to try to cover all such families' needs. Programme B was smaller scale, working initially with ten families in a large, relatively isolated coastal town. Although the programme's approach was based on co-production and tailored to each family's needs, its support tended to focus on pragmatic issues such as education, mental health and emotional well-being, employment and securing benefits, alongside meeting day to day needs such as accompanying families to medical appointments. This was intended to help them become more self-reliant and improve their resilience and well-being without requiring extensive funding at a time when funding was being reduced. Both programmes were explicitly non-judgmental and regarded schools, early years' settings, social services and other agencies working with families as partners in provision.

The research into Programme A involved semi-structured individual and group interviews with 83 professionals and practitioners (from schools and other agencies) and in-depth case studies of nine families involved in the programme. Programme B's research involved semi-structured interviews with 32 professionals and practitioners (including school staff and social workers) and 20 case studies of families. The data were analysed using thematic analysis (Boyatzis, 1998) and theory of change models specifically developed to evaluate the programmes. The findings reported in this chapter summarise some of the findings from these research projects.

Benefits and impacts

Assessment of the impact of both programmes was central to the funders of the research, both to inform their further development and to underpin applications for further funding. This meant that part of our research had to focus on assessing the extent to which various *hard* impact measures had been met. In Programme A, the local authority was focused on ambitious, transformative outcomes at the system level. In the family case studies, this included improving families' well-being and promoting their resilience by re-engaging young people in school and improving their attendance and achievement, and preventing child protection plans from being implemented and de-escalating those that were already in place. In Programme B, our analysis suggested that the programme prevented at least nine children from going into care, representing an estimated saving of almost £300,000 per year; and was associated with a significant reduction of children on child protection and child in need plans. However, these and other positive outcomes were achieved in the face of a number of systemic local and national challenges, which were likely to affect the extent to which they could be sustained in the longer term. Our intention in this chapter is to explore some of the factors which affected their success, using Smith's (2013) analysis as a theoretical framework against which to measure the extent to which improvements to families' well-being were mediated, or moderated, by collaboration and partnership between education and social work professionals.

Factors affecting inter-agency collaboration

Common purpose

As already stated, Programme A's ambitious objective was to support and improve the well-being of all vulnerable families in the city. This was underpinned by an ethos of inter-agency collaboration and working in partnership with families, although this was not as explicit or successful as the co-production approach adopted by Programme B, the smaller size of which made this more achievable. Some progress was made towards achieving effective collaboration between partners, notably between schools and elements of Programme A, such as the Schools Families Support Service (SFSS), which was able to extend the programme's reach in its key role *between* schools and other services. Families involved in the research felt that Programme A was more effective in providing the *right kind of support* than previous programmes in which they had been involved. This was a mix of one to one emotional support as well as practical support, delivered in their own homes and reflects Featherstone et al.'s (2014) identification of the value of locating ordinary help for families in their own communities. Family support workers often visited families daily and were well placed to undertake a monitoring role and respond to the early warning signs which are so often indicative of larger issues, such as reductions in children's attendance at school. The more holistic approach (all families) adopted by the programme to improving families' well-being allowed professionals to make such small adjustments in vulnerable young people's lives, distinct from the depersonalised, *nudge* approach criticised by Crossley (2017). Specifically, they monitored issues such as families' mental and emotional health and well-being, relationships and dynamics within them, and the domestic environment. However, collaboration was largely limited to professionals. We found little evidence of common purpose developed or decision-making shared with families, particularly listening and giving voice to children and young people, which has been associated with improving provision for vulnerable families (Crowther and Cohen, 2011) and collaborative or co-productive approaches. This may have been the result of the time it takes to introduce such collaborative approaches, as well as prevailing, disempowering policy rhetoric (already highlighted) of *turning families around*, which does not allow the time or conceptual space necessary to engage with or listen to families and, particularly, young people.

The smaller-scale focus of Programme B made its strong emphasis on co-producing interventions and outcomes with families more achievable. One of the primary headteachers interviewed emphasised taking a longer term, more holistic approach to working with families in this way, rather than focusing on symptoms such as children's behaviour in school:

> In education, traditionally interventions have been with the child. So, the behaviour team will come in and work with the child but the parents aren't involved in that at all. Whereas this [programme] is very much about the whole family being part of that because quite often as we know the child may have a difficulty that's not actually a difficulty for the child. It's actually a family system issue and that's what they address.

She also emphasised that "It's giving them the skills, the strategies and the confidence to do that them-selves. And that's not a quick fix". These types of transactional, relationship-based approaches were very different from those envisaged in the UK Government's approach to family policy in England where the policy and rhetoric shifted responsibility on to so-called *troubled* or *anti-social* families (Hayden and Jenkins, 2015). The fact that the much smaller-scale Programme B was more successful in meeting its purpose of increasing families' sense of agency and encouraging them to take more responsibility for changing their own behaviour emphasises the difficulty of achieving this at scale and over time.

Individual/group task

How would you go about building consensus and purpose among colleagues you work with to improve families' and children's well-being and promote their resilience? What kind of things would you do initially?

Mediation

The negative emphasis of the troubled families' agenda, which was the policy background to both of these programmes, inextricably in the case of Programme A, has sometimes encouraged support agencies to attempt to take control of families' lives. However, both programmes were successful when they were able to adopt a mediating role between families and the agencies and institutions with which they were engaged. For example, in Programme A its introduction of the SFSS, which had an explicit mediatory role, played a key part in creating the neutral space which helped ensure that children remained in mainstream education and did not have to move to alternative provision in four of the nine case studies. It is often difficult for children and young people to move back into main-stream education from alternative provision, which is also much more expensive. This was important because the research also found that schools were more comfortable referring vulnerable families to other agencies than acting as *lead professional* in initiating support for them, despite the exten-sive training which the programme offered. They were reluctant to coordinate support for a family because they were not confident about working with specialist services such as mental health ser-vices or talking to families about non-educational problems which affect their well-being such as finan-cial or domestic issues (Fitzgerald and Kay, 2008). Thus, mediation operated at different levels, with the SFSS mediating between schools and other services, as well as between families and a range of agencies. Furthermore, the programme's complexity, with its multiple sub-programmes, made it difficult for many professionals to develop an understanding of it as a whole. Professionals outside education were unlikely to have heard of the SFSS and schools were not always clear what would happen when its support ended. Since school staff could be required to act as (mediating) lead pro-fessional at that point, their reluctance to develop a better understanding of the programme overall and their collaborative role in it prevented them from being able to do this effectively. As one case study parent emphasised, schools' reluctance to recognise there was an issue created tensions:

> I don't want to slag the school off because it is a really great school, but I wouldn't be confident now like going in and speaking to someone. They just think there's nothing wrong with him and he can't behave himself but I think there's a little bit more to it definitely.

The programme itself also fulfilled a mediating role in Programme B. At times this was at odds with the inflexibility of school approaches, but schools were able to accommodate themselves to this, as one of the Education Welfare Officers interviewed commented:

> Sometimes [the programme's] agenda to support families is maybe at odds with the behaviour and discipline policy in the school, but I think because we've got good working relationships with the workers, we've managed to overcome some of the more difficult obstacles you're going to get in any organisation.

Her experience was that previously schools had found it difficult to engage children from vulnerable families. While schools had made home visits, they would not have been able to develop the kind of relationship with the family necessary to reintegrate them into school. Similarly, social workers would have offered them support, but would not have worked sufficiently closely with schools to be able to promote the importance of education effectively. Again, it was often very simple mediatory things undertaken by the programme, such as reminding parents in the morning that they needed to get their children up for school or ensure they had clean clothes that made the difference and significantly improved families' well-being. The challenge for research is to find ways to evaluate the importance of such relatively minor actions.

Acknowledging conflict and complexity

Both programmes took their complexity, and the complex lives of the families with whom they worked, as their starting point. In attempting to achieve consensus, and overcome conflict, the importance of professionals adopting the non-judgmental approach both of the reforms promoted was repeatedly emphasised. Such an approach is rare. Several of the families involved in Programme A felt that interactions with social workers had previously intimidated them and left them feeling powerless. Where effective relationships were developed, for example with family support workers, families felt that the relationships they developed with the workers were sufficiently robust to allow them both to challenge and support them. Their non-judgmental approach was very different from their prior experiences with social care professionals and, in many cases, came to characterise collaborative relationships between social workers and education professionals, which made a significant contribution to improving their well-being. However, when tensions arose, this was often because families were frustrated about how long it often took to receive support from the programme.

One of the care workers involved in Programme B explicitly highlighted the importance of the programme's neutrality: "It's about looking from the outside-in and being able to give that advice in a non-judgmental way". Focusing on building relationships in order to understand where families were and how to work with them to improve their situation had enabled professionals, from both social services and education, to develop high levels of trust very quickly, as the following section underlines. One of the Education Welfare Officers emphasised that she felt that the concentrated nature of the programme allowed professionals from different areas to join together to offer support consistently in a way that prevented conflict from escalating:

> In this case [the programme] was able to pull together a raft of other professionals to support the family members. So, Mum got support with her health, Dad got support with his addiction

and also his mental health. [...] It was a joined-up approach over an extended period of time. And that's what made the difference.

Respecting families and gaining their trust was key to this and much more difficult to achieve in Programme A.

Trust

The importance, and difficulty, of establishing and maintaining trust between professionals and families, as well as among professionals themselves, was a key factor affecting the programmes' effectiveness. Due to lack of space, we use issues surrounding communication as proxy indicators of how trust functioned in different ways in the programmes. The complexity and size of Programme A meant that communication issues consistently created tension. Families found it difficult to find out what services were available in their area, despite the creation of a new services directory. While there was evidence of improved understanding among professionals of the range of services other agencies offered and cross-agency meetings to combine expertise and coordinate services around a family became more common, this did not automatically lead to trust or cohesion (Featherstone et al., 2014). Consistency was an issue as professionals in all the agencies involved were concerned that reducing budgets resulted in thresholds for services being raised, therefore excluding families from support and affecting families' trust in the support on offer.

The smaller size of Programme B made it easier for professionals involved to meet families' needs and expectations consistently: "They don't overpromise, they don't under-deliver. If they say something's going to happen, it does happen" (Education Welfare Officer). One of the headteachers interviewed emphasised the importance of having a single social worker communicating with and coordinating all support for the family, rather than being repeatedly moved between professionals with whom they had to start from scratch. This enabled the social worker to develop a trusting relationship that was deep enough to enable them to identify support that anticipated, rather than merely meet, families' articulated needs: "They had to try to find a way in to give them the support they needed that they didn't actually say they wanted. They were very good at that". This allowed professionals in the programme to build trust at different levels, including among professionals, as one special educational needs coordinator commented: "I've felt much more that I trust services that are working to support young people. I haven't always felt that in the past". As a result, different agencies were able to work closely together in ways that were not always apparent in the much larger Programme A. Again, this highlights the fact that, although applicable to small scale interventions in a range of contexts, it is difficult to sustain these kinds of approaches, especially at scale, because they depend so much on professionals being trained and prepared to build the kind of consistent and trusting relationships with vulnerable children and their families that are so crucial to improving their well-being and resilience.

Individual/group task

As we have emphasised, building trust among professionals and families is much easier said than done. How do we go about developing and maintaining trust with vulnerable families and individuals?

Conclusion: implications for improving vulnerable families' well-being and resilience

Although the capabilities-based approaches adopted (to different degrees) by the two programmes we have explored can be difficult to evaluate, both in terms of their impact and the values on which they are based (Ecclestone and Lewis, 2014), it appeared that they allowed professionals to develop an understanding of where families were and used that knowledge to build strong relationships with them. Alongside the agencies' mediating role, in many cases this allowed the programmes to increase families' confidence, the benefits of which are likely to have been longer term improvements in their well-being and resilience to cope with the challenges they continued to face. The short-term nature of the research that is undertaken into such interventions makes it impossible to make more than a tentative claim for this. However, it is also clear from the research that, as Warmington et al. (2004) highlighted, tensions are an inevitable part of interagency working, including between education and social work, and this needs to be anticipated and built into its implementation and evaluation.

It is also important to emphasise the limitations that continue to characterise interagency collaboration. Despite their emphasis on co-production and close partnership with families, both programmes struggled to achieve the 'co-configuration' (Warmington et al., 2004, p.4) in which "ongoing customisation of services is achieved through dynamic, reciprocal relationships between providers and clients". The failure to move forward in allowing families, including children and young people, to have a voice in their own support (Tucker et al., 2015) may be a consequence of the rhetoric of blame that has blighted policies such as the troubled families programme. Co-production, as co-configuration tends now to be termed, remains much more common in adult social care services than in children's services, despite advances in many areas. In particular, young people are rarely listened to or involved in decisions about support that is designed to improve their well-being and promote resilience. Doing so may in itself have a positive effect on their well-being; the importance of listening to children and young people, and associated influence on their well-being is explored further in Chapter 4. This suggests that interagency collaboration needs to focus on the importance of developing a deeper understanding of the *empirical realities* of the children and young people they work with, particularly in schools which are increasingly being required to take on more responsibility for vulnerable children and young people in the face of enduring budget reductions. The success of interventions like the SFSS in Programme A, which facilitated better joint working between social work and schools, indicates the value of reconfiguring professional roles and services to promote mediation and collaboration which involves, as well as supports, vulnerable families and promotes their well-being and resilience.

Summary points

- Supporting families and children's well-being and promoting their resilience is complex, affected by multiple independent factors, and requires multi-agency collaboration, such as between education and social work, to mediate between services and build trust.
- Effective multi-agency collaboration still rarely involves families or young people as partners, despite the emphasis placed on approaches which are co-produced or co-configured. In particular, young people are rarely listened to, which itself has negative effects on their well-being and resilience.
- Deficit perceptions of vulnerable families continue to have a negative effect on vulnerable children's and families' well-being and resilience, and support structures and systems are still too often influenced by such attitudes.

Recommended reading

Brown, K., Ecclestone, K., and Emmel, N. (2017) Review article: The many faces of vulnerability, *Social Policy and Society*, **16**(3), 497–510.
Jopling, M. and Vincent, S. (2016) *Vulnerable Children: Needs and Provision in the Primary Phase*. York: Cambridge Primary Review Trust.
Potter, T. and Brotherton, G. (2013) What do we mean when we talk about "vulnerability"? In Brotherton, G. and Cronin, M. (eds.) *Working with Vulnerable Children, Young People and Families*. London: Routledge, pp. 1–15.
Smith, R. (2013) Working together: Why it's important and why it's difficult. In Littlechild, B. and Smith, R. (eds.) *A Handbook for Interprofessional Practice in the Human Services*. Harlow: Pearson, 12–22.

References

Ahgren, B., Axelsson, S.B., and Axelsson, R. (2009) Evaluating intersectoral collaboration: A model for assessment by service users, *International Journal of Integrated Care*, **9**(26), 1–10.
Boyatzis, R. E. (1998) *Transforming Qualitative Information: Thematic Analysis and Code Development*. Thousand Oaks, CA: Sage.
Brown, K., Ecclestone, K., and Emmel, N. (2017) Review article: The many faces of vulnerability, *Social Policy and Society*, **16**(3), 497–510.
Crossley, S. (2017) *In their Place. The Imagined Geographies of Poverty*. London: Pluto.
Crowther, K. and Cohen, G. (2011) *Effective relationships with vulnerable parents to improve outcomes for children and young people: Final study report*. London: Action for Children.
Department for Education and Skills (2004) *Every Child Matters: Change for Children*. London: TSO.
Ecclestone, K. (2016) Behaviour change policy agendas for "vulnerable" subjectivities: the dangers of therapeutic governance and its new entrepreneurs. *Journal of Education Policy*, **32**(1), 48–62.
Ecclestone, K. and Lewis, L. (2014) Interventions for resilience in educational settings: Challenging policy discourses of risk and vulnerability. *Journal of Education Policy*, **29**(2), 195–216.
Featherstone, B., White, S., and Morris, K. (2014) *Reimagining Child Protection: Towards Humane Social Work with Families*. Bristol: The Policy Press.
Fitzgerald, D. and Kay, J. (2008) *Working together in children's services*. Abingdon: David Fulton.
Frawley, A. (2015). *The semiotics of happiness: The rhetorical beginnings of a social problem*. London: Bloomsbury.
Hayden, C. and Jenkins, C. (2015) Children taken into care and custody and the "troubled families" agenda in England. *Child & Family Social Work*, **20**(4), 459–469.
Hesjedal, E., Hetland, H., and Iversen, A.C. (2015) Interprofessional collaboration: Self-reported successful collaboration by teachers and social workers in multidisciplinary teams, *Child & Family Social Work*, **20**(4), 437–445.
Jopling, M. and Vincent, S. (2020) Vulnerable families: Policy, practice and social justice. In Papa, R. (ed.) *Springer Handbook on Promoting Social Justice in Education*. Berlin and Heidelberg: Springer, 725–746.
Powell, M. and Glendinning, C. (2002) Introduction. In Glendinning, C., Powell, M., and Rummery, K. (eds.) *Partnerships, New Labour and the Governance of Welfare*. London: The Policy Press, pp. 1–15.
Rincon-Gallardo, S. and Fullan, M. (2016) Essential features of effective networks in education, *Journal of Professional Capital and Community*, **1**(1), 5–22.
Taylor, J. and Thoburn, J. (2016) *Collaborative Practice with Vulnerable Children and their Families*. Boca Raton, FL: CRC Press.
Tucker, S., Trotman, D., and Martyn, M. (2015) Vulnerability: The role of schools in supporting young people exposed to challenging environments and situations, *International Journal of Educational Development*, **41**, 301–306.
Warmington, P., Daniels, H., Edwards, A., Brown, S., Leadbetter, J., Martin, D., and Middleton, D. (2004) *Interagency Collaboration: A Review of the Literature*. Bath: Learning in and for Interagency Working Project.
Willumsen, E., Ahgren, B., and Ødegard, A. (2012) A conceptual framework for assessing interorganizational integration and interprofessional collaboration. *Journal of Interprofessional Care*, **26**, 198–204.

11 Solution-focused resilience work

From the fantastical to the real

Dean-David Holyoake

…when people asked me if school made me resilient, I say hell no, school steals resilience and its one of the most fun things to watch…

Rob (16)

…the real world ate me alive, even though I was mostly empty…

Claire (15)

Introduction: background and aims

Solution-focused (SF) psychotherapy started during the 1980s and has at its core a future-focused agenda. It relies very much on the notion that people know most about their own lives and can be trusted to make change. Unlike other approaches, it attempts to disrupt client's typical thinking by employing tactics of curiosity, collaboration and confidence. So, resilience may have a past, but it's the future that matters to young people like Robert, Claire and Judy (names changed) who were participants in my clinical work. My aim in this chapter is to explore how the nature of SF practice helps them envisage, engage and subsequently enact with theirs. My reflexion on how SF practice provides a number of skills known as skeleton keys which offer ways for clients to reimagine their futures and reformulate resilient change, Young people have always experienced difficult times, but during the past ten years I have noticed how they have more despondent futures and little hope of achieving a sense of sovereign responsibility to call their own. It has been my experience that resilience, like their future, is progressive demanding a degree of suffering, a can-do attitude and a lifelong supply of disruptive creativity. To help me think things through I have the following three aims:

(1) Apply the case studies of Robert, Claire and Judy to introduce SF practice.
(2) Provide examples of key skills the reader can consider for their own organisations and personal practice.
(3) Offer some suggestions as to the interplay of confidence, motivation and acceptance as poignant concepts in my work with resilience.

Introducing ten principles of solution-focused practice and their relationship with resilience

SF practice is now an established approach to working with children and young people in many health, social care and educational settings. Teachers, social workers, nurses and service users recognise traces of SF in their practice with approaches including brief intervention, acceptance and narrative strategies which are becoming more popular. I have intentionally attempted to reduce the amount of theory here but for those who might want to pursue the approach I would suggest the work of Steve de Shazer (1991, 1994), Dolan (1998), O'Connell and Palmer (2003), O'Hanlon (1999), Selekman (1997), Lines (2011), Macdonald (2011) and Sharry (2001). Each of these cover a wide range of theory and technique for the curious. My aim here is to suggest that referral to Child and Adolescent Mental Health Services (CAMHS) represents the most intensive of health settings for young people suffering from mental health issues and usually embodies part of a long scary, serious and life-threatening ordeal for young people and their families. In my experience, it is suffering, which usually is extensive, complex and requiring any number of interventions such as SF. The three young people (Rob aged 16, Claire 15 and Judy 15) who helped me think about resilience as an important concept for imagining new futures all accessed in-patient CAMHS and would see me weekly for an hour session in what Claire termed a 'checking up on' and by Rob who affectionately referred to me as 'the shrink' or 'mind police'.

So, I take as my starting point the idea that resilience and our interest in it is a good thing and something young people have capacity to orchestrate to their advantage. Chapter 5 refers to and discusses the work of writers on resilience such as Luthar et al. (2000) and Southwick et al. (2014) referring to resilience issues being about bouncing back and adapting to adversity, These qualities are those sought by SF practitioners who actively search with clients like Rob, Claire and Judy for successes relating to any number of life events, perceived failures and interestingly, something called chance. I am reluctant to use official diagnosis because in my SF sessions (which usually amount to a total of 6) I try and surprise young people by not referring to previous self-image because such identification signified by official diagnosis hinder possibilities, predetermines hopes and upholds expert worldviews instead of encouraging resilience through a process of re-thinking. Therefore, disrupting how Rob, Claire and Judy think of resilience is my first strategy to stimulate new SF relationships with resilience and the possibility that the future for them is different to their past. As a prelude, I list the guiding principles to my work and hopefully your future appreciation (see Tables 11.1 and 11.2). In addition, my intention at the start of each session is to establish goals which utilise skills and strengths young people already sense they command. During sessions, I ask the following type of question: "What is the goal of this conversation for you?" "How will you know this session has been useful?" "How will you know when enough is enough?" "What would you like to see instead of the problem?" "What are your best hopes?" "What are the differences you hope for?" "What would be different tomorrow if today is successful?" "What do you want to do differently?" "How else?" "Who else?" "What would others notice is different about you?" "What needs to happen so that we no longer need to meet up?" I have devised the following ten points I use to establish resilience in my work and you can see that apart from these questions my overall aim is one of enabling new imagine futures, getting young people to notice parts of these futures and then experiment in order to make a small change.

Table 11.1   Guiding principles of SF

1. **Future-focused potential and capacity** (All acts of resilience will occur in the future. Noticing success is dynamically contextual best served through identifying best hopes, goals and the recognition of previous success.)
2. **The mundane and detailed** (Resilience requires degrees of certainty and believability therefore, leaving no stone unturned to establish the simplest of detail is a useful strategy. I use the question 'what else?' to achieve this.)
3. **Descriptive and noticed** (Rather than seek the depth of explanation young people are encouraged to describe their hopes, their preferred futures, their strengths and the notice the things that are 'going well', that they 'would not want to change'.)
4. **Confidence and motivation** (These are the experiences that make the next thing happen, they are the building blocks of resilience.)
5. **Sovereign responsibility** (Resilience is founded on a sense of autonomy, self-respect, self-identity and notions of duty, reputation and simple acts of overcoming struggle.)
6. **Goal setting and outcome orientation** (Overcoming struggle is the human condition, resilience is less about minimising obstacles, but setting goals and smashing through them.)
7. **Pragmatic emergence** (Rather than searching for the depth advocated by approaches favouring emotion and cognition, SF emphasises useful behavioural change which is both feasible and sustainable.)
8. **Contextuality and connectivity** (SF resilience is not only about strengthening essential qualities but also noticing support systems and connections already existing for the young person.)
9. **The imagined and believable** (The distinction between fact and fiction is established only to frame future action. That which might happen usually turns into can happen.)
10. **Resilience is not reflecting, it is reflexive** (Resilience requires all of the above because of its reflexive nature. Young people respond, adapt and establish themselves despite of themselves.)

Table 11.2   Each encounter (10 E's to enact) route-map.

1. Establishing future goals
2. Exploring best future hopes
3. Encouraging imagery, visualisation and disruption
4. Expectation and collaboration
5. Extract detail
6. Exact description
7. Emerge possibilities
8. Eliminate distraction for motivation
9. Entrust/Earmark levels of confidence, sovereignty
10. Experiment and task

Individual/group task

A One-Minute Question: what SF two-worded question can open any discussion about resilience?

...after you'd asked me about miracles, I took noticing seriously. I'm no longer just a self-harmer, I'm much more

Judy (15)

The skeletons, route-maps and performance of SF practice"

"What's better"? I said, "Since last time".
"The last time we met you made me start something new", said Judy.
"To appreciate things, you tend not to notice", I said, "So what's better now?"
"Well", she paused looking up to help her think.

So, my approach to building resilience is entangled with complex ideas, skills and collaborative dynamics which flex back and forth in a messy process leaving novices feeling out of their depth. Yet in principle, I approach every session using my ten Encounters route-map (see Table 11.2 – remembering that the map is not the terrain) in a co-authoring effort to move the young person from establishing goals to actual change task (see Table 11.3). My work with Judy is a perfect example of how I started off by purposefully ignoring her self-harm diagnosis to disrupt her usual way of regarding herself.

"So what needs to happen here today so that you know it was worth you coming?"
After some deliberation, "To keep a check on my cutting".
"What else?"

Table 11.3 Stages in the SF design of R (the facts and fictions of SF resilience)

- Noticing and monitoring behaviour rather than feelings and cognitions
- Setting realistic goals rather than preferred desires
- Sticking to details rather than bigger ideals
- Employing description rather than explanation
- Deploying purposefully disruptive strategies to encourage new resilience
- Employing imaginative visualising and thus more possibilities
- Evaluating one's successes and rejecting expert centralise authority
- Appreciating success, indirect complimenting of unnoticed achievements, pacing and matching collaboratively
- Motivation, confidence
- Actively give messages, tasks and experiments

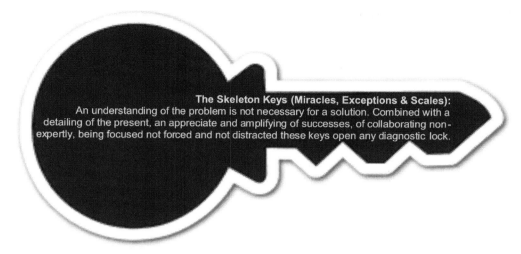

The Skeleton Keys (Miracles, Exceptions & Scales):
An understanding of the problem is not necessary for a solution. Combined with a detailing of the present, an appreciate and amplifying of successes, of collaborating non-expertly, being focused not forced and not distracted these keys open any diagnostic lock.

Figure 11.1   The skeleton keys (miracles, exceptions and scales).

The question what else? (sometimes referred to as the detail question or as my colleague Dave Bell terms 'elsies'). They act as add-on's and range from the grand tour such as "describe what happened" and "what happened next?" to the more specific about successes "what else did you do to achieve that?" and "then what?"

Resilience for Judy is not about having goals in themselves, but about generating hopes, examining possibilities and taking what might be otherwise ignored out of the dark and into the light. By asking "what else?" I'm suggesting that Judy has strengths, her own ideas, able to voice more fragments and resources which represent her daily mundane experiences. With questions such as "what else?" or "what would your teachers say you were good at that you're too embarrassed to admit?" I'm hooking into potential, capacities, alternatives, subtly complimenting and laying the foundations for our consideration of futures and resilience-work. We enter a contracted space which is expectant, collaborative and consultative rather than expert driven. She is the expert in her own life and as a result the setting is set for her to step up in the guise of a resilient mind-set.

Initiating and setting the scene for helping young people feel they can emerge resilience requires integrated skills by the practitioner to establish context which generates a 'get and go' dynamic underlying confidence building and stimulating motivation rather than finding out the causes of problems. Even though we think of ourselves in terms of our past experiences for SF, the building of resilience starts with identifying goals, imagining what they might look like and then assessing how confident and motivated we are to achieve them). In the broadest sense, the past may be useful for 'seeking exceptions' and 'ascertaining ranges of possibility', especially when combined with the often-untapped resource of imagining possible new futures. This is where resilience-work can really come into its own using 'skeleton keys' (skeleton key is the term used to describe a range of interventions which are not concerned with the exploring the problems a young person brings to the session. In this respect, the idea is that the same key can unlock any number of locks regardless) as shown in my work with Claire:

"You've got some good reasons why you want to be more in control of your weight and body image", I said acknowledging her resources, "So I have a strange question which requires some imagination. Some say it has helped them think outside the box about what their future might look like, do you want to hear it?"

It is at this point that young people like Claire get their curiosity awoken. Such engagement strategies use enticing claims and explanation to get them starting to believe that there is hope and a purpose for their attendance. I then ask what is known as the classic 'miracle question'.

"Suppose", I purposefully pause and pretend to think, "Suppose, that when you leave here today and you go to sleep tonight and a miracle happens meaning that the issue that brought you here was resolved", I pause again,

> But you're asleep so you don't know the miracle has occurred and then you wake up. Curiously, you start to notice small things, the way people talk to you and stuff like that. What would these small things you notice be? Things so different that you say to yourself, 'hmmmm that's strange, a miracle must have happened'?

Individual/group task: take one minute to consider

Can you imagine what you would do next if you had everlasting resilience?
What would be the first thing I'd see you doing?
Who else in your life would notice that some type of miracle must have occurred?

Over the years, there have been many adaptions to the miracle question so what I offer here is the typical way I ask it, but I'd encourage others to learn it by rote. That means saying it over and over again 100 times until you know it backwards (no pun intended) to build confidence, enabling you to adapt and link it to other skeleton keys and 'add-ons' and to start structuring your encouraging of young people to visualise, reimagine and describe what is up to this point, just fantasy and unbelievable Using the work of Todorov (1970) – what I term 'the fantastic'.

"Hmmmm, I don't know, I've never been asked this before", said Claire, but my experience tells me this initial response requires some prompting and patience.
"I know, it is a strange question", I said, "But I dare you, go on give it a go, what would I see you doing?"
"Hmmmm, I guess I'd eat more and feel less anxious".
"Uhuuu, and what else?" my desire for detail never ends because I need her to be specific so that she can start to believe the smallest of change is possible. I want trajectory towards her initial identified goal to 'feel more in control over her eating'.

It can be daunting for CAMHS young people to take charge of their own lives. So, getting them to imagine miracles and future goals requires a lot of resilience in itself. Yet, ideas of the fantastic dovetail well with many of the techniques highlighted in literature about resilience. The aim is to first get them imagining and only then start assessing how confident and motivated they are at achieving this. Thus, on my route-map my concern is to extract detail, description and emerge alternative possibilities like my 'exception seeking' work with Rob.

"So, there have been times when this depression thing has not got the better of you", I acknowledged being careful to maintain distinction between the 'thing termed depression' and Rob himself, "What happened next, when you first noticed?" My only intention at this point is to identify trajectory and get him sticking with the detail. I needed him to say it out loud, to help him think, to help us collaborate and emerge something new. He no longer needed to wallow in his captivating problem in order to move towards focused solutions. All he required was detail to start believing he could possibly do the next thing. Take the smallest of steps towards overcoming his depressive ordeal.

"It was like I was happy for the first time in ages", he said.
"What did you look like when this happened? I mean, what did you do, who noticed?"

Exception seeking acknowledges how young people like Rob tend to notice only the things which upset them. Yet, for every problem noticed there will be an equivalent number of alternatives, substitutes and exceptions. In SF psychotherapy, there is a general agreement that every problem has at least one solution that can be sought. Exceptions have add-ons (questions that can be used linking skeleton keys) elicit future focused visualisations and 'fragments' by describing 'little bits', 'small sparkling moments' and 'differences'. Examples that I add-on to my scaling, exception seeking and miracle question include "What is different?", "What are small glimpses of the miracle you've witnessed?", "How is now different from then?", "What's the one new thing that's different?" The 'miracle question' and 'exception seeking' are called skeleton keys because like a key that can open any lock, they are not diagnosis specific, but rather interchangeable, aligned and do at least three things. First, they encourage the child to dream, imagine and be creative. That is, envisage what they might be doing in the future. As with all skeleton keys there is a hopeful expectation of change which promotes a forward moving sense of progress towards future orientated goals. Second, practitioners work with detail and descriptions as opposed to explanations of cause which aims to extract exact goals, pin-point possibilities and start motivating towards pragmatic achievable outcomes. These are not about feelings or cognitions, but actual behaviours which can be witnessed by the young person and significant others (note how my questions are about the observable). As a result, all SF terminology is framed with resilience comments such as "What would you see yourself doing when you achieve your goal?" Finally, SF assesses levels of confidence and motivation using a range of exception seeking keys, miracle questions and scaling techniques in order to help the child realise that their reimagining, reordering, reconsidering can be made real from the fantastic through any number of secret experiments and noticing tasks. Thus, when combined with a collaborative can-do and expectant approach the unbelievable can be envisaged real as metaphorically, I walk alongside them gently tapping them on the shoulder should they be tempted to wander off into the past, problem saturated or resilient impossible.

Scaling best hopes, resilient-focused cultures and context

CAMHS young people rarely present with a single diagnosis. They can even copy, and gain new ones as they wrestle to explain things to themselves and others). My SF work with resilience building is now confronting challenges which even a decade ago would be unbelievable. My work with Judy and her chronic self-harming behaviours is typical of how young people today are exposed to cyberbullying, addictions of the pixelated kind, sexual antics, lack of mastery over job security,

0 hour futures, excessive educational expectations, which reflect future global trials somehow positioning their resilience and sense of identity somewhere between the hardiness of Teflon, flexibility and alertness of digital security whilst appearing sophisticated, capable and 'totally unified'. It seems to me that only the resilient survive in an age where resilience is no longer about being tough and non-emotional.

> "So how will you begin to scale the challenge ahead of you?" I said being careful to future focus my words.
> "To be honest, I don't know if I longer care," said Judy, "You get to a point when you might dream the miracle but know that it'll never come true".
> "Yep, you bet", I said, "But let's say on a scale from one to ten, where ten represents your first evening without cutting?"

Scaling Questions are Skeleton Keys and easily add-on to the others, but they are particularly good for allowing young people to visualise and think through what 'needs to happen'. By fixing a score of say '3', I am able to ask "How come a 3?" and raise an awareness of confidence and motivation.

> If the miracle/goal/personal aim/thing that brought you here today is a 10 and the moment, place, person, relationship difficulty/the moment when your teacher made this appointment is just the worst is a 0, where on that scale are you now?

"How come?" "What would I see you doing at that number?" "What does a 10 look like?" "How would you be able to move up 1 point?" "What would your teachers see you doing differently?" "What else?" "Where would you be satisfied?" "How confident are you that you will achieve that leap?" "Sounds like a big jump, so how often are you at number 7?" "What is already working in the right direction?"

Thus, resilience is a sense of connection. Scaling how confident Rob is about attending his school for a complete day is like asking him to appraise any number of associated resilience qualities. I could ask scales about self-esteem, ask him to detail what he does to maintain positive senses of identity, safety, mastery and insight. I have found that measuring oneself on scales starts to become second nature to young people and they freely offer their opinions about their perceived chances to achieve transformation and change. Yet, scales show up how resilience is not only connective but also dynamic, contextual and constituting. Like something live, it transforms and is transformative in that at different times in a young person's life it flexes. This sits nicely with the contextual and systemic make up of SF practice in that resilience is impacted by family, the afore-mentioned personal qualities such as self-respect, peers, school and wider community commitments. These dynamic nature means that learning from past mistakes, problem-solving, appreciating personal qualities, setting realistic goals, living independently, negotiating risk, sustaining mutually beneficial relationships, communicating well and self-reflecting all come down to a complex set of jostling markers and scalable markers, exceptions and miracles young people have to negotiate in today's fast-paced resilience demanding existence. Sovereignty is a demonstration of all these qualities in measures and conditions which are rarely stable, always shifting and constantly transforming everyday experiences.

So many young people like Rob find that services tend to focus on the 'I am' type resilience themes rather the 'I can' ones.

'So Far', moving beyond the fantastic means 'If' becomes 'When'

Helping young people transform scales, exceptions and miracles into new behaviours requires not only pacing by a patient collaborator, a grasp of confidence, empathetic of what motivates but also, some type of putting theory into action. Resilience is dynamic and requires proof. Young people like Rob, Claire and Judy are not stupid. They know what is good and bad for themselves and understand there is nothing more than the elixir of looking in the mirror and feeling proud that they have achieved something. We can all feel and think as much as we want as noted by Judy, "But unless I'm prepared to get back up when I fail there's no point," she concluded, "I mean, at first it was difficult, but I did the experiment and found that I kind of liked it."

"So you did the task?" I said.
"Sort of, I did part of it".
"You're so smart", I said, "You even adapted the experiment we came up with".
"Well", she said, "Your ideas are too old fashioned".

There are a number of SF experiments I use to help transform hopes into change and Judy's wish to control her 'delicate cutting' required putting ideas into action. Young people like the idea of experiments and definable tasks and as such, in the previous session I'd suggested,

"So there are a few small parts of your miracle ready for testing?"
"I suppose", she'd said.
"So, go home and imagine that the miracle has occurred for the first hour of everyday. Imagine
   that you are totally in control of the cutting monster and see what happens".

This experimental task related to session goals and imagined future hopes. It was bite-sized and achievable allowing for a sense of achievement.

"So, what did your mom say?" I said, "You, know, when she saw you smiling and in a school uniform?"
"She almost died of shock", said Judy, "She was like, Oh My God, but she didn't know I was only
   in control for an hour".
"What else?"
"She was like so happy and hugging me, it was all so", she paused, "So yuk".
"Uhu, who else noticed?"

Suffice to say that resilience makes the fantastical real through action, continued confidence and some way of making a start. This means experiments which kick-start a sense of sovereign pride. A sense of self-identity which can be described as self-efficient, consistently responsible, valued, respected, with favourable reputation, adaptive, dutiful, able to meet contextual demands, be a locus of control and mastery. In my sessions, young people also identify the opinion of others as being significant to how they respect themselves. To their perceived abilities, levels of effort and in some cases, the luck of being in the right place at the right time. This reflexive feedback, as a means of identifying the limits of themselves, is a resilience relationship with appraising performance, noticing confidence, motivating achievement, satisfaction (sense of worth, uniqueness, essential, fulfilment, significance, progress), productivity and a 'get up and go' interwoven with hints of arousal, instinct and an act of 'doing something new' like that for Claire.

> "I tried eating more often, but making sure that my mother knew it", she paused, "To keep her off my back".
> "Clever", I said, "Who else?"
> "My teachers, they have to be proactive, you know, giving me special space to eat dinner, so I thought, you know what sod this, treat me the same as everyone else".

Summary points

My intention here takes into account at least ten simultaneous principles which show themselves in all SF practice. As with all of the conversations in this chapter, you will see how my collaboration has been about:

In the previous session, I'd asked Claire "to scale 3 things she'd not want to change about her life". I will use these tasks and 'add-ons' as solution focused techniques to help me sum up my discussion of how resilience is less about a thing in itself and how behaviour can easily escalate into any number of new possibilities somewhere between fact and fiction. To help me with this, I use a number of competency questions:

"Hmmmm, it sounds like you're battling through, how do you do that?", "How do you keep going?", "What are those things you've got in the locker enabling you to get this far?", "Gee it makes me wonder how come things aren't worse?" "You're smart, how come you know so much?" "You've got good reason to be upset with your friend, I'm curious what you'll do next?" "What will be that one small change/difference?"

"I guess I've learnt resilience has to be done starting with the fantastic and then in real", she said.

Recommended reading

Brown, Z. and Daly, J. (2017) The complexities of childhood resilience, in, Brown, Z. and Ward, S. (eds.) *Contemporary Issues in Childhood: A Bio-ecological Approach*. London: Routledge, pp. 43–54.

References

de Shazer, S. (1991) *Putting difference to work*. New York: Norton.
de Shazer, S. (1994) *Words were originally magic*. New York: Norton.
Dolan, Y. (1998) *One small step*. Watsonville, CA: Papier-Mache.
Lines, D. (2011) *Brief counselling in schools: Working with young people from 11 to 18*. London: Sage.
Luthar, S., Cicchetti, D., and Becker, B. (2000) The Construct of Resilience: A Critical Evaluation and Guidelines for Future Work. *Child Development*, **71**(3), pp. 543–562.
Macdonald, A.J. (2011) *Solution focused therapy: Theory, research and practice* (2nd Edition). London: Sage.
O'Connell, B. and Palmer, S. (eds.) (2003) *Handbook of Solution Focused Therapy*. London: Sage Books.
O'Hanlon, B. (1999) *Do one thing different: Ten simple ways to change your life*. New York: Quill.
Selekman, M.D. (1997) *Solution-focused therapy with children: Harnessing family strengths for systemic change*. New York: The Guildford Press.
Sharry, J. (2001) *Solution-focused groupwork*. London: Sage.
Southwick, S.M., Bonanno, G.A., Masten, A.S., Panter Brick, C., and Yehuda, R. (2014) Resilience Definitions Theory and Challenge Interdisciplinary Perspectives. *European Journal of Psychotraumatology*. **5**, Oct 2014, pp. 1–19.
Todorov, T. (1970) *Introduction à la littérature fantastique* (trans: Richard Howard as The Fantastic: A Structural Approach to a Literary Genre in 1973). Paris: Le Seuil.

Section 4

Societal and cultural influences upon children's and young people's well-being and resilience

12 The flourishing practitioner

Zenna Kingdon

Introduction

In this chapter, I discuss notions of flourishing (Seligman, 2011; Kingdon and Gourd, 2014, 2017). The chapter opens with a discussion of what constitutes flourishing. This is followed by a discussion of why flourishing is important, particularly in educational settings and specifically with regards to practitioners. It would seem that many discussions of flourishing and well-being in early childhood settings focus on the children and fail to consider the practitioners who deliver the pedagogy.

Individual/group task

Before you read the chapter, please consider what you think a flourishing practitioner would look like in practice?

What is flourishing?

> Flourishing comes from values and relationships developed and deepened over time that develop and strengthen the receptive capacities of the brain that enable an individual to appropriately emotionally respond to life events.
>
> (Kingdon and Gourd, 2017, p. 12)

Over two texts, Kingdon and Gourd (2014, 2017) developed the notion of flourishing as a concept to support children, families and practitioners in early childhood settings. Initially, they (ibid., 2014, 2017) drew on the work of Seligman (2011) to describe flourishing using an approach that is underpinned by PERMA.

Personal Enjoyment: the pleasant life
Engagement: a flow state in which thought and feeling are usually absent
(Positive) **R**elationships: relationships are key to the development of all humans
Meaning: belonging to and serving something that is bigger than the self.
Accomplishment: the pursuit of success, achievement, and mastery for its own sake

(Seligman, 2011)

He (ibid., 2011) suggests that when these five elements are in place then a person is likely to flourish. Moreover, he argues that these features may actually be, "...one of our best weapons against mental disorder" (Seligman, 2007, p. 5). Flourishing and well-being can be considered to be interrelated. An individual that enjoys good mental health is likely to demonstrate a range of behaviours including: being confident, having good self-esteem, is able to build and maintain positive relationships and cope with the stresses of everyday life (Mind, 2016). As Kingdon and Gourd (2017) developed their work, they drew on a wider range of theory and recognised the linkages between flourishing, well-being, happiness and pleasure to form the basis of their definition. They (ibid., 2017) maintain that aspects of happiness are significant contributory factors to long-term flourishing; however, moments of happiness in themselves do not necessarily lead to it. Furthermore, they (ibid., 2017) recognise that a number of theorists do not necessarily discuss flourishing but do discuss its constituent attributes including happiness, resilience, self-esteem, interpersonal relationships and values, are essential to their definition. In work on self-determination, Ryan and Deci (2001) argue that there are three psychological needs that must be met if an individual is to grow psychologically and these are autonomy, competence and relatedness. These elements are essential for a person to flourish. Referring to Chapter 2, which critiques the political rationale behind children's need for resilience, the same rhetoric can be applied to practitioners who would benefit from being supported to flourish. Autonomy can be more difficult to achieve in settings driven by the need to quantify and measure outcomes in order to justify investment and perpetuate neo-liberal agendas. Practitioners need to feel that their professional competence is recognised, that they are achieving. They also need a sense of belonging, being part of a community within a school or setting.

In educational terms, notions of flourishing are most closely associated with notions of mental well-being that is promoted through a holistic pedagogy (McLaughlin, 2008). Seemingly, it is the integration of what we know about psychology, neuroscience and counselling that affect a child's ability to flourish and develop resilience "the implications for how teaching, learning and relating are conducted are very profound" (McLaughlin, 2008, p. 358). Educational settings that prioritise happiness, it would seem, support the flourishing of both the individual and the community. It is to be hoped that happiness for adults and children should be an aim of education (Noddings, 2003). Additionally, as noted by Scoffham and Barnes (2011, p.547), "... happy people are rarely mean, violent or cruel". Therefore, it would appear that whilst happiness and flourishing are not one and the same it is unlikely that an individual or community can flourish with an absence of happiness. Happiness, should therefore, be considered to be a serious goal. It is neither measurable nor recordable in any quantitative sense but qualitatively it must be a priority. The development of flourishing is holistic and all aspects of a person's life contribute to their ability to flourish. In terms of educational settings, it is essential that there is an ethos within the setting and the community that values this approach. The concept of flourishing is now being considered within educational settings alongside notions of well-being and resilience. Flourishing is a term that incorporates some of these ideas (Seligman, 2011; Kingdon and Gourd, 2017).

Individual/group task

Consider the content detailed in Chapters 1 and 2 on well-being and resilience and the content in this chapter on flourishing. How do you think notions of flourishing, well-being and resilience are considered alongside one another in educational setting?

Why does flourishing matter?

Inevitably, what is revealed is that if practitioners are not supported to flourish then they cannot genuinely deliver a syllabus that supports flourishing. Undoubtedly, if children and young people are to enjoy an experience of flourishing in their schools and settings, then it must follow that those practitioners who are responsible for them need also to flourish. The development of critically reflective practice has been seen as an essential skill for early years' practitioners and teachers, it is one of the competencies laid down by government. It also aids them in developing an understanding of their own roles, values and professional responsibilities (Chalke, 2013; Lea, 2014). Opportunities for practitioners to engage in dialogue or critically reflective practice, whereby they talk about their work, share stories, observe each other, learn from each other and constantly challenge the quality of their practice, will support them in developing their self-knowledge and self-esteem which leads to flourishing (Brighouse, 2006). Happiness, '… can include calm reflection, curiosity, fascination, exhilaration, and ecstasy' (Scoffham and Barnes, 2011, p. 537).

In research conducted by Ikegami and Agbenyega (2014, p. 53), they noted that one finding stood out above any of the others and, "…that is happiness is a strong relational concept which can make a significant contribution to the quality of early childhood education when it is used to drive program planning and implementation". They (ibid., 2014) considered how quality and happiness in Early Childhood were related. Their study was conducted within a group of settings that had adopted a Buddhist philosophy. These Japanese settings were subject to governmental standards of quality but predicated their provision on happiness. Their findings suggested that, "… by framing the quality of early childhood education in happiness, educators and children can engage deeply with learning that has the potential to influence the whole child and their full participation in society" (Ikegami and Agbenyega, 2014, p. 46). Such an approach that links directly with notions of flourishing in which happiness is at the centre, supports an understanding of why flourishing is important. The need for happiness to be placed ahead of rigid outcomes is reflected in the work of Ikegami and Agbenyega (2014), reflecting the need for settings to be spaces in which both the children and the practitioners are enabled to flourish. For many engaged in the caring professions, including early childhood education and care and teaching, opportunities for emotional support within the workplace are rarely offered (Buckler, 2017). This lack of support can lead to burn-out and other negative issues. Therefore, it is essential that practitioners are supported to find ways to counteract this negative experience and to flourish in their work place.

The study

Previous research suggests that the voice of the practitioner is often over-looked or ignored. Here, I report on a small-scale Feminist Participatory Action Research study that I conducted with a small group of early childhood education and care practitioners. The study is situated in an interpretivist paradigm in which the individuals were encouraged to share their experiences and social realities.

The study appeared to demonstrate that in order for practitioners to flourish a number of challenges need to be faced. What was clear though was that the practitioners are willing to develop creative approaches in practice which enable them to have their needs met and therefore to flourish. Importantly, they believe there are messages that policy makers need to hear, including a recognition of the gendered nature of the workforce and also the need to provide appropriate support for on-going professional development.

Having engaged in previous research concerned with flourishing (Kingdon and Gourd, 2014, 2017), it had become apparent to me that whilst there is a significant focus on how we can support children and young people to flourish, there is considerably less attention paid to the practitioners who work with them. That is not to say that no interest has been shown for the workforce; quite the contrary. However, interest has focussed on an up-skilling and professionalising agenda that has often left individuals feeling de-valued; as though what they had to offer was of no value. The implication from the language was that what went before was in some way deficit and not good enough (McGillivray, 2008). The workforce had seemingly been constructed in two ways; as a form of redemption for society and as chaotic and disorderly (Osgood, 2009). This latter construction led to notions of the need for professionalisation. Seemingly the government had a vested interest in constructing the workforce in deficit terms (Osgood, 2012). This then ensured that there was a need for radical reform. The new policy focus led to questions about the practitioners own responses to debates about education (McGillivray, 2008). It was apparent that the voice of the practitioner was often overlooked in the political discussions and notions of flourishing were absent. This small-scale study was intended to provide a first insight into how practitioners working with the youngest children could be supported to flourish.

The research was framed within Feminist Participatory Action Research which draws on the approaches of Feminist research, participatory action research and action research. All of which are, "…critical approaches that focus on democratising the research process, acknowledging lived experiences, and contributing to social justice agendas to counter prevailing ideologies and power relations…." (Reid and Frisby, 2013, p. 93). The early childhood education and care workforce remains at over 98% women, despite government attempts to change the gender balance and therefore taking a feminist perspective appeared particularly salient (Davies, 2017).

Through attending an early childhood conference, a range of practitioners were invited to engage in the research. Participants were self-selecting, choosing to participate in the research and then deciding their own anonymised names. The participants were a range of practitioners and setting managers from a variety of both voluntary and maintained organisations across the West Midlands. The practitioners were invited to consider some of the ways in which practitioners can develop both professionally and personally. The intention was to try to identify some ways in which practitioners can develop autonomy and self-determination, a sense of relatedness or affiliation which will enable them to flourish. It also served to inform policy makers of the ways in which they can consider how this could be absorbed into daily practice.

The methods

Qualitative research is concerned with utilising data collection methods that enable the researcher to gather thick, that is detailed and rich, descriptions (Geertz, 1973). Similarly, it is recognised there are many different experiences of life and therefore a broad range of data collection methods generate data that reflect and illuminate these different perspectives (Cohen et al., 2013). Having established that I would be using Feminist Participatory Action Research (Reid and Frisby, 2013), it was my intention to gather data in a way that would diminish the power relationship between researcher and research participant. Power dynamics between researcher and researched often remain even where there is an attempt to minimise these (Grover, 2004). With this in mind, I adopted two forms of data collection; narrative discussion groups and semi-structured interviews. Narrative discussion is usually used when participants are being asked to tell their story. It requires the researcher to provide a question that is broad enough to enable the participants to talk and tell their story; however, it also needs to be sufficiently focused that the data elicited will enable the researcher to answer the research question (Midgley, 2013). Given that I was interested in the practitioners' experiences of flourishing, it was necessary to provide a broad platform from which they could begin their narrative discussion. Semi-structured interviews are similarly open-ended; however, they allow the researcher to introduce a degree of structure to the conversation (Flick, 2006). These two data collection methods appeared appropriate for the research project and therefore they were adopted.

The research began with a focus group in which I acted as a facilitator, "…moderating, monitoring and recording group interaction" (Punch, 2009, p. 147). The participants developed the focus group discussion drawing on some of the principles of narrative discussion groups in which the practitioners were initially invited to set out the parameters for the discussion and to tell their stories (Midgley, 2013). Whilst there were some open-ended questions that I used to frame the discussion, in the main practitioners themselves led the discussion, often picking up on comments that their peers had made in order to pursue ideas and areas for discussion. Engaging the practitioners in the process actually helped them to frame the research and to become co-researchers rather than simply research respondents. Asking them to engage in creating the parameters of the discussion demonstrated which of the issues were of most significance to them. Following on from the narrative discussion group some practitioners then agreed to participate in semi-structured interviews. These enabled me to gather further data from individuals and to follow-up from the themes that were introduced in the narrative discussion.

The data

In total five practitioners participated in the research: below is a brief pen portrait of each of them. Some of them discussed their qualifications, however, they were not asked what they were and some told me whilst others did not.

FREYA: Works in a Foundation setting in a maintained setting. She is a qualified teacher and has been in practice for more than 20 years.

LAURA: Is the manager of a pack-away pre-school in the voluntary sector. She has a degree and Early Years Professional Status.

JANINE: Works as a practitioner in a private day nursery. She has worked in early childhood for less than 5 years.

HELEN: Works as a room leader in a private day-care setting, she has a degree and Early Years Teacher Status, she has worked in early childhood settings for more than 5 years.

CARA: Works as practitioner in a private day-care setting, she has worked in early childhood for more than 5 years.

The findings

Both the narrative discussion and the semi-structured interviews were framed with questions that focused on flourishing. Practitioners were asked about the ways in which they described flourishing, what enabled them to flourish both personally and professionally and the ways in which they are given voice. The semi-structured interviews provided an opportunity to ask how as an individual they could be supported to flourish. Four key themes began to emerge from the data analysis: money, professional respect, the gendered nature of the workforce, and team moral and team building.

Money

Training

Whilst this was a central issue, it was not first and foremost about pay, this was seen as a secondary issue. The practitioners were concerned about training. All of them felt that it was an essential element for them to develop and to flourish. They also discussed the fact that money was a constant barrier to their participation in training. In the narrative discussion, Laura stated '*training is my priority*', however, she then went on to say that because as a voluntary sector pre-school that there was no money for training, so, "*…staff have to have webinars and join with other settings. We use free courses but we can only send two staff at a time*". All of the practitioners appeared to recognise that where training was provided for free there remained the issue of how to cover that member of staff whilst they were off-site. Helen's setting appeared to have some better access to training, however, it remained limited. She explained, "*…those that have been on training then develop that training into practice and share it with other staff. We all try to reflect on it*". Laura responded to this saying that this appeared to be, "*… a good way of doing it and a good use of funding*". Whilst the practitioners did appear to be concerned about their lack of access to budget which could fund training, they were clearly willing to consider creative ways in which they could access the training they wanted and they felt would support their professional development. Freya acknowledged that, "*…there is no money to train; training costs £250 per day. We use free education shows and seminars*". All of the practitioners who were part of the research had accessed the early childhood education and care conference run for free at my university. This conference is free to participants; however, it occurs on a Saturday and therefore is something that they must attend in their own time. It therefore becomes apparent that these practitioners recognise the importance of professional development and are willing to invest their own time into doing so.

Pay

Given that money was discussed there was inevitably some reference to pay. Whilst this was not one of the leading concerns raised in their discussion, they acknowledged that they are paid considerably less than teachers; this included those practitioners in the private and voluntary sector who had completed a relevant degree. Helen commented that, "*we're not seen as teachers due to the age of the children that we work with*". She then went on to say, "*we're not in it for the money*", a sentiment that was echoed by all of the other participants. They went on to discuss the lack of men in the sector (98% women in the UK) stating that this was an issue that supports lowered wages. Janine reported a conversation that she had with a father who was dropping off his child one day in which he said to her, "*…you don't deserve to get paid as teachers, you're a woman, it's what you do*". All of the participants were shocked by these comments; however, they recognised that some of the under-lying sentiment is reflective of the way in which the sector is viewed and potentially under-valued, and that this is subsequently reflected in their remuneration. Some of the participants are often expected to do things in their own time for no pay – including training and staff meetings. Janine asked the group, "*do your staff get paid for extra time and staff meetings?*" Laura stated that she had managed to, "*pay staff for undertaking an NVQ in their own time*". Helen said that settings '*needed to*'. What was evident was that many staff were being paid at an hourly rate for their contact hours only. This was a contentious issue that furthered some of the feelings that early childhood is not respected as an important stage of a child's life. Several felt that this was a reflection of the gendered nature of the workforce.

The gendered nature of the workforce

In the UK, unlike other European countries, the workforce remains predominantly female and whilst there has been a focus on up-skilling over the last two decades many settings do not have graduates in place. The practitioners suggested that the gendered nature of the workforce was one of the reasons the sector is not always treated positively. Laura stated her belief that,

> ECEC (Early Childhood Education and Care) is thought of dimly because there are no men. Because they think it's a woman's job, all we do is play with kids. What other sector would they [the government] … they set our funding and then how much we can charge, how many children we can have? Our voice is not being heard by government.

The practitioners appeared to suggest that the workforce as a whole was not treated well because voicing concerns was seen as complaint. Following on from Laura's comments Freya stated, "*The government think that we will get on with whatever they impose and we will sort it out*". The practitioners all demonstrated their understanding of the importance of early childhood and the way in which it had a long-term impact on the child's achievement. There was general agreement that their opinions were not being listened to, Freya commented, "*It is taking a long time for our voices to be heard. We need to be shouting*". There was a perception that the gendered nature of the workforce led to the lack of professional respect within wider society that many of them had experienced.

Professional respect

The practitioners reflected on issues around professional respect demonstrating how they were often treated in ways that appeared to lack common courtesy let alone respect for their professional knowledge. Freya who leads Foundation stage in a primary school commented that, "*SLT [Senior Leadership Team] looks down on Early Years. We only play in early years…*", the importance of play in child development were not acknowledged. Freya, who has Qualified Teacher Status, mentioned that a parent had asked whether she was, "*able to teach in the rest of the school*" and had demonstrated surprise when Freya had stated that she was qualified to do so. All of the participants discussed notions of hierarchy and how this frames them as lacking competence. Laura discussed meeting up with a Reception teacher shortly after a group of her pre-school children had joined the school, the teacher said to her, "*…you were spot on with all of them*". Laura said that to begin with she felt pleased, but then felt rather annoyed because the teacher had clearly not expected her to be. Helen responded stating, "*… teachers don't expect you to know how to do it*".

Freya replied stating that, "*everyone plays a vital role in preparing the children for school and onwards right up to university*". Helen acknowledged that there is a, "*… a slow recognition of Early Childhood Education and Care*". All of the practitioners felt that in order for them to flourish there needed to be a good sense of moral and teamwork within their settings.

Team moral and team building

Individual/group task

Before reading on do you think these findings present any possible implications for policy and practice?

Once the practitioners began to discuss moral and team building, evidence of their ability to flourish in the work place became evident. The practitioners discussed the need to feel motivation towards their work and acknowledged that they need to want to come to work. Laura suggested that her team needs to be enabled to flourish before she can flourish. Likewise Freya said that, "*… I go and ask [the practitioners] at least once a week if they're happy*". Janine seemed to feel that this was a really positive approach and stated that, "*just asking the question is important*". In her semi-structured interview, Freya said that in order to flourish she needed, "*… the trust of the Year 1 teacher, the trust of the Headteacher and Ofsted*". She went on to say that she thought it was really important that, "*I'm happy and the children are happy*". Cara suggested that, "*having a mentor*", would help her in building her confidence and morale, likewise Freya suggested that opportunities for, "*mentoring and coaching, talking and support, workplace buddies*", all helped raise morale and enabled practitioners to work as a team. Furthermore Helen stated that she felt, "*… intrinsic motivation, not by pay, but by my value*". She went on to say that, "*having completed Early Years teacher status, I feel valued*". Laura argued that it was not simply what happened inside the setting that was important. She said, "*…it's important to see each other as a group not with the children. It's important for morale. You can forget that you are actually people*". The practitioners felt that it was this broad range of practices that support morale and can lead to flourishing.

Implications for policy and practice

Practitioners who are enabled to engage with each other to talk, to reflect, to develop are enabled to flourish (Brighouse, 2006; Chalke, 2013; Lea, 2014). The needs of the workforce must be met in order that they do not become demoralised. A workforce that comprises of flourishing practitioners is one that is able to support our children and their families. There can be no debate about the gendered nature of the workforce in the UK. It would seem that due to the gendered nature of the workforce, certain assumptions are made about the practitioners working within it (McGillivray, 2008; Osgood, 2012). The up-skilling agenda has often framed the workforce in deficit terms. However, practitioners themselves acknowledge that access to training is vital if they are to flourish personally and professionally. Therefore, it would seem that policy makers need to acknowledge the professional nature of the Early Childhood Education and Care workforce and the importance of the work that they do (Lea, 2014). The practitioners discussed positively the ways in which they could flourish and suggested creative ways that this could be possible. Professional recognition and respect for what they do is considered to be essential (Osgood, 2012; Lea, 2014). Thus, it would seem that practitioners can be supported to flourish – particularly if they are shown respect for their contribution. Whilst the practitioners did not directly discuss emotional labour (Brooker, 2010; Gourd, 2014), there was an undercurrent of this in their discussions about morale and desire for professional respect. They were all aware of the impact that flourishing has on their practice. Freya maintained that, *"If you are positive the children have a good day, if the children have a good day, you have a good day"*. In this way, both the practitioners and the children are enabled to flourish.

Conclusion

In this chapter, I have reported on a small-scale research project that focussed on the notion of flourishing and how practitioners in early childhood education and care settings believe that they can flourish and the conditions that need to be in place for this to occur. I have demonstrated that whilst the term flourishing has been seen to have links to happiness, it is more complex (Seligman, 2011; Kingdon and Gourd, 2014, 2017). Evidence suggests that in pedagogical terms flourishing is associated with well-being and can be considered to support resilience.

The findings from the research demonstrate that there are some common themes which all the practitioners felt were important if they were to be enabled to flourish. They need regular access to on-going professional development. They need to have their expertise recognised and acknowledged. The gendered nature of the workforce needs to be accepted, particularly by policy-makers. There need to be opportunities for individual and team-morale to be raised.

In settings where flourishing is considered by the management, they are able to flourish. Flourishing needs to be considered to be important in all settings. In this way, practitioners are supported which has a positive impact on the children with whom they work.

Summary points

- Many discussions of flourishing and well-being in early childhood settings fail to consider the practitioners who deliver the pedagogy.
- Flourishing and well-being can be considered to be interrelated.
- If practitioners are not supported to flourish then they cannot deliver a syllabus that supports flourishing.
- Practitioners need regular access to on-going professional development and they need their expertise recognised and acknowledged.
- The gendered nature of the workforce needs to be accepted, particularly by policy-makers.
- Opportunities need to be made available to raise individual and team-morale in settings.
- In settings, where flourishing is considered by the management, practitioners are able to flourish.

References

Brighouse, T. (2006) Essential pieces: The jigsaw of the successful school. www.rtuni.org/usefiles/TimBrighouseBook.pdf. [accessed 22 February 2016].

Brooker, L. (2010) Constructing the triangle of care: Power and professionalism in practitioner/parent relationships', *British Journal of Educational Studies*, **58** (2), pp. 181–196.

Buckler, S. (2017) 'Risk taking and ethical practice to support flourishing', in Kingdon, Z. Gourd, J., and Gasper, M. (eds.) *Flourishing in the Early Years: Context, Practices and Futures*. London: Routledge, pp. 68–84.

Chalke, J. (2013) 'Will the early years professional please stand up? Professionalism in the early childhood workforce in England', *Contemporary Issues in Early Childhood*, **14** (3), pp. 212–222.

Cohen, L. Manion, L. Morrison, K. (2013) *Research Methods in Education 8e*. Abingdon: Routledge.

Davies, J. (2017) *How Can We Attract More Men into London's Early Years Workforce?* Fatherhood Institute. http://www.fatherhoodinstitute.org/wp-content/uploads/2017/09/MITEY-2017-London-report-1.pdf [accessed 21 October 2019].

Flick, U. (2006) *An Introduction to Qualitative Research 3e*. London: Sage.

Geertz, C. (1973) *Interpretation of Cultures*. New York: Basic Books.

Gourd, J. (2014) 'Future policy and impact of societal change', in Kingdon, Z. and Gourd, J. (eds.) *Early Years Policy: The Impact on Practice*. London: Routledge, pp. 95–114.

Grover, S. (2004) 'Why don't they listen to us? On giving power and voice to children participating in social research', *Childhood*, **11** (1), pp. 81–93.

Ikegami, K. and Agbenyega, J. (2014) 'How does learning through happiness promote quality early childhood education?' in *Australasian Journal of Early Childhood*, **39**(3), pp. 46–55.

Kingdon, Z. and Gourd, J. (2014) *Early Years Policy: The Impact on Practice*. London: Routledge.

Kingdon, Z and Gourd, J. (2017) 'The conceptualisation of flourishing', in Kingdon, Z. Gourd, J. and Gasper, M. (eds.) *Flourishing in the Early Years: Contexts, Practices and Futures*. London: Routledge, pp. 11–27.

Lea, S. (2014) 'Early years work professionalism and the translation of policy into practice', in Kingdon, Z. and Gourd, J. (eds.) *Early Years Policy: The Impact on Practice*. London: Routledge, pp. 13–32.

McGillivray, G. (2008) 'Nannies, nursery nurses and early years professionals: Constructions of professional identity in the early years workforce in England', *European Early Childhood Education Research Journal*, **16** (2), pp. 242–254.

McLaughlin, C. (2008) 'Emotional well-being and its relationship to schools and classrooms: A critical reflection', *British Journal of Guidance & Counselling*, **36** (4), pp.353–366.

Midgley, W. (2013) 'Participants and research method design: The development of narrative discussion group method', in Midgley, W. Danaher, P. and Baguley, M. (eds.) *The Role of Participants in Education Research: Ethics, Epistemologies and Methods*. London: Routledge, pp. 182–191.

Mind (2016) *Understanding Mental Health Problems*. London: Mind.

Noddings, N. (2003) *Happiness and Education*. Cambridge: Cambridge University Press.

Osgood, J. (2009) 'Childcare workforce reform in England and "the early years professional": A critical discourse analysis', *Journal of Education Policy*, **24** (6) pp. 733–751.

Osgood, J. (2012) *Narratives from the Nursery: Negotiating Professional Identities in Early Childhood*. London: Routledge.

Punch, K. (2009) *Introduction to Research Methods in Education*. London: Sage.

Reid, C. and Frisby, W. (2013) 'Continuing the journey: Articulating dimensions of feminist participatory action research', in Reason, P. and Bradbury, H. (eds.) *Sage Handbook of Action Research 2e*. London: Sage, pp. 93–105.

Ryan, R.M. and Deci, E.L. (2001) On happiness and human potentials: A review of research on hedonic and eudaimonic well-being. *Annual Reivew of Psychology*, **52** pp. 141–166. doi:10.1146/annurev.psych.52.1.141

Scoffham, S. and Barnes, J. (2011) 'Happiness matters: Towards a pedagogy of happiness and well-being', *The Cambridge Journal*, **12** (4), pp. 535–438.

Seligman, M. (2007) *The Optimistic Child: A Proven Programme to Safeguard Children Against Depression and Build Life-long Resilience*. New York: Houghton Mifflin Company.

Seligman, M. (2011) *Flourish*. London: Nicholas Brealey Publishing.

13 Developing a resilient nation
Devolution and the Welsh approach to enhancing well-being

Caroline Lewis

Introduction

This chapter seeks to provide an overview of the work undertaken since devolution to support the well-being of children and young people within Wales. In areas such as the former mining communities, there exists a culture of defeatism combined with high levels of child poverty and low educational attainment. The challenge for Welsh Government, as well as key stakeholders and third sector organisations, has been to develop policy that supports and promotes resilience and facilitate upward social mobility. Revised curriculum proposals, higher education student finance arrangements, as well as the Well-Being of Future Generations Act (2015) are just some of the initiatives aimed at redressing imbalances and developing a resilient population. Through a case-study approach, the chapter offers an insight into how such a policy has been developed and enacted. In particular, it considers the implications that this has for educational practice.

Devolution in Wales

Wales is one of three devolved nations alongside Scotland and Northern Ireland within the UK, as voted for in the 1997 referendum. By a majority of 50.3%, the Welsh people voted in favour of devolving powers from Westminster to what would be the new National Assembly for Wales, which was officially opened in Cardiff Bay in 1999, with 60 Assembly Members (AMs), elected. At this time, the National Assembly for Wales did not hold any primary law-making powers which meant that key decisions were still the remit of the UK government; however, the National Assembly were able to enact secondary legislation in relation to a number of defined areas. These included agriculture, culture, economic development, education and training, the environment, health, sport, economic development, education and student loans, the environment, health, local government and housing, sport, social services, transport and the Welsh language. Secondary legislative powers meant that ministers had the power to decide how primary legislation such as acts of parliament were applied in practice within the Welsh context, to make amendments to existing laws, or to set dates on which parliamentary acts become law.

Individual/group task

Before you read the rest of the chapter, think about what might have been the priorities for the National Assembly at this time in relation to education and why? Are these priorities any different to the rest of the UK and why do you think that might be?

In 2006, the Governance of Wales Act devolved further powers to the Assembly for Wales and formally separated the National Assembly for Wales and the Welsh Government to clarify the different roles held. It allowed for the appointment of Welsh ministers within the Welsh Government who could make decisions, develop and implement policies within their areas, which are then scrutinised and approved by the AMs within the National Assembly. In addition, AMs can hold ministers to account as well as approve budgets and can implement 'assembly measures', a type of low level primary legislative powers devolved under the act.

In 2011, a referendum held on further transfer of law-making powers returned a 'yes' vote and resulted in primary legislative responsibilities granted to Wales in a number of areas including education. The Welsh Assembly Government was then officially renamed the Welsh Government under the Wales Act (2014). Initially, considered by some to be the weaker of the devolved nations, Wales now possesses a significant body of legislation within its own right, with well-being now utilised to underpin wider policy within the country (Wallace, 2018).

Further research

For further information on the Welsh Government, its functions, responsibilities and structure see www.gov.wales

Background on Wales

As a nation, Wales faces a number of challenges. From a geographical perspective, the large amount of mountainous terrain makes it difficult to establish good transport and communication links between the north and south and concerns are often raised in relation to the amount of infrastructure and investment seen in the south and southeast of the country compared to elsewhere. There is a significant and dispersed rural population and a heavy dependence on farming and agriculture in such areas. The south Wales valleys are particularly problematic since the loss of the coal mines in the 1980s on which these areas were mainly solely dependent in terms of jobs and opportunities. Despite this loss, the steel industry in areas such as Port Talbot in the south still exists, but the future is precarious in the face of competition from overseas. Meanwhile, urban areas such as Cardiff and others along the M4 corridor are expanding and developing significantly. Coastal areas within Wales rely heavily on the tourism industry while becoming an attractive prospect for retirees and holiday homeowners.

In terms of population, statistics place the population of Wales in 2018 as 3.138 million (statswales.gov.wales. 2019), the smallest of the mainland UK nations. There is an increasing population of those aged over 45 while the younger population distribution noted as decreasing over time.

Pause for reflection

Before reading any further, what challenges might the issues above raise in relation to well-being as you see it? What might be the impact on communities or children and young people for example? What about jobs and skills?

Poverty and well-being in Wales

Broad research into the impact of poverty including Gould (2006) and Bradshaw (2016) note the key link between poverty, mental health and well-being. Bramley et al. (2016) outline the deep psychological as well as material harm caused by poverty for those who experience it while Dickerson and Popli (2016) consider the timing of the poverty experience within the lifespan as well as its duration as a central issue. Ivinson et al. (2018) noted in their report that poverty was very much a taboo area, with children and young people often striving to hide the mitigating effects where possible.

Within Wales, poverty is a significant driver for change in relation to policy development as well as for third sector organisations and other key stakeholders. Where possible, Welsh Government engages proactively with such stakeholders to work in partnership to address the poverty and well-being agenda for children and young people. The 2018 report 'Poverty in Wales' by the Joseph Rowntree Organisation highlighted a number of key points in relation to the growth of poverty within the country and noted the key link between poverty and physical/mental health (Joseph Rowntree Foundation, 2018). It noted that the attainment of pupils clearly correlated with their socio-economic circumstance. For example, of the pupils eligible to receive free school meal at Key Stage 2, only 77.9% were attaining their expected reading level in comparison with 92.1% of pupils who were ineligible. However, it is at GCSE level that the widest gap exists between groups according to the research. The Pupil Deprivation Grant (PDG) introduced in 2012 to provide funding to schools based on the eligible amount of free school meals pupils or Looked After Children (LAC) enrolled has gone some way to help this gap but by itself is not enough to redress the balance.

Children in Wales are an umbrella third-sector organisation for those who work with children and young people whilst offering a range of activities to support their members. Their annual survey undertaken since 2015 provides key insights into the challenges relating to poverty within Wales and the impact that this has on children and young people. Within the 2015 survey, 100% of respondents cited welfare reform as a key concern with 80.5% seeing it as more of a concern since 2014. About 95% of respondents highlighted food poverty as an issue with 86.7% of those seeing it as more of a concern since 2014. Concerns over levels of debt as well as the potential impact of these factors on mental health as well as the emotional support needed for families were also cited (Children in Wales, 2015).

Further surveys conducted in 2016 and 2018 saw no significant decrease in concerns over the issues raised in 2015 although both reports indicated a greater increase in references to the impact of poverty on well-being for children, young people as well as parents and carers. The 2018 report in particular highlighted the concern over the lack of trained counsellors and mental health support within schools along with trained youth workers (Children in Wales, 2016, 2018, 2019). This correlates with research by Pitchforth et al. (2019), highlighting the marked growth in concerns over the well-being and mental health of children and young people within the UK along with an increasing demand for support services.

In 2015, Public Health Wales in collaboration with Liverpool John Moore's University outlined findings from a study undertaken of 2,000 people surveyed who were residential in Wales in relation to Adverse Childhood Experiences (ACES) (Bellis et al., 2015). The study aimed to identify the relationship between childhood ACES and their subsequent impact on well-being in adulthood and outlined that 47% of those surveyed reported having experienced one ACE while 14% had suffered four or more. Such childhood stressors can have a significant impact on health-harming behaviours in adulthood with the report also highlighting recent research considering how chronic stress in early life can alter development in terms of hormonal, immunological and neurological functions. Such changes can see individuals reach a stage of heightened awareness for danger and can significantly impact well-being throughout the future life course.

Adverse childhood experiences include the following childhood stressors

- sexual abuse
- physical abuse
- verbal abuse
- domestic violence
- parental separation
- mental illness
- alcohol abuse
- drug abuse
- incarceration

Welsh Government and policy development

Clearly, the issue of well-being within Wales significant and stems from a range of sources such as poverty, exacerbated by the challenges faced in terms of the resources available plus the historical context of economic and geographical development. The situation is complicated further when considering the individual experiences of children and young people within Wales and the impact that poverty and ACES can have on well-being. Therefore, the challenge in addressing these multifaceted issues within Wales is significant. As a newly devolved administration, in 1999 the Welsh Government was in a position to address such issues utilising the powers granted under the terms of devolution. Further extensions of power in 2006 and 2011 to encompass primary legislative powers allowing the opportunity to propose robust policy that truly puts the children and young people of Wales central within the agenda. Beyond Wales, the United Nations has placed the eradication of child poverty along with universal primary education and access to secondary education as human rights issues and goals (McKinney, 2014). A commitment to children's rights alongside strategies to address poverty has formed the basis of key Welsh Government policy initiatives in recent years also. Minujin and Hardy (2012) outline how children are the key to breaking the cycle of poverty and by formulating policy that supports and develops their well-being is central to societal well-being as a whole. It is to these policies that this chapter now turns to provide an outline of some of the key developments.

Building Welsh policy

Following devolution, the new responsibilities of Wales required a clear recognition of the challenges ahead. The result was 'The Learning Country', a paving document confirming the direction to be taken within Wales in relation to key areas concerning education and lifelong learning (National Assembly for Wales, 2001). The ministerial foreword by Jane Davison spoke of the work needed to enhance the health and well-being of all within Wales and the potential consequences should we fail to respond to these issues. Although, as Aasen and Waters (2006) notes, Welsh Government do not actually clearly define at that point what well-being is, the drive to centralise its position within education policy such as the Foundation Phase is a significant step. Addressing education and learning in its entirety, the Learning Country set a 10-year plan for change and development across the sector emphasising equality for all. Establishing Wales as a learning country where education is embraced as a medium of change by all was a central tenet to this bold statement of intent.

In 2006, 'Vision into Action' outlined the progress to date on the objectives set in the Learning Country and adjusting where necessary the initial objectives set. Making more explicit the need to develop educational policy that has a meaningful link with the child poverty agenda, it clarified how Welsh Government saw their role in tackling the poverty of educational opportunity and raising standards (DELLS, 2006). Jane Davison described the role of Vision into Action as intrinsic to addressing the issues of child poverty. The document outlined how a child within Wales would have access to a wide range of opportunities to aid their progress and development. High-quality childcare, education, parental support and appropriate career guidance would work to support well-being and foster a lifelong love of learning as well as economic security throughout the lifespan for all.

Policy into action

As we can see, the commitment towards developing policy that addresses issues of poverty, educational attainment and well-being are of increasing importance within Wales. Research by Wallace (2018) highlights two ways in which we can understand and measure social progress within the context of well-being, either through personal well-being or through societal well-being. Within Wales, societal well-being is central, with reform of the public sector and partnership across services, institutions and communities key to the development of a strong, resilient nation. This is in line with the approach taken in Scotland where similar challenges exist for people and communities. The focus on society as a whole acknowledges the cyclical nature of poverty, which can persist across generations as evidenced by Blanden and Gibbons (2006) in their study, which examined the impact of family background on later outcomes for children and young people. Hirsch and Spencer (2010) as well as Tomlinson and Walker (2010) corroborate this and evidence the impact of intergenerational poverty on the life chances of children and young people.

Four of the key principle-tackling poverty developed by Welsh Government are as follows:

(1) **Flying Start** – aims to promote a range of services to families in designated areas to provide the best start in life to children.
(2) **Families First** – seeks to improve outcomes for children, young people and their families through early intervention and multi-agency working.
(3) **Communities First** – a place-based approach to tacking poverty within areas of high deprivation.
(4) **Supporting People** – early intervention to support vulnerable people to live independently and provide safe, suitable accommodation.

Individual/group task

Research each of the above initiatives and consider the following:

- Who were they aimed at helping and why?
- How successful have they been? What has been the impact of each of them?

Further policy developments include the Children and Families (Wales) Measure 2010, which set out the aim of Welsh Government to the eradication of child poverty. It placed obligations on local authorities to put services in place to tackle child poverty and support children and young people in Wales. Additionally, it ensured that children and young people had a voice in relation to the choices local authorities made that may affect them directly. Additionally, provision of adequate play opportunities, suitable childcare as well as integrated family support teams alongside improving standards in social work were all highlighted within the policy. Consequently, Wales became the first UK nation to place into law a responsibility to address child poverty and placed a duty on ministers to develop a strategy, released as the Child Poverty Strategy for Wales in 2011 (Welsh Government 2011). Outlining ways in which Welsh Government can practically improve outcomes for children and young people, three key objectives were set of reducing the number of workless households while increasing skills and reducing inequalities with a vision to prevent poverty occurring within the most at risk households. The strategy was reviewed and updated in 2015 and added two further objectives in relation to securing a stronger economy and labour market and to increase the income of households in poverty through debt and financial advice and tackling the 'poverty premium' (Welsh Government 2015b). The Tacking Poverty Action Plan (Welsh Government 2012) further set out plans to address poverty across all years groups and established targets for key Welsh Government departments when it was refreshed in 2013.

The Well-being of Future Generations Act (Wales) 2015

In 2012, initial consultation plans began for a new well-being act within Wales. In preparation, a National Conversation began in 2014 and engaged nearly 7,000 people from across Wales. The resultant report 'The Wales We Want' was published the following year and outlined the views of participants in terms of how they would like Wales to look by 2050 and what the country's priorities should be. The report highlighted concerns such as education, natural resources, climate change, along with the need to build strong communities.

Individual/group task

Access a copy of 'The Wales We Want' and consider if you agree with the findings of the report. Are there any that you think are more relevant than others are within the document?

The Well-being of Future Generations Act passed in 2015 and became the first law of its kind within the world. Utilising the concept of sustainability to promote the economic, social, environmental and cultural well-being of Wales, it outlined seven well-being goals seen as essential to the future prosperity of Wales for generations to come.

Goals of the well-being of future generations act (Wales) 2015

- A prosperous Wales
- A resilient Wales
- A healthier Wales
- A more equal Wales
- A globally responsible Wales
- A Wales of vibrant culture and thriving Welsh Language
- A Wales of cohesive communities

It places a legal obligation on public bodies within Wales to work on improving the economic, social, cultural and environmental well-being of Wales. Each public body must undertake sustainable development towards all of the well-being goals as well as set and publish well-being objectives to show how they plan to do this. They must also publish a statement outlining their objectives and an annual report to identify progress made towards achieving their objectives. Utilising the concept of sustainability the Act states:

In this Act *'sustainable development; means the process of improving the economic, social, environmental and cultural well-being of Wales by taking action, in accordance with the sustainable development principle, aimed at achieving the well-being goals'* (Well-Being of Future Generations (Wales) Act, 2015).

The Act also outlines five ways of working to ensure that each public body thinks differently when making decisions and to show how they have applied the sustainable development principle.

(1) **Long term** – the need to balance short-term needs with the ability to meet long-term requirements.
(2) **Prevention** – how acting to prevent problems occurring or getting worse may be useful in helping public bodies meet their objectives.

Table 13.1   A list of affected public bodies

Public bodies included in the well-being of future generations act (Wales) 2015

Welsh ministers	Local authorities	Local health boards
Public health Wales NHS trust	Velindre NHS trust	National park authorities
Fire and rescue authorities	Natural resources Wales	National museum of Wales
The arts council of Wales	Sports council of Wales	National library of Wales
The higher education funding council for Wales		

(3) **Integration** – considering how the objectives of each public body may affect their other objectives or those of different public bodies as well as the impact on the well-being goals themselves.

(4) **Collaboration** – working with others to help achieve the objectives

(5) **Involvement** – ensuring they involve people that reflect the diversity of their area and have an interest in achieving the well-being goals.

(www.futuregenerations.wales, 2019)

Whilst the Act is only legally binding to public bodies, it is clear that having a commitment to the goals and working together across a range of bodies and organisations within Wales can help turn the goals into a reality.

The Future Generations Commissioner

The Act also provided for a Future Generations Commissioner to be appointed in order to hold public bodies to account for their decisions and to help ensure that the long-term impact of decisions is considered by the public bodies. The first Commissioner appointed within Wales was Sophie Howe, elected to the role in 2016. Additional responsibilities of the Commissioner are to be a role model of best practice as well as undertake any necessary reviews and to work with others to drive forward the changes needed. Prior to her current role, Sophie Howe was the first Deputy Police and Crime Commissioner for South Wales. She was responsible for leading programmes to tackle violence against women and girls and led the first police programme designed to address childhood adversities. Previously, she was an elected Councillor for a number of years as well as an Adviser to two Welsh First Ministers and described by the Big Issue as one of the leading Change makers within the UK (The Big Issue, 2019).

> ### Further reading
>
> Look at https://futuregenerations.wales for further information on the Well-being of Future Generations (Wales) Act 2015 and the work of the Commissioner.

'Taking Wales Forward' published in 2016 outlined the four key cross cutting strategies that would help deliver the promise of the Well-being of Future Generations Act up until 2021 with a view to transforming the education and skills sector as one of these. "*The Future Generations Act presents an opportunity to work differently and engage with others to develop innovative solutions to the challenges we face*" (Welsh Government, 2016). "Prosperity for All: the national strategy" (2017) takes the objectives set in 'Taking Wales Forward' and outlines how they can be placed in a wider long-term context and how this fits with the wider work of public services within Wales and establishes the strategy for delivering on the promises made (Welsh Government 2017b). To ensure that our children and young people are equipped with the necessary skills and provided with the opportunity to prosper and succeed is central to these policies.

The future of well-being in Wales

So far, we have seen a clear commitment to safeguarding the future for children and young people in Wales articulated by Welsh Government. The link between prosperity, well-being and education clearly established since the early days of devolution is now clearly enshrined in policy, strategy and national objectives. We have seen in recent years a number of educational initiatives with well-being and attainment at the core. The 2015 report, 'Qualified for Life' set out aims to reform education through increasing the skills of learners and teachers in response to continually poor results from the Programme for International Student Assessment (PISA) tests Welsh Government. (2015a).

Further to this, the 2015 'Successful Futures' report by Professor Graham Donaldson outlined the vision for a new curriculum within state maintained schools within Wales. The report acknowledged the skills shortage within Wales and the need to ensure we are developing learners prepared for an uncertain future who are resilient and adaptable to change. Professor Donaldson noted the effect that disadvantage has on educational attainment and well-being of learners and the shortfall within the existing curriculum to address the future needs of Welsh learners. Hughes and Davies (2019) highlight in their survey of trainee teachers the role poverty has on the attainment of children and acknowledges schools themselves have a key role in addressing this however there is no quick resolution. 'Education Our National Mission' (Welsh Government, 2017a) set out an action plan for 2017–21 for delivery and implementation of the new curriculum and recognises that a strong education system is central to the prosperity and well-being of Wales while directly outlining the role of the Well-being of Future Generations Act within this.

Within higher education, revised funding models for learners in terms of undergraduate and postgraduate study as well as greater diversity of provision aim to increase accessibility for all. An undergraduate funding model for students focusing on providing a living wage is unique when many students are struggling to balance their financial and educational commitments during a time of national austerity. Students from Wales are entitled to apply for a means-tested loan that contributes to their living costs regardless of where they study within the UK. A non-repayable grant regardless of household income is available to all students with a higher amount paid to those from households with a lower income, enabling all learners to access the skills and knowledge development they require for future prosperity.

Conclusion

In conclusion, we can see how since devolution, Wales has taken a unique direction in its approach to addressing education, well-being and prosperity within the country through shifting from reactive to proactive policies and initiatives. The Welsh Government has made bold decisions and promises that it is striving to uphold for the benefit of current and future generations. Davies and Parken (2017) acknowledge that while it is too early to tell conclusively if the Well-being of Future Generations Act is having the desired impact, the Future Generations Commissioner has set the challenge for other countries to follow. Such developments are bold, putting the children and young people of Wales at the heart of their goals and designed to support well-being across the life course utilising education as the key vehicle for change. While we are still a long way from eradicating child poverty, we are making positive steps to mitigate against its effects to allow for equity within the learning experiences that our children and young people can access. While the future direction of the UK is uncertain, there is hope that where Wales leads that others will follow in setting the agenda for a sustainable future for all.

Summary points

*   As one of three devolved nations within the United Kingdom, child poverty within Wales is problematic and long established, caused by a range of historical, societal and economic factors.
*   Links between experiencing poverty in childhood and the impact this has on future life chances are clear and as such, Welsh Government has made the eradication of childhood poverty a key priority in terms of government policy and future direction.
*   The Well-Being of Future Generations Act (2015) is the first act of its kind in the world aiming to safeguard the well-being and interests of current and future children and young people within Wales.
*   Welsh Government view education and access to education as key drivers of change in the alleviation of poverty and the promotion of positive well-being for all and the development of opportunities for as many people to access the education they want and need is of paramount importance.

Recommended reading

Bradshaw, J. (eds.) (2016) *The Well-Being of Children in the UK*. Bristol: Policy Press.
Donaldson, G. (2015) *Successful Futures: Independent Review of Curriculum and Assessment Arrangements in Wales*. Cardiff: Welsh Assembly Government.
Wallace, J. (2018) *Wellbeing and Devolution*. New York: Springer Berlin Heidelberg.

References

Aasen, W. and Waters, J. (2006) The new curriculum in Wales: A new view of the child? *Education 3–13*, **34**(2), pp. 123–129.
Bellis, M.A., Ashton, K., Hughes, K., Ford, K., Bishop, J., Paranjothy, S., and Public Health Wales (2015) *Adverse Childhood Experiences and their Impact on Health-harming Behaviours in the Welsh Adult Population: Alcohol Use, Drug Use, Violence, Sexual Behaviour, Incarceration, Smoking and Poor Diet*. Cardiff: Public Health Wales NHS Trust.
The Big Issue. (2019) *The Big Issue*. [online] Available at: https://www.bigissue.com/ [Accessed 10 Oct. 2019].
Blanden, J., and Gibbons, S. (2006) *The Persistence of Poverty across Generations: A View from Two British Cohorts*. York: Joseph Rowntree Foundation.
Bradshaw. J. (eds.) (2016) *The Well-being of Children in the UK*. Bristol: Policy Press.
Bramley, G. et al. (2016) *Counting the Cost of UK Poverty*. York: Joseph Rowntree Foundation.
Children in Wales (2015) *Child and Family Poverty in Wales: Results from the Child and Family Survey 2015*. [online] Cardiff. Available at: http://www.childreninwales.org.uk/resources/poverty/ [Accessed 18 Aug. 2019].

Children in Wales (2016) *Child and Family Poverty in Wales: Results from the Child and Family Survey 2015.* [online] Cardiff. Available at: http://www.childreninwales.org.uk/resources/poverty/ [Accessed 18 Aug. 2019].

Children in Wales (2018) *Child and Family Poverty in Wales: Results from the Child and Family Survey 2015.* [online] Cardiff. Available at: http://www.childreninwales.org.uk/resources/poverty/ [Accessed 18 Aug. 2019].

Children in Wales. (2019) *Home-Children in Wales.* [online] Available at: http://www.childreninwales.org.uk/ [Accessed 17 Jul. 2019].

Davies, R. and Parken, A. (2017) Devolution, recession and the alleviation of inequality in wales, in Fée, D. and Kober-Smith, A. (Eds.) *Inequalities in the UK.* Emerald Publishing Limited, pp. 323–340.

DELLS. (2006) *The Learning Country: Vision into Action.* Cardiff: Welsh Assembly Government.

Dickerson, A., and Popli, G. (2016) Persistent poverty and children's cognitive development: Evidence from the UK millennium cohort study. *Journal of the Royal Statistical Society A,* **179**(Part 2), pp. 535–558.

Donaldson, G. (2015) *Successful Futures: Independent Review of Curriculum and Assessment Arrangements in Wales.* Cardiff: Welsh Assembly Government.

Futuregenerations.wales. (2019) [online] Available at: https://futuregenerations.wales/wp-content/uploads/2017/02/150623-guide-to-the-fg-act-en.pdf [Accessed 17 Aug. 2019].

Gould, N. (2006) *Mental Health and Child Poverty.* York: Joseph Rowntree Foundation.

Hirsch, D. and Spencer, N. (2010) *Unhealthy Lives: Intergenerational Links between Child Poverty and Poor Health in the UK.* London: End Child Poverty.

Hughes, S. and Davies, G. (2019) 'Childhood poverty in Wales and its implications for schools – A survey of trainee teachers' perceptions', *Teacher Advancement Network Journal,* **11**(1), pp. 25–36.

Ivinson, G., Thompson, I., Beckett, L., Egan, D., Leitch, R., and McKinney, S. (2018) 'Learning the price of poverty across the UK', *Policy Futures in Education,* **16**(2), pp. 130–143.

Joseph Rowntree Foundation (2018) *Poverty in Wales 2018.* [online] Available at https://www.jrf.org.uk/report/poverty-wales-2018 [Accessed 18 Aug. 2019].

McKinney, S. (2014) 'The relationship of child poverty to school education', *Improving Schools,* **17**(3), pp. 203–216.

Minujin, A., and Nandy, S. (eds.) (2012) *Global Child Poverty and Well-being Measurement, Concepts, Policy and Action.* Bristol: Policy Press.

National Assembly for Wales. (2001) *The Learning Country a Paving Document: A Comprehensive Education and Lifelong Learning Programme to 2010 in Wales.* Cardiff: National Assembly for Wales.

Pitchforth, J., Fahy, K., Ford, T., Wolpert, M., Viner, R.M., and Hargreaves, D.S. (2019) Mental health and well-being trends among children and young people in the UK, 1995–2014: analysis of repeated cross sectional national health surveys. *Psychological Medicine,* **49**, 1275–1285.

Statswales.gov.wales. (2019) [online] Available at: https://statswales.gov.wales/ [Accessed 14 Aug. 2019].

Tomlinson, M. and Walker, R. (2010) 'Poverty, adolescent well-being and outcomes later in life', *Journal of International Development,* **22**, 1162–1182.

Wallace, J. (2018) *Wellbeing and Devolution.* New York: Springer Berlin Heidelberg.

Well-being of Future Generations (Wales) Act 2015, c.2. Available at http://www.legislation.gov.uk/anaw/2015/2/contents/enacted (Accessed 19 August 2019).

Welsh Government. (2011) *Written Statement – Child Poverty Strategy and Delivery Plan for Wales* [Accessed 18 July 2018].

Welsh Government. (2012) *Tackling Poverty Action Plan 2012–16* [Accessed 17 July 2018].

Welsh Government. (2015a) *Qualified for Life: A Curriculum for Wales: A Curriculum for Life* [Accessed 28 July 2019].

Welsh Government. (2015b) *Child Poverty Strategy for Wales* [Accessed 16 Aug. 2018].

Welsh Government. (2016) *Taking Wales Forward 2016–2021* [Accessed 18 July 2019].

Welsh Government. (2017a) *Education in Wales: Our National Mission. Action plan 2017–21* [Accessed 28 Aug. 2019].

Welsh Government. (2017b) *Prosperity for All: The National Strategy* [Accessed 18 Aug. 2019].

14 Well-being as a right

Challenging the role of educational professionals in supporting children in Italian schools

Elisabetta Biffi, Cristina Palmieri and
Maria Benedetta Gambacorti-Passerini

Introduction

Within article 3 of the Convention on the Rights of the Child (UN, 1989), it states the 'best interest of the child' is the primary goal to every action taken related to children. It is specified that: "State Parties undertake to ensure the child such protection and care as is necessary for his or her well-being". In these terms, the 'well-being' of the child can be considered as a fundamental part of his/her 'best interest' (Toczydlowska and Bruckauf, 2017)., in all its possible declinations (e.g. care, protection, health) (Fundamental Rights Agency, 2019; Sen, 2009). This is particularly true in situations where children are more vulnerable and their ability for developing resilience to possible mental health conditions must be developed. In fact, strengthening an aptitude for resilience is fundamental in relation to the concept of mental health, as discussed in Chapter 2, in order to prevent mental health difficulties. The contribution of educational professionals is pivotal for working in these directions, with the aim of ensuring children's well-being. Based on a children's rights perspective, this chapter will explore the role of educational professionals (teachers, educators, social workers) in guaranteeing children's well-being within the field of mental health vulnerability, and the conditions that can promote their resilience, with reference to the Italian effort to take care of Special Educational Needs in schools.

Mental well-being as a right for children: supporting of children with special educational needs in Italian schools

As previously mentioned, the UNCRC stated in Article 3 the fundamental role of States is to ensure children's well-being. This means for States to ensure that

> the institutions, services and facilities responsible for the care or protection of children shall conform with the standards established by competent authorities, particularly in the areas of safety, health, in the number and suitability of their staff, as well as competent supervision.
>
> (UNCRC, art. 3.2)

The UNCRC is, indeed, a formal act which has the means to direct all countries involved in order to develop adequate welfare systems which can be able to protect and support children in their own development. For this reason, the focus given by the Convention to the services and institutions is expected, as those are the first target of the Convention itself. Specifically, the right of the child to be protected and guaranteed in their well-being is under the responsibility of services and institutions in charge of education and care tasks (UNICEF Office of Research, 2017).

A child's well-being is, indeed, related to their physical development, as well as being related to the general environment where the child is growing and which provides necessary care and protection. In this respect, well-being itself can be considered a dimension for assessing the best progress of the child (Beltman et al., 2016). From this perspective, it is necessary to further examine the single case, to consider the individual life story of the child whilst maintaining an overview of the formal framework offered by the institutional dimension. Professionals involved require a high level of competency to understand the complexity of the child and their life story within the constraints and resources of their general environment. Focusing on the Italian context, it is interesting to consider the efforts to care for the well-being of children with Special Educational Needs in schools. The term 'Special Educational Needs' was proposed by Ianes (2006), and it covers all the difficulties that children could develop in their schooling experience which influence their learning process. It is based on the International Classification of Functioning, Disability and Health, dated 2001.

Nowadays, in Italy there is a distinct regulatory framework that orientates professionals' acting in taking care of these difficulties:

- Ministerial Directive, 27 December 2012, "Instruments for intervention with students having Special Educational Needs and local organisation for inclusion at school".
- Notice n. 8, 27 June 2013, focused on clarifying how to realise the Directive, 27 December 2012.
- Notice, 22 November 2013, "Instruments for intervention with students having Special Educational Needs, scholastic year 2013–2014: clarification".

These Directives were proposed by the ministry with the aim of offering regulatory interventions to schools, in order to evaluate and, eventually, change their ways of delivering education to become more inclusive. In fact, as Ianes stated, working towards an inclusive perspective isn't only related to teaching; it includes different accredited interventions for children who experience learning difficulties. Working in an inclusive way requires special education to be the norm rather than a separate pedagogy or culture: this implies a continuous questioning about the best interventions to promote learning for that unique child, in that unique classroom. In doing this it's important to have knowledge of specialist interventions and techniques, but also to adapt them to the context and its particular demands (Ianes, 2006).

The Italian system has particularly considered a re-evaluation of the core duties of special needs teachers in order to create good practices for inclusion and well-being. The idea of Index for Inclusion, proposed by Booth and Hawkins (2001), focuses on functions of 'supporting diversity' implemented by all teachers and professionals working in schools, projecting and realising activities in order to comply with students' needs. Strengthening this change in direction and emphasis, the effort is to re-think the role both of special needs teachers and of the curricular teachers, trying to produce well-structured didactic tools, creating the conditions for individual and unique learning processes for students. In this sense, Italian schools are trying to enhance the role of special needs teachers, profiling them as professionals with specific educational competencies to collaborate with curricular teachers in order to create a learning context able to address every student's needs. Furthermore, special needs teachers are required to have skills to understand how to modify organisational and curricular aspects of schooling, focusing on the particular characteristics of children.

All these aspects, necessary for scholastic inclusion, are generated and supported by a political and legislative legitimacy and by a curricular and special needs teachers' training that create individual dispositions and competences to work in an inclusive direction.

Finally, it's important to note that the attention in Italian scholastic system is oriented also to strengthen the children's capabilities to cope with their special educational needs: in this sense, it is important to deepen the concept of resilience and recovery that are fundamental to developing an inclusive way of schooling.

Individual/group task

From the information provided about the taking care of children with Special Educational Needs in Italian schools, can you identify differences and similarities with your country?

Resilience and recovery as resources for well-being: an educational point of view

Resilience is a complex term with multiple definitions utilised appropriately to individual practice, as discussed in earlier chapters. It often relates to *bouncing back* in the face of adversity. The Italian perspective is that it is fundamental to strengthen and train this aptitude in children in order to promote well-being and prevent mental health difficulties escalating, although it is recognised that internationally it is disputed whether resilience is a skill which can be taught.

The concept of recovery, within the area of mental health and well-being, is strictly connected to the process of progression and restoration after experiencing a mental illness and it is based on capabilities and characteristics that could be trained and reinforced in children and adults, in order to promote his/her well-being and to prevent recurring illness. The process of recovery in mental health refers to the word "healing", but it is not intended as the restoration of the situation that was present before the distress. In fact, it implies a changing movement that accompanies the person to a new adjustment for their existential conditions, discovering and learning to use their competencies. Recovery is a personal process, where the person actively tries to regain potential and aspirations (Maone and D'Avanzo, 2015). In this sense, the idea of recovery in mental health is intended more as an ongoing process, than as a final result, and it can last for a person's entire lifespan.

Being in recovery implies to create a new way of considering the experience of suffering, not representing it as something unspeakable, but as something to be recognised and faced. It is a process of firstly investing in personal identity, deconstructing and re-constructing it in the changing of life conditions. Trying to recover implies both an effort in reducing the effects of poor mental health and its malicious effects on life in an attempt to understand how it can be possible to coexist with these effects and learning how to manage it during the time. Following these directions, the concept of recovery refers to a model of educational practice aimed at considering every person suffering from mental distress as the protagonist of their life project, based on the child's personal interests and wishes (Davidson et al., 2009).

The innovative educational aspect of such an approach is represented by treating the experiential dimension as formative: every experience, including the illness, can bring a generative changing process, able to produce learning, self-knowledge and awareness about possible existential conditions. A child's early self-awareness relating to their well-being can promote a changing process through a shared re-elaboration of experience. Key elements of the recovery process are concerned with the development of hope and empowerment (Duffy et al., 2016).

Being able to hope involves thinking that is oriented to the future, considering the possibility to orientate and project everyone's own life process. It involves personal capabilities to perceive the need to change and also to recognise the difficulties this might invoke, in order to consider them in projecting and promoting the existential movement. In this sense, hope is strictly linked to personal aspirations.

Empowerment is a multi-faceted concept, which is strongly articulated on the possibility of having an active control on life. Increasing people's empowerment can focus on different aspects, but it always implies getting the energies and the power to actively promote real change in personal life (Barnes and Bowl, 2001). Referring to children, training them to develop resilience, hope and personal empowerment can surely be an educational strategy in order to prepare them in facing all the difficulties they will experience (Atkins and Rodger, 2016).

The role of educational professionals in school and services is pivotal in this direction: being aware and trained in the subjects of resilience and recovery can represent a valid starting point in order to thematise, project and propose educational actions of well-being promotion and primary prevention of mental health illnesses (Mazzer and Rickwood, 2015; Carr et al., 2018; Guerra, Rajan and Roberts, 2019). Specifically, children with Special Educational Needs can be more predicated to poor mental health, and their well-being can be at risk in terms of exclusion and feeling vulnerable.

In this sense, the practice of educational professionals in schools, following the afore-mentioned directives, can be articulated in inclusive ways, focussing on strengthening children's resilience and empowerment in the learning process, as mentioned in the first paragraph.

Individual/group task

How do you understand the concept of recovery?
How can you arrange activities in schools and educational services that promote children's well-being?

The role of educational professionals in supporting children's mental well-being

In order to understand how educators can promote and guarantee children's well-being, the first step is to clarify from a pedagogical point of view the meanings of well-being.

The notion of well-being is, as already discussed, complex and is related to the whole concept of health. It doesn't refer simply to the absence of distress or suffering but to the possibility to cultivate individual life perspectives (WHO, 1986) and to plan independent living (ONU, 2006). This involves discovering and enhancing the unique and specific potentialities that each person has, taking into account both strengths and weaknesses. Assuming this definition in a pedagogical perspective suggests, it is necessary to create the conditions through which children and adults can discover their limits and potentialities through lived educational experiences that test their well-being in protected contexts. Being put to the test means to be challenged by experience: therefore, it isn't a well-being experience in itself, but it is an experience that allows children and adults to identify and understand their personal and relational resources, to be more aware of their weakness and capabilities, to be able to ask for help in order to face the distress that the educational experience causes. To reach these competencies is the first step in order to build resilience and to live in a situation of good well-being (Benard, 1991; Cyrulnik and Ferron, 2001).

Living such educational experience is most important for children: it allows them to acquire the emotional and cognitive skills needed to face both their evolution tasks and the all the challenges and troubles that living implies, for instance small and big separations, frustrations, limitations; personal, relational and contextual changes; social requests and aspirations. Therefore, for educators, to protect children and guarantee their well-being doesn't mean to restrict them from the difficulties of life, but to help them to face difficulties, starting to live challenging experiences that can support them in it.

The educators' role deals with the principal task of planning, carrying out, evaluating and re-planning such educational experiences (Dewey, 1938). According to Dewey (1938), an experience is 'educational' when it can open up other and richer experiences, so that children can grow with a passion for educating themselves. Therefore, when an educator plans this experience, he/she has to consider two dimensions: the learning experience that the child can live – the *subjective* experience – that is linked with the previous experiences he/she lived, and the situation – the *objective* experience – that refers to the interactions that children have with the environment. Planning an educational experience, therefore, requires creation of a situation that stimulates the children's learning subjective experience: this is the condition through which an educator can safeguard the children's liberty to explore the context and themselves in it (*ibidem*, Montessori, 1999) enhancing their awareness of their limits and potentialities, avoiding direct on their decisions and their behaviours, and giving them times and spaces where they can learn to choose.

Planning such situation requires the Educator to take into account both the material and immaterial dimensions that compose it: spaces, times, objects, rituals, languages, roles, rules, symbols, gestures, postures, etc. This is important in order to provide a dynamic context where children can discover new meanings and experience new emotions and relations (Biesta, 2006, p. 100–116). In order to fulfil that task, educators must have a pedagogical strategy: a methodical way to combine all these elements with the features of both the situation and the children, in order to obtain a learning effect that supports the building of children's resilience and well-being.

In this framework, the educators' role is a very complex one. Educators have to be present in situation, playing their 'part': quoting Goffman (1969), they have 'to influence' children in order to involve them in the experience, and to change their attitude, posture, gestures and relation on the basis of both the educational goal of the situation and the children's needs. At the same time, educators have to manage and monitor the development of the situation as 'directors': they have to change for instance times, spaces, rituals, languages, rules, roles, contexts and relation, in order to make the experience a real educational one.

Focusing on Special Educational Need of children in schools we can note that the concept of ICF encourages professionals in the effort of considering the functioning of every child, in order to understand their eventual special needs and plan-specific learning and educational situations for their well-being.

Referring to our discussions about well-being, utilising the ICF framework and the indications of the above-mentioned Italian directives in an educational way can orient teachers and educators to act in different directions. First, teachers and educators must be able to create material and organisational conditions in order to support an inclusive way of making school, planning effective strategies for every student. Second, in doing this this, they must change their way of teaching in order to promote learning by experience, identifying the most adequate practices for the range of different ways of children's learning and being (Florian, 2008). Third, they must enhance the children's capabilities to feel, manifest, think about and process what they live inside and outside the school. In this sense, the effort is to create a school that can be a positive educational opportunity for everyone, a place where all the students can experience, recognise and know how to face their educational needs, less or more special.

Case study: working in an educational inclusive way with children with special educational needs in Italian School

Focusing on operative aspects, Italian schools try to take care of Children with Special Educational Needs both on a didactic level and an institutional one.

The didactic system implies the chance to create a personalized educational path for Children with Special Educational Needs, giving value first to their capabilities and personal resources. This action requests the setting up not only of individualized teaching processes (with a one-by-one relationship), but also of learning processes able to modify scholastic contexts and to support everyone's educational path.

The "Didactic Personalised Plan" supports teachers and educational professionals in this direction. It involves teachers, health services and children's families in its definition, and is focused on both knowing the children's characteristics and needs, and on identifying the material and immaterial elements of the contexts that must change in order to enhance accessible learning experiences.

With the aim to provide constant attention on Special Educational Needs, the Italian system also foresees that every school establishes a Working Group for Inclusion with the following tasks:

- Notification of Special Educational Needs.
- Collection of the documentation about Didactic Personalized Plans.
- Supporting and discussing with colleagues about working with Special Educational Needs.
- Monitoring the level of inclusion of the school.
- Proposing an annual plan for inclusion, evaluating the activities proposed in the past year.

Conclusion

In conclusion, the educational role is pivotal in promoting and guaranteeing children's well-being and resilience: planning and fulfilling educational experience in all the contexts educators' work can help children in both a preventative and in a rehabilitative way. But it is a very complex role that needs to be recognised and supported by adequate policies and cultural and social awareness: educators act indirectly, and the results of their work needs time to be evident. If the child's well-being is considered as a fundamental right of the child, this means to design political strategies in order to support professionals in coping with this sensitive task, by implementing an adequate system of child protection, care and education, as well as by developing professional training approaches able to support them. The effort undertaken by the Italian system in order to support children with Special Educational Needs, in this sense, can be considered as a good practice oriented in guaranteeing their well-being and resilience.

Summary points

- The "well-being" of the child can be considered as a fundamental part of their "best interest", in all its possible declinations and it is particularly true in the situation where children are more vulnerable, as experiencing Special Educational Needs in Schooling.
- The concept of recovery, within the area of mental health, is strictly connected to the process of going on after experiencing a mental illness and it is based on capabilities and characteristics that could be trained and reinforced in every person, also in children.
- The role of educational professionals in school and services is pivotal in this direction: being aware and trained on resilience and recovery aspects can represent a valid starting point in order to thematise, plan and propose educational actions of well-being promotion and primary prevention about mental health issues.
- For educators and teachers, to protect children and guarantee their well-being doesn't mean to restrict them from the difficulties of life, but to help them to face difficulties, starting to live challenging experiences that can train them in it.
- The effort undertaken by the Italian system in order to take care of children's Special Educational Needs is presented as a good practice oriented in guaranteeing their well-being and resilience.

Recommended reading

Boardman, J., Currie, A., Killaspy, H., and Mezey, G. (Eds.) (2010) *Social inclusion and mental health.* Glasgow: RCPsych Publications.
Waller, R.J. (Ed.) (2016) *Mental health promotion in schools. Special topics, special challenges.* Sharjah: Bentham Books.
WHO (2001). *International classification of functioning, disability and health.* Geneva: World Health Organization Press.

References

Atkins, M.A. and Rodger, S. (2016). Pre-service teacher education for mental health and inclusion in schools. *Exceptionality Education International*, **26**: 93–118.
Barnes, M. and Bowl, R. (2001). *Taking over the asylum: Empowerment and mental health.* London: Palgrave Macmillan.
Beltman, D., Kalverboer, M.E., Zijlstra, A.E., Van Os, E.C.C., and Zevulun, D. (2016). The legal effect of best-interests-of-the-child reports in judicial migration proceedings: A qualitative analysis of five cases. *The United Nations Convention on the Rights of the Child: Taking Stock After*, **25**: 655–680.
Benard, B. (1991). *Fostering resiliency in kids: Protective factors in the family, school and community.* Portland, OR: Western Centre for Drug-Free Schools and Communities.
Biesta, J.J. (2006). *Beyond learning. Democratic education for a human future.* Boulder, CO: Paradigm Publisher.

Booth, T. and Hawkins, K. (2001). *Developing and index for inclusion with countries of the south.* Paris: UNESCO.

Carr, W., Wei, Y., Kutcher, S., and Heffernan, A. (2018). Preparing for the classroom: Mental health knowledge improvement, stigma reduction and enhanced help-seeking efficacy in Canadian preservice teachers. *Canadian Journal of School Psychology*, **33**(4): 314–326.

Cyrulnik, B. and Ferron, C. (2000). A proposito del concetto di resilienza. *La salute umana*, **174**: 7–9.

Davidson, L., Rakfeldt, J., and Strauss, J. (2009). *The roots of the recovery movement in psychiatry.* Oxford: Wiley-Blackwell.

Dewey, J. (1938) *Experience and education.* New York: Kappa Delta Pl.

Duffy, J., Davidson, G., and Kavanagh, D. (2016). Applying the recovery approach to the interface between mental health and child protection services. *Child Care in Practice*, **22**(1): 35–49.

Florian, L. (2008) Special and inclusive education: Future trends. *British Journal of Special Education*, **35**(4): 202–208.

Fundamental Rights Agency (2019). *Fundamental rights report 2019.* https://doi.org/10.2811/303379 (consulted on 06 August 2019).

Goffman, E. (1969). *The presentation of self in everyday life.* Garden City: Doubleday & Company.

Guerra, L.A., Rajan, S., and Roberts, K.J. (2019) The implementation of mental health policies and practices in schools: An examination of school and state factors. *Journal of School Health*, **89**: 328–338.

Ianes, D. (2006). *La speciale normalità. Strategie di integrazione e di inclusione per le disabilità e i Bisogni Educativi Speciali*, Trento: Erickson.

Maone, A. and D'Avanzo, B. (Eds.) (2015). *Recovery. Nuovi paradigmi per la salute mentale.* Milano: Raffaello Cortina Editore.

Mazzer, K. and Rickwood, D. (2015) Teachers' role breadth and perceived efficacy in supporting student mental health. *Advances in School Mental Health Promotion*, **8**(1): 29–41.

Montessori, M. (1999). *La scoperta del bambino.* Milano: Garzanti (or. Ed. 1948, The MontessoriPerson Estates).

ONU (2006). *United Nations convention on the rights of Persons with disabilities,* https://www.un.org/development/desa/disabilities/convention-on-the-rights-of-persons-with-disabilities.html (consulted on 6 August 2019).

Sen, A. (2009). *The Idea of Justice.* London: Allen Lane.

Toczydlowska, E. and Bruckauf, Z. (2017). Growing inequality and unequal opportunities in rich countries. *Innocenti Research Brief 2017–16*, 1–5. https://www.unicef-irc.org/publications/pdf/RESEARCH BRIEF 2017-16 FINAL.pdf.

UN (1989), Convention on the Rights of the Child, available on https://www.ohchr.org/en/professionalinterest/pages/crc.aspx

UNICEF Office of Research (2017). *Building the future: Children and the sustainable development goals in rich countries. Innocenti Report Card* (Vol. 14). https://www.unicef-irc.org/publications/pdf/RC14_eng.pdf.

WHO (1986). *The Ottawa charter for health promotion.* https://www.who.int/healthpromotion/conferences/previous/ottawa/en/ (consulted on 6 August 2019).

15 The role of the kindergarten in children's well-being and resilience

The case of Norway

Maria Dardanou and Eirin Gamst-Nergård

Introduction

In this chapter, we discuss the various terms and arguments in policy documents relating to children's well-being and resilience in the context of the Norwegian kindergarten. Research has shown growing attention on young children's well-being and happiness in the Norwegian context (Seland and Sandseter, 2015; Dahle et al., 2016; Koch, 2018). This chapter aims to investigate the role of policy documents and kindergarten practices in promoting children's social relations and competence, life skills, and health through active participation and varied experiences, challenges and achievements. With this in mind, this chapter supports readers to reflect upon their understanding of well-being and resilience in early childhood everyday practices.

The Norwegian context and welfare system

Authorities organise the welfare system in Norway with central and local services. The child welfare services are responsible for providing advice and guidance, undertaking investigations, and making administrative decisions according to the Child Welfare Services Act (Ministry of Children, Equality and Social Inclusion, 2013). The service also prepares cases for consideration by the county social welfare board and implementing and following up child welfare measures (Ministry of Children and Families, 2019). The kindergarten is highlighted as the first stage of the Norwegian educational system and operates as a part of a flexible welfare system. Parental leave benefits allow parents to choose to stay at home with their new-born child between 49 weeks of full earnings and 59 weeks of 80% earnings (NAV, 2019). If the parents choose the full earning-program of 49 weeks of parental leave, 15 weeks are reserved for the father, while as 19 weeks if they choose the 80% earning. The mother has the same percentage of weeks reserved for her. For the remaining weeks of parental leave (19 or 21), it is for the parents to decide who stays at home with the child. To determine by law that part of the parental leave is for the father only, the Norwegian government states the importance of both parents to bond and form attachment with the child. According to Musgrave (2017), being attached to your child, the parents are likely to protect and care for the baby and prevent harm from occurring. Having developed a secure attachment early in life is essential for growing healthy self-esteem and better self-reliance. Those are important skills aspects for a person's well-being and resilience. For the well-being of a family, it can be of importance that both parents share the responsibility of taking care of the child during the child's first year. Both parents can pursue their careers even though they become parents, and it is no longer for the mother only to stay at home and take care of children and household. Therefore, because of the parental leave, most children do not attend kindergarten before the age of one.

Municipalities (County) are responsible for the kindergartens and facilitate a coordinated admission process. The Norwegian government has set the maximum cost for full time participation for each child to 3040 Norwegian kroner (NOK) per month (around 270 British pounds), whether it is a municipal or non-municipal kindergarten. In 2015, the funding system expanded to include children between 3, 4, and 5 years in low-income families, a scheme providing 20 hours of free kindergarten a week. In August 2019, this right expanded to include children from the age of 2 years (Ministry of Education and Research, 2014).

Individual/group task

- Discuss the welfare system related to parental leave and kindergarten funding in your country.
- How do the authorities organise Early Childhood Education and Care (ECEC) systems in relation to these two aspects?

The Norwegian kindergarten

In the Norwegian kindergarten, there are children aged between 1 and 5 years. The Norwegian kindergarten is not mandatory for children, but 91.8% of children between the ages 1 and 5 years attend (Statistics Norway, 2019). The kindergarten follows the Kindergarten Act that was implemented in 2005 and has incorporated regulations related to the laws and rules of the kindergarten's operation (Ministry of Education and Research, 2005). Children in kindergarten are usually divided into mixed age groups. The Norwegian kindergarten aims to promote children's creativity, sense of wonder and search of knowledge, and is based on values such as democracy, respect and inclusion (Norwegian Directorate of Education and Training, 2017). The Kindergarten Act legally binds all Norwegian kindergartens to follow its regulation (Ministry of Education and Research, 2005).

Additionally, kindergarten staff must ensure that all children find safety, belongingness, and well-being (Norwegian Directorate of Education and Training, 2017). The opening hours can vary, but most of the kindergartens are open between 07.30 am and 16.30 pm. The head teachers and pedagogical leaders in a Norwegian kindergarten must be trained pre-school teachers or have formal pedagogical qualifications (a bachelor's degree). In line with regulations, there must be one official qualified teacher for every seventh child under the age of 3. In age groups over the age of 3 that have daily residence over 6 hours, the ratio of a qualified teacher is 1 to every 14th child (Utdanningsdirektoratet, 2018).

In 2017, the framework for kindergartens content and tasks was revised. The revision emphasised the responsibility of kindergartens to ensure a good childhood, underlining the importance of well-being, friendships through playing and active participation (Norwegian Directorate of Education and Training, 2017). The framework distinguished between seven interdisciplinary areas of learning:

- Body, movement, food and health
- Art, culture and creativity

- Nature, environment and technology
- Ethics, religion and philosophy
- Local community and society
- Quantities, spaces and shapes

Norway has an indigenous group, the Sámi people. There are around 100,000 Sámi in Norway (Rasmussen and Nolan, 2011). Most Sámi live in the northern part of Norway, but there is also a significant group living in and around the capital city Oslo. Traditionally, the Sámi people lived a semi-nomadic lifestyle depending on herding reindeer, hunting and harvesting the nature. Along the coast, the Sámi population support themselves through fishing and livestock farming. According to the Sámi culture, there is a close bond between Sámi people and nature. The Sámi culture has their own unique forms of expressions like the characteristic song the 'Joik' and craftwork tradition called 'Duoddji'. It includes woodcarving, making knives, sewing clothes, shoes, etc. from the reindeer leather. 'Duoddji' also has its own unique embroidery and weaving. For many years (1860–1960), the official policy was to assimilate the Sámi people to become Norwegian citizens (Nergård, 2019). When at school, the teaching was in Norwegian only, and the Sámi children had no permission to speak their own language even during breaks and playtime. Due to this, the Sámi language disappeared in many areas. Since the 1970s, the Sámi culture and language has experienced revitalisation (Nergård, 2019). Gradually, the language and culture has been introduced in schools and kindergartens. The Framework for kindergarten states that kindergartens for Sámi children and in Sámi districts were to be an integrated part of Sámi society (Norwegian Directorate of Education and Training, 2017). For kindergartens located outside of a typical Sámi district, parents and children are entitled to expect staff to be familiar with Sámi culture as well as to emphasise on it as part of the kindergartens' daily practices. To integrate Sámi culture involves learning children about Duoddji and sharing traditional Sámi tales and Sámi lifestyle.

Individual/group task

From the information provided about the Norwegian kindergarten, can you see differences and similarities with the early childhood institutions in your country?

Participation as a main concept of the framework

The UN Convention on the Rights of the Child (UNICEF, 1989) obliges national states to acknowledge children's rights, respecting the view and voices of children. The Norwegian Framework for kindergartens has the UN Convention as its founding starting point. Kindergartens shall and must recognise children's right to participation over their well-being. An essential part of the legal framework dictates and highlights the importance of children's active involvement explicitly 'in planning and assessing the kindergarten's activities regularly' (Norwegian Directorate of Education and Training, 2017, p. 27).

Moreover, the Norwegian framework for Kindergartens underlines the importance of children's participation must be in accordance with their age and their premises (Norwegian Directorate of Education and Training, 2017). The concepts of involvement and active participation are complex.

Nevertheless, the framework considers as a democratic right the encouragement of children to self-play an active role in self-determination, codetermination, as well as the involvement in everyday situations and experiences (Jansen, 2019). A study by Seland and Sandseter (2015) indicated a strong correlation between experienced happiness and well-being in 1- to 3-year olds when devoting themselves to social interactions with others as opposed to being deeply concentrated in play and exploration alone. Practices of inclusion and participation in the kindergarten provide all children opportunities to express themselves, to be heard and practice values of democracy and resistance. Significantly, children's interactions during play are promoting social skills and emotional competence, as those activities are arenas for practicing those values (Pettersvold, 2017).

In line with Drawn and Goleman (1995), emotional learning occurring in the first 3 years of the child's development is affected by the caregiver's and other participants' role as well as the cultural context of the environment. Based on the study of Dahle et al. (2016), the feeling of belonging in respect of social relations and participation in playing activities, are essential for very young children's life quality and well-being. Additionally, the kindergarten teacher's "experiences of participation in the planning of daily activities seemed crucial for children's learning, and well-being" (Alvestad et al., 2014, p. 682).

Individual/group task

- Can you give some examples of everyday practices in the kindergarten where children's participation and inclusion are the focus?
- In what way can the kindergarten staff ensure children's resistance and negotiation in everyday activities?

Holistic learning and inclusion

A holistic approach to learning is an expression used to distinguish between the pedagogical perspectives formulated in the Norwegian Framework for Kindergartens. The framework differentiates between care, formation, play, knowledge, social competence, communication, and language, and it should be understood in context as the Kindergarten's contribution to children's holistic development (Norwegian Directorate of Education and Training, 2017). The framework considers these aspects of a child's development and recognises the child as an active learner. Social interaction and play-based activities are essential for children's social and emotional development and learning. Play is essential to children's development and learning, social, and linguistic interactions. Universal values such as responsibility, egalitarianism, freedom of mind, and tolerance are explicit and underlined in the framework. Children's participation presupposes that kindergarten teachers must listen to children's views and use these in the planning (Jensen, 2009). One example can be a meeting in the morning circle where the kindergarten teacher asks the children what they would like to do today (for example draw, play in different rooms or outdoors with other children). The teacher takes into consideration children's ideas, wishes, and plans the day according to them. However, as Koch (2018) argues, children have their specific agenda for happiness outplayed by experimenting. Challenging their limits, for example in-play or outdoor activities provide them opportunities for feelings of control, accomplishment, and emotional well-being.

Inclusion is fundamental for the establishment of positive social relationships among children in kindergarten so that every child will experience authentic practices of engagement, participation, and achievement. Consequently, inclusion for kindergarten children is related to their involvement and influence in kindergarten everyday activities as a part of its democratic values, ideals and practices (Jansen, 2019). Additionally, kindergarten is a place where democracy must generate culture for dialogue and constant discussion or negotiations about valid perspectives and positions (Ødegaard, 2012).

Individual/group task

How do you understand the concept of holistic learning and how can you arrange activities in the kindergarten that promote children's learning in a holistic perspective?

Well-being as a concept in Norway

The concept of well-being has several definitions (see Chapter 1). Dodge et al. (2012) portray the multitude of definitions as challenging to define, as it may be easier to describe the idea than provide a definition of the term. The concept of well-being was recently introduced in Norwegian intellectual discussions and public health research communities (Helsedirektoratet, 2015). However, due to its definitional complexity, the term 'well-being' is often referred to in English, even when applied in Norwegian. Nevertheless, the sense of 'well-being' is a product of several other concepts such as happiness, emotions, mental and physical health, feelings, and social interactions and has a political dimension. This dimension can be connected to the role of the individual as a member of the society that can participate actively in the forming of its functions. 'Well-being' is sometimes considered as an individual and subjective perspective. Silberfeld (2016) related the feeling of well-being as profoundly connected to the perception of 'a good life' and right living conditions. Well-being is intimately close to prosperity and good mental and physical health that affects emotional development and the feeling of 'having a good time' (Silberfeld, 2016).

The World Health Organization (WHO) has tried to define 'well-being' concerning health. Through HEALTH 2020, European countries have been challenged to "significantly improve the health and well-being of population" (World Health Organization, 2013, p. xii). Quality of life is part of 'Well-being'. WHO defined the quality of life as:

> An individual's perception of their position in life in the context of the culture and value systems in which they live and concerning their goals, expectations, standards, and concerns. It is a broad-ranging concept affected in a complex way by the person's physical health, psychological state, personal beliefs, social relationships and their relationship to salient features of their environment.
>
> (World Health Organization, 1997).

Research on children's well-being is limited as it is not easy to know very young children's own understanding of health and well-being (Musgrave, 2017). According to a report made by UNICEF (2013), Norway is listed at the top of the list among 29 countries related to different aspects of child well-being, such as material well-being, health, and safety, educational well-being. Thus, well-being is a subjective experience of having a good life. What this means, however, depends on the individual's values, views of life, backgrounds and how one relates to more or less explicitly expressed expectations in the social and cultural contexts (Eide et al., 2019).

Moser et al. (2017) point out cultural and societal perspective to understand children's well-being. Well-being is dependent on education and the extent to which ECEC institutions are available, accessible, acceptable for, and adaptable to the needs of children and their families. The Norwegian Framework for the kindergarten (Norwegian Directorate of Education and Training, 2017, p. 11) underlines that kindergartens "shall promote physical and mental health in the children. They shall contribute to the children's well-being, happiness, attainment, and feeling of self-worth, and they shall combat harassment and bullying". Therefore, kindergarten staff must adjust their practices to fulfil the claims of the framework. For example, by developing close relationships and being an active participant in children's daily life in kindergarten. Well-being is, therefore, about developing as a person physically, emotionally and socially.

Individual/group task

Discuss your understanding of the concept of well-being

- What does this mean to you?
- Why is it an important consideration when working with young children?
- How does developing and supporting well-being in England compare to Norway?

Resilience in Norway

Resilience is about coping with life and life experiences. Miljević-Ridički1 et al. (2017) define resilience as strength in emotion regulation and prosocial skills. Another definition is when a child can cope despite encountering difficult situations or adverse events, and to return to almost the same level of emotional well-being as before the negative experience (Cahill et al., 2014, see also Chapter 2).

Being resilient can help to promote both social and emotional well-being. Whether a child experiences trauma or is growing up in a high-risk environment, being resilient can have a protective effect. For some children who experience maltreatment kindergarten can play an important role in functioning as an environment providing both resilience and well-being. A positive teacher–child relation can enhance a child's social well-being and resilience. Having close ties with one adult, this adult can function as the significant other and therefore provide resilience and well-being. Thus, early childhood systems like Norwegian kindergarten can promote good health for children. The framework for Norwegian kindergartens emphasizes the importance of providing for every child's outcome in terms of social and cognitive development. According to the Framework plan, kindergartens should place emphasis on children's development and learning, and stimulate the child's linguistic and communicative competence (Norwegian Directorate of Education and Training, 2017). One of the main goals with the kindergartens is to reduce social differences. The Framework also states what the employees are to do to ensure that the children attending kindergarten thrive and develop. By supervising and supporting children's play and social interactions, the kindergarten teachers provide for all the children to have the opportunity to play with peers and develop their social skills. The seven interdisciplinary areas of learning described in the framework is an example on how resilience and well-being can be promoted in Norwegian kindergartens. The teachers in the kindergarten are supposed to schedule activities to ensure that the children develop physical, emotional, cognitive, academic and motorial skills. By providing for a variety of activities, children who attend kindergarten are not depending on their family's income alone in order to thrive and develop. Focusing on children's resilience and well-being, the kindergarten staff can guide and advise parents on stress-related problems. The framework states that the children must experience a variety of both success and failure in order to cope and regulate their own emotions. Through activities and play, children also learn about their own and others' emotions (Norwegian Directorate of Education and Training, 2017).

High peer status is beneficial for children's overall adaptation (Luthar and Cicchetti, 2000). During playtime and daily activities in kindergarten, there is a focus on how children interact and relate to peers. The kindergarten staff is required to provide time and help to initiate play activities that can enhance children's emotional and social development. Developing social competence is emphasized as important for children in Norwegian kindergartens. Focusing on a child's social and emotional development can result in resilient adaptation and behaviour.

Individual/group task

Different skills linked to resilience are coping with stress, emotional regulation, self-control and prosocial skills.

- How can kindergartens develop these skills to enhance children's resilience?
- How does the concept of resilience in Norway compare to the concept in England?

Kindergarten practices that promote well-being

Principles in Norwegian kindergarten encourage values such as learning, democratic ideals and solidarity through children's active participation in kindergarten's everyday activities. The focus is on children's experiences that facilitate social interactions and expose children in responsibilities and independence. Being a part of a group and acknowledging that the contribution of each one is necessary and vital in the whole group's enjoyment, play and 'having a good time'. Through participating in a variety of activities – spontaneous or planned – children have opportunities to experience a sense of inclusion, belonging and promotion of autonomy (Pettersvold, 2018). Therefore, their involvement with indoor and outdoor activities provides sensory experiences social interactions in the sense of freedom in open spaces (Rose et al., 2016).

The Norwegian kindergarten, as well as Norwegian culture in general, are distinguished by influences of the Sámi culture where nature is a resource for different aspects of everyday life. Consequently, the kindergartens "shall build on a Sámi understanding of nature and Sámi Culture" (Norwegian Directorate of Education and Training, 2017, p. 25). Findings from Estola et al. (2014) indicate well-being also included understanding about the influence of one's environment and experiences. Teaching children to influence their everyday life in kindergarten, through their interactions with other children, can provide children with a feeling of self-value. Thus, it is a vital starting point for active participation in one's cultural and social community.

The following case study provides an example of children's active participation and responsibilities that can emerge while planning a trip to a nearby forest.

Case study

A group of 12 children (aged between 4 and 5) together with their two kindergarten teachers are planning their weekly trip to the nearby forest. It is mid-October, and the weather is rainy and wet. During the circle time in the morning of the trip, the teachers ask the children what they need to bring along for this half-day trip.

- Monica (kindergarten teacher): So, it is raining today, what kind of clothes do you think we should wear?
- Johan (four years old): We need rain-coats and outdoor trousers! My mother said I should wear my outdoor trousers and my wet-play gloves!
- Monica: That's right, Johan! Is there anything else we need to bring as well?
- Christina (4–5 years old): We need to have our water bottles! And our packed lunches.
- Monica: Yes, you need to bring your water bottles. But we will barbeque at the wooden house in the forest like we did last time, do you remember? What do we need to bring along for the barbeque?
- Johan: We need wood! To make a bonfire! And matches.
- Monica: Yes, we need wood. So, who wants to fix wood for the trip? (addressing to all the children). Christina, Emil, Johan and I will fix the barbeque. Everyone check that there is a water bottle in his/her bag and extra clothes for changing! Let's get busy!

Individual/group task

Can you think of other examples from kindergarten's everyday life that provide children opportunities to take responsibilities and an active role in the planning and carrying through different activities?

Conclusion

Children's experiences in kindergarten should include both the immediate feelings of happiness, joy, belongingness and engagement in exciting and challenging activities of participation that support the individual child in growing up as a healthy, competent, respected, valued and democratic citizen (Moser et al., 2017). Playful activities have intrinsic value for children, and it is through such experience children meet with inclusiveness in social relations and practices.

Good attachment is vital for children's short- and long-term emotional well-being and for improving mental health in childhood and adulthood. Having developed a secure attachment early in life is essential for growing healthy self-esteem and better self-reliance. Those are important skills aspects for a person's well-being and resilience (Musgrave, 2017).

To conclude, well-being is a positive physical, mental and social state. Nevertheless, it is difficult to measure these conditions on a family level. However, almost 92% of the Norwegian children attend kindergarten and have therefore opportunities to experience the same or similar practices that enhance the concepts of well-being and resilience. It is enhanced by conditions that include positive personal relationships with adults and peers in an environment that promotes challenging indoor and outdoor play activities. An inclusive community that allows the child to experience joy and happiness, to unfold his/her potential and to express his/her view on the ongoing activities, places kindergarten as an essential setting in young children's life.

Summary points

This chapter provides

- An understanding of the concept of well-being and resilience in the Norwegian early childhood context.
- An insight of kindergarten's everyday practices that promote aspects related to young children's well-being and resilience, such as participation and inclusion as stated by policy documents such as the Kindergarten Act (2005) and the framework for the Norwegian kindergarten (2017).
- A holistic approach to children's experiences provide opportunities for play, learning, social and emotional development.

Recommended reading

Fiore, L. (2019) *Grit, Resilience, and Motivation in Early Childhood*. New York and Oxon: Routledge.
Traynor, M. (2019) *Stories of Resilience in Nursing: Tales from the Frontline of Nursing*. London: Routledge.

References

Alvestad, T., Bergem, H., Eide, B., Johansson, J.-E., Os, E., Pálmadóttir, H., Pramling Samuelsson, I., and Winger, N. (2014) 'Challenges and dilemmas expressed by teachers working in toddler groups in the Nordic countries'. *Early Child Development and Care*, **184**(5), 671–688. [online] Available at: https://doi.org/10.1080/03004430.2013.807607 [Viewed 3 July 2019].
Cahill, H., Beadle, S., Farrelly, A., Forster, R., and Smith, K. (2014). *Building resilience in children and young people: A literature review for the deaapartment ofeducation and early childhood development (DEECD)*. Melbourne, VIC, Australia: Youth Research Centre, Melbourne Graduate School of Education,University of Melbourne. Available at: http://www.education.vic.gov.au/Documents/about/department/resiliencelitreview.pdf [Viewed 16 July 2019].
Dahle, H.F., Eide, B., Winger, N., and Wolf, K. D. (2016) 'Livskvalitet for de yngste barna i barnehagen' [Life quality for the youngest children in kindergarten]. In Gulpinar, T., Hernes, L., and Winger, N. (Eds.) *Blikk fra barnehagen* [Glance from the kindergarten]. Bergen: Fagbokforlaget, pp. 43–67.
Dodge, R., Daly, A., Huyton, J., and Sanders, L. (2012) 'The challenge of defining wellbeing'. *International Journal of Wellbeing*, **2**(3), 222–235. [online] Available at: doi:10.5502/ijw.v2i3.4 [Viewed 3 July 2019].
Eide, B. J., Winger, N., and Wolf, K. D. (2019) 'Alt henger sammen – Hverdagslogistikk og små barns muligheter for tilhørighet i barnehagen' [Everything is connected – Everyday logistics and young children's opportunities for belonging in the kindergarten]. *Nordic Early Childhood Education Research Journal*, **18**(1), 1–15. [online] Available at: https://doi.org/10.7577/nbf.2688 [Viewed 1 July 2019].
Estola, E., Farquhar, S., and Puroila, A.-M. (2014) 'Well-being narratives and young children'. *Educational Philosophy and Theory*, **46**(8), 929–941. [online] Available at: https://doi.org/10.1080/00131857.2013.785922 [Viewed 1 July 2019].

Goleman, D. (1995) *Emotional Intelligence.* New York: Bantam Books.

Helsedirektoratet. (2015) *Well-being på norsk* [Well-being in Norwegian]. Oslo: Helsedirektoratet.

Jansen, K. E. (2019) *Medvirkning i praksis. Deltakelse og danning i barnehagens hverdagsliv* [Participation in practice. Participation and formation in kindergarten's everyday life]. Bergen: Fagbokforlaget.

Jensen, B. (2009) 'A Nordic approach to early childhood education (ECE) and socially endangered children'. *European Early Childhood Education Research Journal,* **17**(1), 7–21, [online] Available at: https://doi. org/10.1080/13502930802688980 [Viewed 5 July 2019].

Koch, A. B. (2018) 'Children's perspectives on happiness and subjective well-being in preschool'. *Children & Society,* **32**, 73–83. [online] Available at: https://doi.org/10.1111/chso.12225 [Viewed 10 July 2019].

Luthar, S. S. and Cicchetti, D. (2000) 'The construct of resilience: Implications for interventions and social policies' *Dev Psychopathol,* **12**(4), 857–885. [online] Available at: doi:10.1017/s0954579400004156.

Miljević-Ridički1, R., Plantak, K., and Bouillet, D. (2017) 'Resilience in preschool children – The perspectives of teachers, parents and children'. *Journal of Emotional Education.* Special Issue, **9**(2), 31–33.

Ministry of Children and Families (2019) *Division of Responsibility in the Child Welfare Services.* [online] Available at: https://www.regjeringen.no/en/topics/families-and-children/child-welfare/allocation-of-responsibilities-related-to-c1/id2353984/ [Viewed 1 July 2019].

Ministry of Children, Equality and Social Inclusion (2013) *The Child Welfare Act.* [online] Available at: https://www.regjeringen.no/contentassets/049114cce0254e56b7017637e04ddf88/the-norwegian-child-welfare-act.pdf [Viewed 26 August 2019].

Ministry of Education and Research (2014) *Funding of Kindergartens.* [online] Available at: https://www.regjeringen.no/en/topics/families-and-children/child-welfare/allocation-of-responsibilities-related-to-c1/id2353984/ [Viewed 29 August 2019].

Ministry of Education and Research (2009) *Kvalitet i barnehagen. (Meld. Nr. 41 2008–2009).* Oslo: Ministry of Education and Research. [online] Available at: https://www.regjeringen.no/contentassets/78fde92c225840 f68bce2ac2715b3def/no/pdfs/stm200820090041000dddpdfs.pdf [Viewed 29 May 2019].

Ministry of Education and Research (2005) *Kindergarten Act.* Oslo: Norwegian Ministry of Education.

Moser, T., Leseman, P., Melhuish, E., Broekhuizen, M., and Slot, P. (2017) *European Framework of Quality and Well-being Indicators.* European Union: CARE Project.

Musgrave, J. (2017) *Supporting Children's Health and Wellbeing.* London, Thousand Oaks, CA, New Delhi, Singapore: SAGE.

NAV (2019) *All informasjon om foreldrepenger* [Information on parents' money]. [online] Available at: https://familie.nav.no/om-foreldrepenger [Viewed 25 November 2019].

Nergård, J.-I. (2019) *Dialoger med Naturen Etnografiske skisser fra Sâpmi* [*Dialogues with nature Ethnographical sketches from Sapmi*]. Oslo: Universitetsforlaget.

Norwegian Directorate of Education and Training (2017) *Framework Plan for the Content and Tasks of Kindergartens.* Oslo: Norwegian Ministry of Education and Research. [online] Available at: https://www.udir.no/globalassets/filer/barnehage/rammeplan/framework-plan-for-kindergartens2-2017.pdf [Viewed 26 May 2019].

Ødegaard, E. E. (2012) 'Meningsskaping i bruk av artefakter' [Meaningmaking in the use of artefacts]. In Ødegaard, E.E. (Ed.) *Barnehagen som danningsarena.* [Kindergarten as an arena for formation] Bergen: Fagbokforlaget, pp. 91–110.

Pettersvold, M. (2018) 'Det demokratiske samfunnsoppdraget' [The democratic assignment of the society]. In Østrem, M. (Ed.) *Barnehagen som samfunnsinstitusjon* [Kindergarten as a society institution]. Oslo: Cappelen Damm Akademisk, pp. 67–85.

Pettersvold, M. (2017) 'Barns motstand i et demokrati-perspektiv' [Children's resistance in a decocracy perespective]. In Øksnes, M. and Samuelsson, M. (Eds.) *Motstand* [Resistance]. Oslo: Cappelen Damm Akademisk, pp. 115–140.

Rasmussen, T. and Nolan, S.J. (2011) 'Reclaiming Sámi languages: Indigenous language emancipation from East to West'. *International Journal of the Sociology of Language,* **209**, 35–55. [online] Available at: https://doi.org/10.1515/ijsl.2011.020 [Viewed 24 November 2019].

Rose, J., Gilbert, L., and Richards, V. (2016) *Health and Well-being in Early Childhood.* Los Angeles, CA, London, New Delhi, Singapore, Washington, DC: SAGE.

Seland, M. and Sandseter, E.B.H. (2015) 'One- to three-year-old children's experience of subjective well-being in day care'. *Contemporary Issues in Early Childhood,* **16**(1), 70–83. [online] Available at: https://doi.org/10.1177/1463949114567272 [Viewed 24 November 2019].

Silberfeld, C. (2016) 'Children's health and well-being'. In Palaiologou, I. (Ed.) *The Early Years Foundation Stage. Theory and Practice* (3rd ed.). Los Angeles, CA, London, New Delhi, Singapore, Washington, DC, Melbourne: SAGE, pp. 280–293.

Statistics Norway (2019) *Kindergartens (2018) Final Figures.* [online] Available at: https://www.ssb.no/en/utdanning/statistikker/barnehager [Viewed 24 May 2019].

Utdanningsdirektoratet (2018) *Bemanningsnorm og skjerpet pedagognorm – hvordan ligger barnehagene an?* [Staffing norms and stricter pedagogy norms – how do kindergartens work?]. [online] Available at: https://www.udir.no/tall-og-forskning/finn-forskning/tema/Statistikknotat-bemanningsnorm-barnehage/ [Viewed 29 May 2019].

UNICEF. (1989) *United Nations Convention on the Rights of the Child.* New York: UNICEF.

UNICEF Office of Research (2013) *Child Well-being in Rich Countries: A Comparative Overview.* Innocenti Report Card 11, UNICEF Office of Research, Florence.

World Health Organization (2013) *The European Health Report 2012: Charting the Way to Well-being.* Copenhagen: World Health Organization Regional Office for Europe.

World Health Organization (1997) *WHOQOL Measuring Quality of Life.* Geneva: World Health Organization.

Conclusion

Sarah Mander and Zeta Williams-Brown

Within our introduction, we outlined the purpose of writing this book; our main aim was to provide students with a resource that brings together theory on childhood well-being and resilience and relates it to current practice. Its naissance was constructed from a few thoughts, discussions and reflections about the importance of well-being for children, young people and their families. We set out to publish a book which allowed students and practitioners to reflect on the importance and potential of well-being to positively influence educational outcomes. This book sought to equip readers with a depth of knowledge and richness in understanding that would inform their well-being work with children and young people. It appeared to us that policy trends and practice delivery had shifted to focus on safeguarding children and young people, and that their well-being was not considered a priority. A contradiction existed between this lack of emphasis on well-being and the emergent mental health crisis. Surely, if well-being was strengthened, the likelihood of developing poor mental health might progress at a slower rate and consequently be less prevalent for some children and young people. This would provide opportunity for earlier intervention and preventative work to prevent escalation of needs and consequently reduce the demand for mental health services. Thanks to the diligence and expertise of our contributing authors a powerful and thought-provoking book has been produced which enables us to explore the educational context of well-being and resilience, gain new knowledge and confidence in the field but also allows for our own judgements and decisions, based on reflection and consideration.

Our valued contributors emanate from a range of disciplines and professional backgrounds, which has brought diversity of knowledge, values, professional cultures and approaches to well-being and resilience. The broad selection of authors has enabled exploration of well-being and resilience on educational outcomes for all age ranges of children and young people, from the early years to higher education students and also including families. Attempts in Section 1 to define well-being and resilience in educational contexts were successfully explored in depth, but the complexity associated with specifying theoretical concepts materialised as these discussions were furthered. The overall conclusion is that for the time being a theory of child well-being is not required, but the reader is tasked with exploring how they might make use of their newly acquired knowledge about well-being and resilience in practice. Important questions have been raised about understanding of well-being and resilience in the context of educational social policy and how this is applied through interventions for building resilience in schools. Readers are challenged to listen to children more often and more effectively in relation to their well-being and to actively promote more opportunities to gain children's voice through a participatory approach to care and education.

Section 2 has identified some of the priorities for children and young people in developing their own well-being and resilience. A key aspect of our learning has been to understand that children benefit when moments of resilience are identified and celebrated with them. Childhood friendships, and both their negative and positive impact on resilience, have taught us that peer relationships are linked to a more positive school experience and higher levels of achievement. Practitioners have a crucial role to play in supporting children to establish and sustain successful friendships by listening to children and promoting opportunity and independence to develop positive peer relationships, guiding and supporting as required. The study of children and young people's relationships viewed through a social media lens has provided insight into digital lives and the ideology which ensues. Safety and risk of online activities have been explored including addiction; risky behaviours such as publishing inappropriate images, posting harmful comments and shunning family and friends; isolation and loneliness which transcends into depression; excessive screen-time which impacts negatively on sleep problems and obesity; social comparisons and fear of missing out which results in peer pressure; cyberbullying; unattainable body images leading to failed perfectionism; self-harm and suicide; and online relationships with strangers which may lead to more sinister activities such as grooming and radicalisation. It seems straightforward to conclude that on balance, digital lives present more harm than good for children and young people. However, as we write this conclusion, we are 2 weeks into the COVID-19 lockdown and digitalisation has presented a lifeline for children and young people at this time. As schools were closed indefinitely (Johnson, 2020), education through home schooling become reliant upon online learning activities. Children and young people and their families experiencing physical isolation of the soft lock-down were able to continue to socialise with their peers and communities through online engagement. During this period, it has become evident that digital lives could become healthier than traditional use has evidenced.

Section 3 demonstrated the strength in multi-disciplinary approaches to children's well-being and resilience. Social work, education and health professionals recounted their case study experiences of building well-being and resilience for children, young people and their families. Readers were asked to consider the potential of the outdoors learning environment to invoke "feelings of wonder, wonderment, awe, joy and inner peace" (Schein, 2018, p. 86). Practitioners considered grit theory (Fiore, 2019) and were challenged to manage risk, and to reflect upon how best we can prepare children for failure and misfortune. The practice of mindfulness was introduced, for all ages from early years to adulthood, and we learnt of its positive impact for children to assist in regulating their emotions and behaviours. Yet again we were reminded that children, young people and families who could benefit from support to develop their well-being and promote their resilience were rarely heard and that this is detrimental to their well-being; a stark reminder for all readers that we need to listen more. Moreover, the reader is challenged to examine their attitudes towards vulnerable families and to shift firmly away from the all too common deficit approach that undermines and erodes support structures and systems which serve to promote well-being and build resilience. We were privileged to gain insight into Child and Adolescent Mental Health Services (CAMHS) and to hear from young people who had participated in solution focussed therapy, but sadly heard that 'school steals resilience'. We therefore request readers reflect upon their practice and implement well thought through and planned actions to return resilience to children and young people whose educational experience should not have been stolen in the first place.

Section 4 provided opportunity for readers to compare and contrast childhood well-being and resilience in different nations. In doing so, policy and legislation were examined as we learnt of the Well-Being of Future Generations Act (2015), the first act of its kind in the world aiming to safeguard the well-being and interests of children and young people within Wales, predicated on improving economic circumstance to reduce levels of child poverty. Holistic learning in Norwegian kindergartens demonstrated how participation is utilised as the main concept for building well-being and promoting resilience in young children whilst the role of professionals to support children's well-being in Italian education provision focussed on an inclusive approach for children experiencing special educational needs. The book would have been incomplete without addressing the necessity for practitioners to give due care and regard for their own well-being; to enable them to flourish. Many discussions around childhood well-being and resilience fail to consider practitioners who deliver the pedagogy. We learned that practitioners must be supported to flourish, through whole school approaches and continuing professional development opportunities. Crucially, practitioner's expertise should be recognised, acknowledged and appreciated.

We now turn to the future, and in going forward start to consider the possibilities and potential for the development in children and young people's well-being and resilience to improve educational outcomes. This book has provided a breadth of content and context to inform our work and we hope it contributes to making a positive difference to educational practice. When considering the future, however, we should take some time to consider the major, unexpected and unprecedented event which has impacted significantly on everyone; the COVID-19 pandemic. Society has shifted from a constant state to a life which is relentlessly and rapidly changing; what we once knew to be certain is no longer assured. The impact this is predicted to have on children and young people's well-being is a gloomy one, to say the least. Individual health concerns are prevalent, economic circumstances have declined, educational opportunities have shrunk and life requires re-building, all of which challenges and stretches children, young people and their families' capacity. Already over-loaded mental health services will struggle to cope with sudden increases in demand. For some, the changes incurred by the pandemic will be too much to manage.

Existing well-being thresholds appear purposeless during the pandemic, but will need to be re-calibrated in a more realistic and meaningful way in the future. We question whether well-being will be measured in an increasingly conservative way, given that some of the greatest life stressors such as bereavement and poverty will be endured by children and young people, and also ponder what potential exists for resilience to develop throughout the pandemic. There is a glimmer of hope, though, in that the pandemic has shown that communities have found strength and comfort through a resurgence of the big society, with volunteering networks formulated, community cohesion strengthened and a general ethos of kindness and compassion. We are reminded of the African proverb referred to in Chapter 5, that *it takes a village to raise a child* and can hope that children and young people's resilience might be strengthened by improved community support throughout such difficult times. The only certainty is that the world is no longer the same as prior to COVID-19. As a consequence, structural changes such as home-schooling, and our individual changes in human behaviours and associated impact on children's well-being and resilience, will be researched, measured and documented for many years to come by Sociologists, Psychologists and Philosophers.

References

Fiore, L. (2019) *Grit, Resilience, and Motivation in Early Childhood.* New York and Oxon: Routledge.

Johnson, B. (2020) *Coronavirus: UK Schools to Close Indefinitely, Says Boris Johnson* [Online video] Available at: https://www.theguardian.com/world/video/2020/mar/18/coronavirus-uk-schools-to-close-indefinitely-says-boris-johnson-video [accessed 18 March 2020].

Schein, D.L. (2018) *Inspiring Wonder, Awe and Empathy: Spiritual Development in Young Children.* St Paul: Redleaf Press.

UK emotional well-being and mental health support organisations for children and young people

Childline

Free 24-hour counselling service for children and young people up to their 19th birthday. Get help and advice about a wide range of issues, call us on 0800 1111, talk to a counsellor online, send Childline an email or post on the message boards.

https://www.childline.org.uk

Mind

Infoline Offers advice and support to service users; has a network of local associations in England and Wales to which people can turn for help.

0300 123 3393, text number: 86463

http://www.mind.org.uk

SANE

Provides practical help, emotional support and specialist information for people aged 16 and over with mental health problems, their family, friends and carers.

0300 304 7000

http://www.sane.org.uk

Supportline

Confidential telephone helpline offering emotional support to any individual on any issue.
01708 765200

http://www.supportline.org.uk

Beat

Provides helplines, self-help groups and online support to anyone affected by eating disorders.
Helpline: 0808 801 0677, Youthline: 0808 801 0711, Studentline: 0808 801 0811

http://www.b-eat.co.uk

The Samaritans

The Samaritans provide a confidential service for people in despair and who feel suicidal. Call free, anytime from any phone on: 116 123

http://www.samaritans.org.uk

NSPCC

Provides helplines and information on child abuse, child protection and safeguarding children. 0808 800 5000

https://www.nspcc.org.uk/

Young Minds

Young Minds has a Parent Helpline that offers free confidential telephone and email support to any adult worried about the wellbeing of a child or young person.

http://www.youngminds.org.uk/for_parents

0808 802 5544

Mental Health Foundation

This website offers a wide range of information about mental health issues.

http://www.mentalhealth.org.uk

Youth Wellbeing Directory

Helps you find support for mental health and wellbeing of young people up to age 25 across the UK.

https://www.annafreud.org/on-my-mind/youth-wellbeing/

Health Talk Online

Aims to provide balanced information about the experience of everyday life with a range of health conditions and issues, what to expect both physically and mentally, overcoming practical difficulties, making decisions about treatment and talking to health professionals. http://www.healthtalk.org/

YouthinMind

YouthinMind is an online resource for information about mental health and offers brief assessments. It also provides links to other useful books, websites and services.

http://youthinmind.info/py/yiminfo/

HaveIGotAProblem.com

Free resource about mental health and addiction issues. It has advice and documents on issues including depression, anxiety, self-harm, bipolar, eating disorders and coping.

http://www.haveigotaproblem.com/

Index

Printed in Great Britain
by Amazon